Diasporic Transformations

Diasporic Transformations

Novels of V.S. Naipaul

Sanjiv Kumar

Rawat Publications
Jaipur • New Delhi • Bangalore • Hyderabad • Guwahati

ISBN 978-81-316-0521-9

Published by
Prem Rawat for **Rawat Publications**
Satyam Apts, Sector 3, Jawahar Nagar, Jaipur 302 004 (India)
Phone: 0141 265 1748 / 7006 Fax: 0141 265 1748
E-mail: info@rawatbooks.com
Website: www.rawatbooks.com

New Delhi Office
4858/24, Ansari Road, Daryaganj, New Delhi 110 002
Phone: 011 2326 3290

Also at *Bangalore, Hyderabad* and *Guwahati*

Typeset by Rawat Computers, Jaipur
Printed at Nice Printing Press, New Delhi

Contents

Preface and Acknowledgements

The entire debate on diaspora studies has taken an altogether different dimension with the economic globalization and subsequent de-territorialization. The geo-spatial boundaries have blurred to the extent that even the concept of 'nation' itself has become a contentious issue and the question of national identity is no more discussed in terms of homogeneous attributes. With the emerging multicultural landscapes, the diasporic literature seems to have lost its validity as now it is no more a literature representing the erstwhile nomads compelled to live ambivalent lives after leaving their homelands to win their bread in an alien territory; rather, in the post-reforms period, the politics of 'home' and 'abroad' is more about falsified depiction of diasporic realities. The Janus-faced diaspora has now perhaps transformed into a cosmopolitan sojourner enjoying the status of a global citizen.

However, V.S. Naipaul's fiction traces the essential transformation in diasporic sensibilities as starting from depicting a forlorn nomad lost in an alien territory and getting nostalgic all the time for his romantic past, he ends up with the fiction where the protagonists seem to have developed a mature outlook towards their diasporic status where they accept the multicultural global realities as they come to them. If his early fiction portrays the shipwrecked and drifted East Indians in Trinidad which for him is no more than 'a dot on the map of the world', his later fiction presents the wider view of global diasporic experiences in tune with his belief that 'my homeland is where I work, and I work everywhere', though with the lingering consciousness of displacement. It is in this context that the present book offers an incisive analysis of Naipaul's fiction to trace the shifting paradigms of diasporic ambivalence.

The book could not have seen the light of the day without the enormous support of my teacher Dr Sanjay Kumar, who made it possible for me to explore the complexities of the theme. Had if I not met Professor Meeta Biswas, Department of English, Himachal Pradesh University, Shimla, I might not have developed my interest in V.S. Naipaul and therefore I acknowledge my sincere thanks to this noble lady.

If someone deserves special mention as a fatherly figure and enlightening soul motivating me to get this work published, it is Professor Mool Chand Sharma, Hon'ble Vice Chancellor of Central University of Haryana whose thought-provoking remarks have strong bearing on me both as a teacher and a researcher. He has always blessed me with his best compliments even for the humblest achievements of mine and this publication is one of them.

Here, I must not forget to acknowledge my thanks to Professor Rajul Bhargava, Professor Anu Shukla, Dr Deepti Dharmani and Mr Pankaj Kumar, who have been a great support to me during my research and after. Professor Hemendra Singh Chandalia, Head, Department of English has been kind enough to provide his valuable inputs during the proof-reading of the script. I must also put on record my thanks for the entire faculty and Deputy Registrar at Central University of Haryana for inspiring me to get this work published.

I have no words for my parents who have always dreamt to see me and my brothers growing and it is their sacrifice and undying commitment to make their children progress that this research could get the desired shape. My brothers Dr Umed Singh (Associate Professor and Head, Department of English, CDLU, Sirsa) and Parveen Kumar (JWO) have always been excessively affectionate to me and provided me all support throughout my academic career. Their love could get doubled with the equal support of my Bhabhis—Poonam and Kamlesh—in my formative years. Exemplary austerity and honesty of my primary teacher Shri Dharam Palji and my father-in-law Shri Shivtaj Singh (Retd SDEO) served as a great source of inspiration for me throughout my academic career. My wife Kalpana and kids—Ayush and Ayushi—have always been anxious about my accomplishments and sacrificed best of their time to see me complete the research.

Last but not the least, I express my deep sense of gratitude for my publishers Rawat Publications, Jaipur who found some worth in my research and published it in the given form. I must also acknowledge Rawat Publications for the books it has published on 'Diaspora' by authors of eminence like Uma Parmeswaran, Prof. Jasbir Jain and Manjeet Inder Singh whom I referred during my research.

My thanks are also due for the all the authors—living or dead—whom I consulted during my research.

Introduction

V.S. Naipaul is considered to be one of the most prominent expatriate novelists having first hand colonial experience. His novels deal with the colonial as well as postcolonial societies with an explicit account of the common complexities inherent among the marginalized societies. Naipaul's work is commonly regarded as an implicit biography of his departure from the narrow background of the Caribbean island to the open cosmopolitan culture of the world at large. He carries three conflicting, and at times, interacting components in his personality of being a Trinidadian colonial, an English metropolitan, and a person of Indian ancestry.

A Trinidadian by birth, Naipaul never acknowledges his association with his native land. Referring to Trinidad, Naipaul admits that he has minimum contacts with members of other races and that he has met people who were outside his ethnic group only in official contexts where it has been extremely necessary. In a characteristic acerbic style, he describes his stay in Trinidad as a complete waste of time. The unpromising land of Trinidad was stifling to his spirit. Trinidadian Hindu family life in its miniature form seemed irrelevant and meaningless. Though Naipaul never relished his Trinidadian roots, he always felt a warm approximation with the members of his family particularly his father whose metaphysical anguish he could easily comprehend and appreciate. His father was his guide, mentor and a constant source of literary inspiration. He aroused in his son the ambition to become a writer and gave him the idea of stories that could be written about colonial and marginalized life in Trinidad. He himself acknowledges his father's contribution: "The ambition to be a writer was given to me by my father."[1] Since his father Seepersad Naipaul himself was a failed writer, Naipaul had immense protective care and affection for him. Viewed perceptively, it seems that it was his father's anguish that spurred in him a writing spirit. Not only this, but it was the direct encouragement of his father that helped young Naipaul set his eyes on the writing career in his formative years. Earning a scholarship at the age of eighteen provided Naipaul an escape route from the constraining limitations of a corroded colonial life. Soon after his flight, he felt that London was the center from where he could launch his literary career. Apart from his father's profligacy, the constant anxiety of living in unstable homes, and ultimately the consciousness of "half-made societies" provided the backdrop to Naipaul's neurosis. Since "neurosis" is seen as a flood gate of creative overture, Naipaul, in his writing career spanning almost fifty years now, has produced a staggering amount of literature ranging from fiction, non-fiction, travelogues and autobiographical essays. In fact, ever since the publication of his first book *The Mystic Masseur* in 1957, he has been seen as a prominent diasporic writer. Quite akin to the spirit and character of his own work, his life reflects queer sense of displacement and restlessness. It is this restlessness of the novelist that helps him portray the postcolonial diasporic angst with intensity and authority. A Trinidadian by birth and Indian by descent from a family of Indian indentured labourers; and a Londoner for his English education and his stay in England, Naipaul cannot call any place his home or cannot take any place for granted. Wherever he went he could, at best remain a visitor. Rootlessness was something that never ceased to haunt Naipaul and he never stopped reminding himself about his Hindu origins and beliefs of his Indian ancestors settled in the Caribbean. The genesis of diaspora, penetration of the writer's consciousness and the resultant expatriate sensibility that gave birth to cross cultural writing, is the context in which Naipaul's love-hate relationship with India and Trinidad is highlighted in his oeuvre.

Naipaul's Indian background is submerged in a mixed culture whose other components are equally threatened. This turbulent relationship finds expression in his passionate concern for the land of his ancestors. His vision being coloured by the diasporic consciousness that gave birth to his quest, he is caught within the ripples of his own making in his first real encounter with India. The India which was the background of his childhood memories was just "historical darkness",[2] a mythical imaginary land from where his ancestors had come as the indentured labourers. His forefathers were predominantly rural and adhered to the traditions of their native land. The East Indian population remained largely distinct from the urban and creolized Afro-Caribbean majority, who despised them for depressing agricultural wages in the sugarcane fields. The clash of cultures was quite evident as both the groups asserted the supremacy of their culture and tradition. Colonized people are highly diverse in their nature and traditions; in cultures they are both rooted in their native cultures and yet exposed to the outside influence. They may be "other" from the colonizers and they are also different from one another owing to their distinct history, tradition and cultural backgrounds. This difference does not allow these groups to get totalized or essentialized through concepts such as black consciousness, Indian consciousness, aboriginal culture and so forth. The colonized people cannot reconstruct their past though an attempt to reclaim the past can obviously be made. Their past may be revisited and realized in partial and fragmented ways only.

There is an interesting similarity in Naipaul's response to the West Indies and to India. The involvement with both is manifested mainly in a violent rejection—a turning away. He has also recorded that he had been brought up in a double world: the closed Hindu world of his grandmother's family and the outside world. Both these worlds were incompatible. It is because most of his books are the outcome of his personal enigma of being a displaced member of a minority race and religion in Trinidad. As it is evident in the works of Naipaul, racial compartmentalization of the Caribbean caused by slavery and colonization, led the earlier West Indian writers to write basically about their communities, who treated the outsiders only as caricatures or figures of fun.

His multiple heritage places him in a position that makes it possible for him to present an objective account of his subjective experiences. Being an Indian by ancestry, Trinidadian by birth and English by intellectual training and residence, Naipaul turns out to be a man with a broader outlook. He seems to negate both Trinidad and India as his possible homes. Though he is generally criticized for being the representative of imperialism, his work condemns this castigating view straightforwardly as he hardly ever shows his inclination or belongingness to England except for momentary comfort after experiencing the torturing expatriate feeling of being unhoused, displaced and alienated in Trinidad. His maturity gets reflected in his fiction and travel writings. His travels to Trinidad, India, Africa, the Islamic world and South America add to his deeper understanding of postcolonial concerns.

Naipaul's literary works acquire a universal connotation as he experiences different cultures to reach to the obvious conclusion that the fragmentation and alienation happen to be the universal predicament of man in the present day world. Though he happens to be concerned with the portrayal of the predicament of man living in a postcolonial society, very often it leads him to be a representative of the predicament of the universal modern man. Thus, from a regional writer, Naipaul rises to the status of a writer who experiences and articulates the concerns of universal humanity. The most important influence that shaped him as a typical diasporic writer was Trinidad, his birthplace consisting of diverse races, cultures, religions and psyches. The society of Trinidad was a fragmented one, comprising heterogeneous people, viz. Africans and Indians inhabiting on the island merely by an accident of history. The society was devoid of any sense of nationality or recognition as the people there were in a perpetual dilemma regarding the uncertainty about their affiliations. They were in a fix whether to feel proud of their original identities or to get themselves readily assimilated with the Trinidadian culture.

The term "diaspora" has varied definitions and connotations associated to it. While in recent times, it refers to the Jewish people residing outside Israel. Diaspora is often associated with Zionism, which is the belief in the Jews' legitimate claim to a homeland, i.e., Palestine. N. Jayaram precisely defines the term:

> Etymologically, the term diaspora is derived from the Greek composite verb *dia*-and *speirein* (infinitive), literally meaning 'to scatter,' 'to spread' or 'to disperse'. It was originally used to refer to the dispersion of Jews after the Babylonian exile in 586 BC and to the aggregate of Jews or Jewish communities scattered in exile outside Palestine. In current parlance, however, the term is applied to describe any group of people who are so dispersed.[3]

Historically, the *diaspora* has undergone different phases; the first significant one occurred in 586 BC when the Babylonians conquered Judah, leading to the enslavement of the Jews. It was the largest Diaspora, which occurred during the first century BC and lasted for more than eighteen hundred years, leading to the displacement of five million Jews. The displacements that have taken place did not necessarily lead to Jews returning to Palestine even after the initial cause of the exile had lost its significance. At the same time, the term *diaspora* has its origin in ancient Greek implying "a scattering or sowing of seeds". Currently the term is being used as the synonym for the "expatriates", "emigrants" or "exiles" in the colonial period when people leave their homelands and settle either in alien land or in the land of colonizer in pursuit of better prospects and individual freedom. "Diaspora" cannot be separated from "colonialism", as this historical condition led to the displacement of people across the world under different circumstances or forms of compulsion. As a result, native population was displaced from their homeland, not only physically but emotionally too; ultimately making them unhoused nomads with a persistent feeling of nostalgia, rootlessness, alienation, ambivalence and cultural insecurity. The link between "diaspora" and "colonialism" is far more complex indeed. The people of the diaspora were settlers, migrants, transported convicts, slaves, or labourers. What is more apparent is the capacity of colonialism to produce so many varied forms of coercive power that compel people to move incessently. Consequently the culture produced by diaspora cannot but contain so many resonances of the movement—the imagination of their homelands, sense of tradition, the circumstances of their removal, and their sense of shame in acknowledging their bond with humble abodes. In fact, it is a Janus-like journey looking backward while moving forward. Janus being a Roman god "having two faces, one looking forward and one back",[4] implies the ambivalent nature of the diaspora.

An expatriate is not only the man who travels across the physical boundaries; rather his imagination, culture, psyche, sociology and anthropology also travel with him, causing a sort of perpetual conflict of fluid identity and alternative centers. According to Jayaram, the immigrants carry with them: "... a sociocultural baggage which among other things consist of (a) a predefined social identity, (b) a set of religious beliefs and practices, (c) a framework of norms and values governing family and kinship organization, and food habits and (d) language".[5] Oscillating between two mutually exclusive worlds, diasporas may be termed as transitional beings because they waver between two cultures. These diasporas, according to Homi K. Bhabha, tend to move in an obvious circle, i.e., from home culture to alien culture leading to an assimilated culture. Edward W. Said also adds to the definition and classification of Diasporas: "The person who finds his homeland sweet is still a tender beginner, he to whom every soil is as his native one is already strong, but he is perfect to whom the entire world is a foreign place ... and a survival in fact is about the connection between things."[6]

Diasporic consciousness in the world of literature is becoming an increasingly dominant phenomenon. It is the mental flight of people constantly trying to reconstruct their present from a past that constantly haunts them. All such attempts, however, are liable to flounder as their own roots re-assert their peculiarities. Their roots strike against a frozen, fractured consciousness forcing them to begin a search for locating the crevices that can warmly encapsulate their ambivalent identities. The search of the émigrés for a permanent foothold is the starting point of diasporic literature. With regard to V.S. Naipaul the seeds of such diasporic ambivalence seem to have been sown quite a few decades prior to his birth.

The enigma of the Indian expatriates in Trinidad has its origin in the abolition of slavery in Trinidad in 1834 and the consequent shortage of labour. The emancipated slaves refused to work on the fields on the predefined conditions. Immigrant workers were imported from Portugal, France, Africa, Madeira, the United States and China as well as from the smaller islands of the Caribbean, but the main supplier of labour then was India. The shift of population between the colonies resulted into the formation of heterogeneous multicultural societies. Gayatri Spivak truly and elaborately comments upon the diasporic Indians:

> Over the centuries we had histories of ... Indian indentured labour being taken to the Afro-Caribbean. After the change of regimes in certain African nations, Indians moved from Africa, then to Britain; then Indians in waves in the early 60's, professional Indians, went to the United States as part of the brain-drain. These Indians who are spread out over the world, for different kinds of historical reasons, they are diasporic ... .[7]

The move of the Indians to West Indies Caribbean Island in late nineteenth century as indentured labourers in the sugarcane fields was the major displacement for those who settled in Trinidad as a separate ethnic group but are still sticking to their native cultural identities. The first Indian immigrants as indentured labourers arrived in Port of Spain on 30 May 1845. The indentured labour emigration was officially sponsored by the colonial government. This form of contractual system of labour began in 1834 and ended in 1920. By 1917, when immigration from India was banned, near about one lac fifty thousand labourers had settled in Trinidad. Most of them came from the provinces of Oudh (now Bihar and Uttar Pradesh). In an essay, David Ormerod narrates: "The indenture scheme is still remembered with bitterness. Trinidad Indians are convinced that they occupy their particular spot on the earth's surface because their forefathers were duped by the planters and the recruiting agents. Conditions were misrepresented ... ."[8]

The return or "reversed migration" of these indentured labourers was made nearly impossible. They were made to work what the slaves had been doing earlier and they were accommodated in the slave barracks. The present population of Trinidad consists of people of Amerindians and the descendants of the people of three continents—Europe, Africa and Asia—who have made this island their uneasy home. Only this confused amalgam of races remains as a witness to the forlorn history of the region.

The expatriates were to live among heterogeneous groups formed by the Africans, native Trinidadians and other displaced groups tormented by the colonizers in one way or the other. The West Indian and East Indian cultures in Trinidad are the byproducts of physical and cultural displacement as a result of exodus in various parts of the world. For an expatriate, the urge to survive becomes the immediate requirement. Their disconnection from traditional cultures left a deep scar on the psyche of the colonized people as in the alien land they found themselves in the painful state of betweenity—constantly searching for an identity and home. It was nothing but the impact of colonization on the minds of the displaced. Bit by bit they are robbed of their originality. Due to this displacement of people from their native land to alien land for one reason or the other, the term "diaspora" came into vogue. Owing to this continual sense of dislocation the colonized people were made to suffer not only in their native land where they were born but also in the alien land where they were forced to migrate because of economic and political compulsions. It is in this sense that diaspora acquires a universal connotation that indeed transcends the boundaries both—temporal and spatial ones. Though the term *diaspora* has always attracted the intellectual attention, it has gained intense currency in the postcolonial era. It is so because postcolonial anguish appears to be inextricably intertwined with the diasporic angst among the people inhabiting the Third World.

Emerging, therefore, as probably the most pivotal intellectual regurgitation, postcolonialism refers to a set of theories in philosophy and literature which has a direct bearing on the legacy of colonial rule. As a literary theory or critical approach, it deals with literature produced in countries that were once colonies of other countries, especially the major European colonial powers like Britain, France, etc. In a very general sense, it is the study of the interactions between European nations and the societies they colonized in the wake of imperial period that lasted till the later half of twentieth century. Postcolonialism as a discourse deals with unequal power relations which existed between the colonizer and the colonized. It also seeks to study the implications of the very ideology which subjugated men and nations in the name of civilizing mission undertaken by the privileged few. The dilemmas of developing a national identity to counter the colonial rule figure prominently in the writings of the postcolonial writers who seek to articulate and even celebrate the indigenous cultural identities. The primary concern of the postcolonial literature is to study the experiences of people who happened to live in colonized countries.

It is in this sense that the term "Postcolonialism" does not only imply the political emancipation of the colonized from the colonizers rather it has varied implications associated to it. It seeks to examine how cultural apparatus have been effectively used by the imperial powers to colonize the people in body and mind. Dennis Walder's opinion adds to the present discussion when he argues:

> 'Postcolonial'... demands a double awareness: of the colonial inheritance as it continues to operate within a specific culture, community or country; and of the changing relations between these cultures, communities and countries in the modern world ... the colonial experience persists despite the withdrawal of political control, as a result of the continuing strategic and economic power of the former colonisers,... however minimal the impact of empire upon a particular people in the long perspective, it has always left its imprint.[9]

Psychological colonization is far more dangerous than the political enslavement as the former persists even after the end of the colonial rule. In his introduction to *West Indian Literature*, Bruce King puts down how postcolonial trends came into vogue among the West-Indian writers. He says:

> West Indian is one of many English literatures, that began under colonialism and emerged after the Second World War, mostly as a result of the social, political and cultural changes which had started in the late 1930s and which picked up speed during the war and with the ending of Empire. As with other new literatures ... its themes and subject-matter have often been the problems resulting from colonialism and independence.[10]

Similarly, colonialism can not be interpreted only as a medium to suppress the colonized economically. Besides the serious damages done to the economy of these countries, colonialism has also caused greater harm to the psyche of the colonized people. Ashis Nandy underscores the same argument:

> This modern colonialism colonises minds in addition to bodies and it releases forces within the colonized societies to alter their cultural priorities once for all. In the process it helps generalize the concept of the modern West from a geographical and temporal entity to a psychological category. The West is now everywhere, within the West and outside, in structures and minds.[11]

It was so because of the presupposition in the minds of the Europeans regarding their superiority and the inferiority of other colonized ethnic societies. The colonizers were well aware that it was imperative to make the colonized people receptive to Western cultural influences in order to establish cultural hegemony. Antonio

Gramsci's concept of "hegemony" also implies that the colonizers could assert their cultural dominance over the colonized not only by using coercive techniques but also by creating willingness among victims through ideology. The colonial subjugation of island had bred only self-disgust among the non-White population and a sense of superiority among the Whites.

The unending quest for past and involuntary assimilation into the alien culture gave way to an important concept in postcolonial theory popularly termed as "ambivalence". Webster's New World College Dictionary defines the term as "simultaneous conflicting feelings toward a person or thing, as love and hate."[12] The term further connotes the "seizure of cultural viscosity"[13] resulting into essential in-betweenness, half-ness, dichotomies, dilemmas and divided-selves of the colonial natives and expatriates. This ambivalent tendency among the colonials is the by-product of the postcolonial concepts like "mimicry", "hybridity", "creolization" and "multiculturalism" which prevail the colonial/postcolonial Third World. "Hybridity" refers to the integration or mingling of cultural signs and practices from the colonizing and the colonized cultures through which people adapt themselves to the necessities and the opportunities of more or less oppressive or invasive cultural impositions. The expatriates, like indentured labourers in Trinidad, live into alien cultural patterns through their own structures of understanding, thus achieving the state of ossification, i.e., maintaining their cultural identity without being insulated from the adapted culture. The assimilation and adaptation of cultural practices, the cross-fertilization of cultures, can be seen as positive, enriching, and dynamic, as well as oppressive. "Hybridity" is also a useful concept for helping to break down the false notion that the colonized or the colonizing cultures are monolithic, having essentially unchanging features. "Hybridity" doesn't allow the displaced people to go home again with the complete realization of their homeliness.

Some of the broad concepts related to postcolonial studies include—the formation of empire, the impact of colonization on postcolonial history, economy, science and culture, the cultural productions of colonized societies, feminism and postcolonialism, agency for marginalized people, and the state of the decolonized states in contemporary economic and cultural contexts. The thinkers/critics like Frantz Fanon, Edward W. Said, George Lamming, Terry Eagleton, Homi K. Bhabha, Ania Loomba, Leela Gandhi, Gayatri Spivak, Benita Parry, Bill Ashcroft, Ashis Nandy, to name only a few, have spelled out their varied interpretations of this diasporic phenomenon which gets reflected in some of the key concepts such as colonialism, postcolonialism and cultural hegemony. Simon During has precisely interpreted postcolonialism which, according to him: "... came to signify something remote from self-determination and autonomy. By deploying categories such as hybridity, mimicry, ambivalence ... all of which laced colonized into colonizing cultures, postcolonialism effectively became a reconciliatory rather than a critical, anti-colonialist category."[14]

Different postcolonial themes like theme of identity crisis, fractured/torn-identities, East-West encounter, rejection, anxiety, love-hate relationship within two cultures, homelessness, expatriate melancholy, rootlessness, etc., reflecting diasporic ambivalence are projected in the writings of almost all the prominent Indian Diaspora writers like V.S. Naipaul, Amitav Ghosh, Jhumpa Lahiri, Anita Desai, Kiran Desai, Salman Rushdie, Rohinton Mistry, Vikram Seth, Chitra Banerjee Divakaruni, Bharati Mukherjee, Amit Chaudhary and Arun Joshi.

Naipaul grew up in the creole society of Trinidad where he never found himself comfortable. But it is also the society that he knows best; the society to which he keeps returning to in his fiction. His love-hate relationship with Trinidad is evident when in *The Middle Passage* he asserts that: "I knew Trinidad to be unimportant, uncreative, cynical ... it was a place where the stories were not stories of success but of failure."[15] But in an interview with Derek Walcott, he acknowledges the contribution of Trinidad in shaping him as a representative writer of West Indian origin. He observes: "I have grown out of Trinidad and in a way I am grateful to the Trinidad I knew as a boy for making me what I am."[16]

Naipaul's initial bitterness for Trinidad and India generated a unique sense of detachment, which helped him in his struggle to establish a connection with Trinidad and India at a time when he felt disillusioned in England. His colonial experience forced him to experience such circumstances that exposed him to three societies and yet left him with a deep sense of homelessness. Naipaul, however, did not confine himself to tackle the problem of rootlessness and enigma of colonial subjects; he went ahead to highlight the suffocating maladies afflicting the people of his homeland and the other Third World societies including India. In this pursuit what inspired him the most were his first-hand encounters with these societies, his keen observation and an objective reaction to this colonial experience. He attempted to understand the countries against the cultural backdrop and had made a well-ordered search for the roots of the maladies that ailed both Trinidad and India. Born into exile and separated from his racial and cultural roots, he was made to experience another exile after his migration to England. In addition to his constant movements between different lands as an expatriate, his travels to Caribbean, India, America, South America, Iran, Malaysia, Pakistan and Indonesia also added intensity to his understanding of diasporic ambivalence. Naipaul's colonial-imperial experiences bring him closer to Edward Said who, according to Patrick Williams: "... lived the combination of being part of the centre (the United States) and the semi-periphery (the Middle East); part of the West, and the non-West ... and part of a fragmented people, scattered, oppressed and ignored; part of the elite, and part of the undistinguished or indistinguishable mass of the majority world ... ."[17]

The genius of Naipaul as a novelist is shaped chiefly by two figures—his father and Joseph Conrad, the writer of *The Heart of Darkness*. Besides, the most important driving force behind Naipaul's work is his childhood years as a member of a large Hindu clan that made him present the angry and anguished response to the half-made colonial society of Trinidad. For him, the large Hindu family was like a crash course in the world. His journalist father was muffled by this family life which never allowed him privacy. He found this family environment critical and disgusting. His father's dejection drew Naipaul closer to him and it made both the father and the son feel the need to protect each other. He reacts:

> In Chaguanas the family had been at the centre of a whole network of Hindu reverences ... our Hindu system began to fail. There were desperate quarrels ... nothing was stable ... . I didn't see my father for days. His nerves deteriorated ... . Disorder within, disorder without. Only my school life was ordered; anything that had happened there I could date at once. But my family life—my family at home or my life in the house, in the street—was jumbled, without sequence.[18]

Since it is not uncommon to discover striking parallels between the writer's life and the fictional world created by him, we find many characters and episodes striking direct affinities with the author's personal experiences. Mr Mohun Biswas and his son Anand in *A House for Mr Biswas* are the exact parallel portrayals of the novelist and his father. In this novel, Naipaul presents the filial bond saying: "Father and son each saw the other as weak and vulnerable, and each felt a responsibility for the other ... ."[19] Naipaul's grandfather, who had been brought to Trinidad as a baby from Eastern Uttar Pradesh at some time in 1880s, grew up to be a Pundit, but Seepersad never wished to be a pundit and experimented with certain odd jobs like sign painting. This job took him to Lion-House at Chaguanas where he met Droaptie who accepted him as her life partner. Being homeless, Seepersad was bound to accept the proposal to settle at Lion-House, and it was here that Naipaul was born in 1932. The same year, Seepersad Naipaul became the Chaguanas' correspondent of the Trinidad Guardian. Two years later, he suffered from a serious nervous breakdown. Naipaul admits that he inherited from his father a tendency to hysteria also: "And what is astonishing to me is that, with the vocation, he so accurately transmitted to me—without saying anything about it—his hysteria from the time when I didn't know him: his fear of extinction. That was his subsidiary gift to me. That fear became mine as well."[20]

Naipaul's early work is a kind of dedication to his father. He says—"a lot of my work-especially my early work—I meant to be dedicated to him."[21] As an act of homage to his father and fulfillment of a promise made to him, Naipaul arranged the publication of a collection of his father's stories in June 1975 with a Forward by himself. The book is *The Adventures of Gurudeva* and in the Forword, Naipaul comes out with moving sentiments about the pain of his father's defeated life. For example, his masterpiece *A House for Mr Biswas* is derived from his father's life-long quest for finding a home in the world after the migration of his family from the Eastern part of India as indentured labourer in Trinidad. *A House for Mr Biswas*, which he considered as closest to his heart, is the autobiographical account of his father's quest for identity in a colonial society. He himself admits in his essay "Foreword to A House for Mr Biswas": "… of all my books, this is the one that is closest to me. It is the most personal, created out of what I saw and felt as a child … . My literary ambition had grown out of my early life; the two were interwined; the tears were for a double innocence,"[22] and he further adds: "it became the story of a man's search for a house and all that the possession of one's own house implies."[23] Similarly, he acknowledges the contribution of Conrad in the last piece "Conrad's Darkness" of *The Return of Eva Peron*: "Conrad's value to me is that he is someone who sixty to seventy years ago meditated on my world, a world I recognize today … . Nothing is rigged in Conrad. He does not remake countries. He chose, as we now know, incidents from real life; and he meditated on them."[24]

Naipaul was born to the parents of Indian descent at Chaguanas in central Trinidad that was one of the British colonies. He could have only the second hand account about the migration of his family from

India. In his essay "Prologue to an Autobiography", he admits: "Indian Immigrants, at the end of their contract, were entitled to a small grant of land or to a free trip back to India with their families. The promise had not always been kept. Many Indians, after they had served out their indenture, had found themselves destitute and homeless."[25] Since his childhood, he was driven by the impulse that he does not belong to Trinidad and this alien feeling stimulated him to win a scholarship at the age of seventeen that enabled him to move to Britian to study at Oxford University. In the same essay he admits how he felt inspired to flee away from Trinidad, his birthplace. He expresses the typical feelings of a colonial mimicking individual aspiring to reach the imperial centre, London. He says: "In 1948, I won a Trinidad Government scholarship ... . I decided to use mine to do English at Oxford. I did not want a degree; I wanted only to get away."[26]

The irresistible fascination for the West and the dreams to have a sense of gratification and achievement mixed with his apathetic attitude towards Trinidad made him settle down among the colonizers. His strong sense of homelessness and "unhoused sensibility" turns out to be extraordinarily intense, as he feels himself twice displaced, i.e., firstly from the land of his ancestors and then from his own birth place to which he never finds himself attached. It was so because he was deprived of a national identity, enthusiasm, dignity and pride in his youth, due to the heritage of colonialism, past of slavery, indentured labour and continual immigration. Like all other diasporic writers, Naipaul's sense of identity and belongingness seemed always at stake. His fractured self asserts itself through his writings from first to last.

Naipaul's drifted self is exposed nakedly through the novel where Mr Biswas, the mouthpiece of writer's father undertakes a war to assert his selfhood and individuality in spite of his fractured self. The novel represents the trauma not only of its protagonist; rather, Mr Biswas represents the diasporic Indians at Trinidad who are prone to the sense of alienation, homelessness and disillusionment. The East-West encounter also comes to the fore within the framework of the novel. King Bruce aptly remarks: "Biswas lives in an impoverished colonial society in which most people do not read, education is not available, English is not always used for conversations, literary models come from abroad and are in appropriate to local society. Literature therefore, seems dead, part of the European past."[27]

V.S. Naipaul has been acclaimed as the greatest Caribbean writer. His ideology about culture is progressive as he admits that the Indians of Trinidad are no longer Asians and he adds that the immigrants cannot be judged by the standards of the culture of their origin as culture is ever evolving. In 1960, when he travelled back to Trinidad for the first time after his emigration, he wrote: "I began to feel all my old fear of Trinidad. I did not want to stay ... I had forgotten nothing."[28] To stress the insignificance of Trinidad, he considers this West Indian Island as a *"dot on the map of the world"*. There are many incidents in *A House for Mr Biswas* which suggest the cultural assimilation, for example, the practice of burying the dead instead of cremating; Mrs Tulsi's sending Sushila to burn candles in the Roman Catholic Church, and putting crucifix in her room; and getting Mr Tulsi's grave cleaned for All Saint's Day. Though Naipaul is nostalgic about his native culture, his sensibility encourages him to accept the progressive idea of culture. The failures of his grandparents and particularly of his father who himself aspired to be a writer with a large number of fond readership, set him in motion with the sole objective to highlight the deep-rooted ambivalence among diasporic people.

His literary acumen and eminence has now been duly acknowledged worldwide as he has received many prestigious awards in his illustrious career spanning over five decades. He was awarded John Llewelyn Rhys Memorial Prize for *The Mystic Masseur* in 1957, followed by Somerset Maugham Award, Hawthornden Prize, W.H. Smith Award, David Cohen British Literature Prize, Booker Prize, Knighthood and ultimately the most prestigious Nobel Prize for Literature in 2001. Undoubtedly, Naipaul is one of the greatest writers with a large number of fictional works, besides scores of travelogues and a handful of autobiographical writings of seminal importance, to his credit. The awards bestowed upon him speak volumes of his monumental contribution to the corpus of literature. In exploring the societies and cultures boasting neither of a glorious past, nor possessing any worthwhile present, he has succeeded in carving a niche for himself in the postcolonial English literary sphere. Despite the cosmopolitan temper of his writing, Naipaul fails to appease the wrath of contemporary writers of West Indies who considered him as an agent of imperial power. Though George Lamming accused Naipaul of being ashamed of his native cultural background and he is generally acknowledged as a conservative and fastidious traveller, Naipaul seems to possess an uncanny insight that helps him perceive and present persistent diasporic ambivalence witnessed in torn-identities of the Third World nationals. This ambivalence comes to surface not only in his fiction but also in his travel writings. His fictional works overflow with his feelings of confusion, ambivalence, torn-self, nomadic existence and a man with an incessant insistence on establishing his identity.

Although many individual and comparative studies have been conducted on the writers of the Indian diaspora, there is a dearth of studies that analyse the diasporic ambivalence and growth of an individual writer within the framework of his continuing encounters with his homeland. Though Naipaul's fictional and non-fictional works have been studied by a few researchers resulting into various critical studies with different perspectives, there appears to be a chasm in the stature of the man of letters and the critical attention he has received particularly with a concentrated focus that takes into account the diverse nuances and subtleties characterizing his fictional world created in almost half a century. It is not only the fictional works of Naipaul that have received tangential endeavour but also his travelogues which, in fact, have more or less escaped the critical scrutiny of the researchers and scholars worldwide. In fact, most of the criticism on Naipaul tends to simplify and categorize him as a "native informer". That is why it is not surprising to observe most of the critics and researchers who have strongly condemned the Nobel Laureate for his apathetic attitude towards the Third World. But to recognize him as a Eurocentric author is obviously erroneous as his literary standpoint is shaped by a variety of experiences he underwent during his brief stay in Caribbean island, India, Argentina, African Countries, and also by his longer stay in England. The book is an enquiry of V.S. Naipaul and his fiction as ever-changing and ever-developing with some predominant preoccupations. Bruce King aptly remarks that: "While there are four recognisable periods of Naipaul's work, characterised by differences in subject matter, manner, technique and complexity, there is a continuity of concerns, themes and certain formal structures in his novels and books of travel."[29] In consonance with King's view, the present work attempts to study Naipaul with noticeable paradigms shaping the diasporic ambivalence in his fictional works. He is studied here not through a jaundiced eye rather his growth is viewed as the result of his extensive and objective observation of the postcolonial scenario from an outsider's point of view. In order to pursue the evolution of literary genius in Naipaul and to trace the paradigmatic shifts in his oeuvre, the book chooses to adopt a wider canvass to validate the essential transformation in Nobel Laureate and his works. All the four important phases of the author's literary voyage have been explored analytically to trace out the shifting paradigms of diasporic ambivalence in his fiction. Two works of fiction are elaborately discussed in each chapter to perceive the novelist's diasporic sensibility which is constantly evolving. Since Naipaul has often eluded facile interpretations, his works are studied by taking into consideration the numerous dimensions involving Naipaul's postcolonial social and political background, travels, and his fictional reproduction inviting critical assessment. The study of his fiction brings out writer's fractured identity owing to his movement from one place to another seeking "a permanent home".

The "Introduction" underlines Naipaul's position as a postcolonial diaspora writer, his age, birth, parentage, influences and the literary background that shaped him as a twice-displaced writer with a unique expatriate sensibility. An attempt has been made to present the factors responsible for the inculcation of the typical diasporic ambivalence in Naipaul. The definitions and the interpretations of the key terms such as postcolonial, colonial, ambivalence and diaspora have also been discussed in detail. Homi K. Bhabha's concept of "transition of culture" aptly describes the persisting confusion among the Indian diaspora in Trinidad. The enactment of Ramayana along with other associated rites concerning marriages, last rites, use of Hindi, etc., are invoked to counter the culture of Caribbean island. The continual change of the houses by his father, i.e., from Chaguanas to Port of Spain in 1938, to Diego Martin in 1940, back again to Port of Spain in 1941 and ultimately to their own house in Nepaul street in 1947, work as the addition of fuel to the fire for Naipaul in strengthening his sense of dislocation in the island.

The first chapter presents the study of the early novels of Naipaul showing his preoccupation with the traumas of displacement and the dilemma of finding a new place in the New World that reaches a climax in his masterpiece *A House for Mr Biswas.* While writing the novels of first phase of his literary career, he seems to look back to Trinidad of his childhood while staying at London. Trinidad and its predicaments preoccupy his Trinidadian tetralogy, viz., *Miguel Street*, *The Mystic Masseur*, *The Suffrage of Elvira* and *A House for Mr Biswas*. The chapter largely focuses on exploring the diasporic ambivalence of the novelist in two of his major early novels *The Mystic Masseur* (1957) and *A House for Mr Biswas* (1961). The childhood days spent in Trinidad, the bond between father and son and the Hindu background are the most influential factors of his personal life and these factors get reflected prominently in his early fiction. In his early fiction, Naipaul records the explicit encounter with his familiar locale and age recreating the society of Trinidad with all pervasive disintegration of the East Indian community. While portraying the disintegration of the East-Indians, he penetrates deeper to expose the inherent ambivalence among the colonials. These East-Indians are shown as the victims of a sort of cultural hysteria and they keep on justifying their native culture even while mimicking the culture and traditions of the West. The obvious conflict between the East-Indian Hindu traditions and West Indian aliens constitutes the core of his early works. It is quite obvious that these displaced people who have lost their native land find themselves in a state of "betweenity". Being displaced from their homelands, the expatriates in Trinidad are disillusioned as they oscillate between two contradictory cultures, i.e., hybrid culture of Trinidad and their native culture. The acculturation of the East-Indians is a major theme in the early novels. For these colonials the only hope lies in their escape from Trinidad. The novelist suggests that for the displaced people like Ganesh and Mr Biswas, owning a house means shaping and ordering of their chaotic life. For him, "house" implies stability, security and coherence. In his fiction of early phase, he presents his indebtedness to his ancestors, birthplace and origins. In these novels, Naipaul is preoccupied with the idea of reproducing his personal experience of displacement in the fictional form.

In the second chapter two major novels of the next phase are analysed to underline the shift in novelist's treatment of diasporic concern. The novels under study in this chapter are: *The Mimic Men* (1967) and *A Flag on the Island* (1967). These fictional works highlight the clash of cultures in a society that readies itself for transition. The inhabitants of the colonial island even doubt the existence of the place and the significance of the flag of their own. The familiar diasporic theme of identity crisis asserts itself even in an independent island. In the novel *The Mimic Men,* Ralph Singh, an exiled colonial minister undergoes the destiny of being a redundant and retired symbol. A creative sense of the self is created through the portrayal of a representative mimic man. His experience of the unfulfilled love, social and cultural commitment and politics later culminate in his writing. The contradictory elements like past and present, chaos and security, and self and otherness are juxtaposed to reach the desired goals. Ralph is presented as the symbol of postcolonial fiction itself—a fake and a pretender. All pervasive Trinidadian colonial experiences of the writer, touched with his stay in London and his travels, influence his fiction of this phase.

The third chapter carries forward the search of paradigmatic shift in the diasporic ambivalence of the novelist. The novels *Guerrillas* (1975) and *A Bend in the River* (1979) are put under close scrutiny in this chapter. In the novel *Guerrillas* a multi-racial

Caribbean island is highlighted where people sense that they are lost. After getting independence from Britishers, a strange feeling of estrangement haunts their minds, as they feel trapped and uncertain. They still aspire to escape from something unknown and to achieve something formless. Jimmy Ahmed, self-proclaimed revolutionary, seeks to establish a new order, but he fails. *A Bend in the River* is a pessimistic novel about Africa which presents the obvious corruptibility of mankind. Salim, the narrator is a Muslim whose family has lived in Africa for hundreds of years. Being an outsider, he ultimately realizes that his meaningful life is almost at its end and he must give up everything. Salim's ambivalence asserts itself through his statement: "I was in Africa one day; I was in Europe the next morning … it was like being in two places at once … . Both places were real; both places were unreal. You could play off one against the other; and you had no feeling of having made a final decision, a great last journey."[30] The protagonists in these novels are alien immigrant minorities uprooted from their homelands. Naipaul at this juncture poses himself as the writer of the world representing the fragmented or torn self of the postcolonials. His depiction of the inward and outward chaos, decay, and futility among the expatriates is remarkable. Agony of an outsider is again the theme of his novels but with the paradigmatic shift, i.e., during this phase the writer seems to have developed the understanding that the feeling of alienation, homelessness, ambivalence and meaninglessness do not only haunt the displaced Indians in Trinidad, but it is also common among the diasporic people in all the colonial societies. The protagonists, in these novels, are men adrift in an alien world and they constantly try to assert their individual self, and hence are in a never-ending conflict with the society.

In the fourth chapter an attempt has been made to trace the progressive shift in Naipaul's treatment of the dominant theme, i.e., the theme of diasporic ambivalence. The novels under discussion are *Half a Life* (2001) and *Magic Seeds* (2004). *Half a Life* explores tensions—racial, cultural, political, linguistic, spiritual, or sexual. Willie Chandran, a writer, like all other protagonists feels partially adrift as he is vulnerable to these obsessing tensions. The novel suggests the incompleteness or the lack of wholeness of life through the word—"half". *Magic Seeds,* declared as the last novel by Naipaul himself, is the continuation of the theme introduced in Naipaul's *Half a Life*—a man of Indian birth who has wandered the world listlessly looking for a meaning in his life. Willie Chandran gets separated from his wife and starts living with his sister in Berlin. He is convinced to go back to India, to realize his purpose by fighting with revolutionaries for the emancipation of lower castes. But to his surprise, he finds among the revolutionaries the people like him who are searching for a meaning in life. The people whom they intend to free are just a medium for their own struggle for liberation from the bondage of dilemma.

In these novels, the writer is very close to have a rather mature outlook because now he finds the theme of diasporic ambivalence prevailing everywhere, i.e., in colonial world as well as in the imperial world. Naipaul here attains a universal understanding after his long stay in London and undertaking the journeys in almost all the parts of the world. Undermining all his nostalgic diasporic longings and desire to belong either to Trinidad, India or England, now he defends assimilation of cultures, though it is quite an obscure idea for an expatriate. His defense of assimilation is based on his understanding of the postcolonial world after traveling far and wide. He seems to have reached to the conclusion that ambivalence, frustration, isolation, uprootedness, alienation, homelessness and sense of insecurity are common traits in all cultures in the modern time and the search for stability is well nigh irrelevent.

The "Conclusion" brings into sharp focus the diverse patterns of ambivalence underlying existential search of "a portion of the earth" that runs beneath Naipaul's fictional works from the beginning to end. An analysis is made as how the past, in Naipaul's fiction, asserts itself through appreciation of tradition and how the former colonial subjects, dispossessed of their native tradition, are obsessed with regaining a distinctive identity. His travels along with his personal experience of rootlessness, made him emphatic in presenting the alienating effects of colonial past on today's postcolonial people. Moreover, his unparalleled emotional bond with India and sometimes Trinidad made him waver continually as to which country he really belongs. The book observes Naipaul's personal displacement from his birth place for a settled life abroad and his consequent "enigma of arrival" at London as an expatriate marking the lives of all the protagonists in his fiction. His aspirations connected to a "promised-land" end in a deep sense of anguish and disillusionment that gets reflected in his works produced in different phases of his literary career.

Notes

1. V.S. Naipaul, "Prolologue to an Autobiography," *Literary Occasions: Essays*, ed. Pankaj Mishra (New Delhi: Picador, 2003) p. 67.
2. Ibid., p. 89.

3. N. Jayaram, *The Indian Diaspora: Dynamics of Migration* (New Delhi: Sage Publications, 2004) p. 16.
4. Denise Dresner and Brigid Avison, eds. *The Hutchinson Encyclopedia*, London, 1998 Edition, p. 567.
5. N. Jayaram, *The Indian Diaspora: Dynamics of Migration*, op. cit., p. 16.
6. Edward W. Said, *Culture and Imperialism* (London: Vintage, 1994) p. 407.
7. Quoted in Manjit Inder Singh, *V.S. Naipaul* (Jaipur and New Delhi: Rawat Publications, 2002) p. 59.
8. David Ormerod, "In a Derelict Land," *Critical Perspectives on V.S. Naipaul*, ed. R.D. Hammer (Washington, D.C.: Three Continents Press, 1977) p. 171.
9. Dennis Walder, *Post-Colonial Literatures in English: History, Language, Theory* (Oxford: Blackwell, 2005) pp. 2–3.
10. Bruce King, "Introduction," *West Indian Literature*, ed. Bruce King (London: Macmillan, 1979) pp. 6–7.
11. Ashis Nandy, "Preface," *The Intimate Enemy: Loss and Recovery of Self Under Colonialism* (New Delhi: Oxford University Press, 1983) p. xi.
12. David B. Guralnic, ed. *Webster's New World College Dictionary*, Third Edition, 1997, p. 43.
13. Tapas K. Roy Choudhury, "Ambivalence, Colonial Text and Tagore," *Summerhill IIAS Review*, Shimla, Vol. XII. No. 2, 2006, p. 25.
14. Quoted in Benita Parry, *Postcolonial Studies: A Materialist Critique* (London: Routledge, 2004) p. 4.
15. V.S. Naipaul, *The Middle Passage* (London: Andre Deutsch, 1962) pp. 43–44.
16. Derek Walcott, "Interview with V.S. Naipaul," *The Sunday Guardian* (Trinidad) 7 March 1965, p. 5.
17. Patrick Williams, "Edward Said: 1935–2003," *Contemporary Critical Theorists: From Lacan to Said*, ed. Jon Simons (Delhi: Atlantic Publishers, 2005) p. 269.
18. V.S. Naipaul, "Prolologue to an Autobiography," *Literary Occasions: Essays*, op. cit., p. 73.
19. V.S. Naipaul, *A House for Mr Biswas* (Harmondsworth: Penguin, 1961) p. 374.
20. V.S. Naipaul, *Finding the Centre* (Harmondsworth: Penguin Books, 1985) p. 72.
21. V.S. Naipaul, interview with Nigel Bingham, *The Listener*, 7 September 1972, p. 306.

22. V.S. Naipaul, "Foreword to A House for Mr Biswas," *Literary Occasions: Essays*, op. cit., p. 128.
23. Ibid., p. 131.
24. V.S. Naipaul, "Conrad's Darkness," *The Return of Eva Peron with the Killings in Trinidad* (Harmondsworth: Penguin, 1981) p. 210.
25. V.S. Naipaul, "Prolologue to an Autobiography," *Literary Occasions: Essays*, op. cit., p. 90.
26. Ibid., p. 77.
27. Bruce King, *V.S. Naipaul* (London: Macmillan, 1993) p. 42.
28. V.S. Naipaul, *The Middle Passage*, op. cit., p. 42.
29. Bruce King, *V.S. Naipaul*, op. cit., p. 2.
30. V.S. Naipaul, *A Bend in the River* (New Delhi: Clarion Books, 1980) p. 246.

1

Colliding with the "Other"

The worldwide cultural, economic and political changes resulted in the emergence of diasporic writing by the prominent writers such as Joseph Conrad, Chinua Achebe, Wole Soyinka, Nadine Gordimer, Derek Walcott, Margaret Atwood, Michael Ondaatje, Salman Rushdie and V.S. Naipaul, to name only a few. These writers represented the generation that had to encounter the struggle that resulted from the withdrawal of imperial order and the resultant cultural confusion. Though all these diasporic writers hold a sway over the perceptive reader, Naipaul seems inimitable among the popular postcolonial novelists because of his exceptional handling of common diasporic experiences. On account of his family and Trinidadian circumstances he is an expatriate who has started with no other resources than his steadfastness and the elegance that he has developed through hard work. For his first twenty years stay in England, he has never felt at home and still recognizes himself as an outsider.

As a sensitive person belonging to the Asian Indian minority in Black-dominated Trinidad, his perspective on decolonization, imperialism, Black-White relations and other themes of postcolonial literatures is more mature and complicated than that of so-called nationalists and their foreign sympathizers. He regards himself as a former colonial who has become a homeless cosmopolitan. Owing to his ability to write more about himself and his past, he can be seen as someone who has projected much of his personal experience of the contemporary world into literature. His unique experience is representative of the major social, psychological, political and cultural changes of our time. His views often have the effect of paradox and surprise necessitating a re-examination of received notions and opinions. He condemns his contemporaries who consider him as a West Indian patronized writer with a parochial vision. A severe critic of India and the shortcomings of the newly independent nations, he is also a nationalist who feels humiliated by the weaknesses and exploitation of the colonized. He maintains an ambivalent attitude towards European imperialism as it accounts for poverty, exploitation and degradation in the formerly colonized countries; but at times he defends it for bringing peace and modern thought to areas of the world that remained uncultured and debilitated by continual local wars. There is a general refusal to sentimentalize England or the former colonies in his works.

Naipaul's early novels represent East-Indian Trinidadian community into which he was born and brought up. The historical experiences of the multicultural Trinidadian community typify the narrowness of a community employed almost exclusively in agricultural labour under indenture system. They carry with them mainly a rural experience of British India, their inherent differences and their native cultural contexts through the migratory process. Their fondness for home culture and its associated implications are integral parts of their being.

Gradually, the emigrant communities that settled as labour class multiplied, and by the mid-twentieth century these expatriates claimed the major portion of the population of Trinidad. Nasser Mustapha has given a data-based account of the Indian immigrants when he observes:

> The majority of Indian immigrants coming to the Caribbean were from the United Provinces (UP) and Bihar .... The Indians who came to the Caribbean tried to recapture their religion as they knew it back in India, and to establish it under the new and challenging circumstances. They viewed the wider Creole society ... with suspicion .... Being separated from their families back in India, religion served as a bond with their homeland during their supposedly temporary sojourn in this strange land. Religion gave their lives direction and a sense of completeness ... .[1]

The concept of acculturation affected the overseas communities in due course, and East-Indian communities of Trinidad underwent a sort of osmosis. In their deliberate efforts to preserve their customs, rites, traditions, religion, language, caste beliefs and their family patterns, they got themselves transformed so as to familiarize themselves to the colonial setting of creolized society of Trinidad. Trinidad being a creole society comprising heterogeneous racial groups, it was impossible for the East Indian expatriates in Trinidad to maintain their homogeneous cultural identity. It was quite obvious that these displaced people, uprooted from their real homes, should find themselves out of place in an alien land. Though East-Indian villagers were initially conservative in their outlook, a noticeable shift was observed even among these isolated rural communities also. The East-Indians of the urban areas in Trinidad, however, became the most deracinated of the group, and their ultimate assimilation into the society in general has been understood as a development of the universal metropolitan setting.

In his early fiction, V.S. Naipaul captures twice-torn and displaced immigrants oscillating between home culture and alien culture on the one hand and obviously fascinated by the sophisticated culture of the Westerners on the other hand. The novels expose the essential ambivalence of East-Indian emigrants at Trinidad seeking belongingness and affiliation there in the West. To present the apparent cultural confusion has been the obsession of diasporic writing, but V.S. Naipaul's account of these dispossessed is based on his first-hand experience and thus seems quite authentic. Jasbir Jain elucidates:

> There is need to realise the significance of the cultural encounter which takes place in diasporic writing, the bicultural pulls and creation of a new culture which finally emerges ... . Diasporic writing has developed ... a double vision ... . The expatriate as he moves from one culture to another may need to locate ... in relation to the centre.[2]

Concerned with the colonized people's quest for order and individuality, Naipaul makes the colonial characteristic features imperative to his fiction. He perceives his characters as desolate and derelict, persistently struggling to come to terms with colonial push and pull while their individuality is questioned. He is for the most part concerned with the fate of individuals in the colonial society where the restlessness imposed by the colonizing culture holds them back. Gurbhagat Singh elaborates the typical concerns of expatriate writers:

> Expatriate writing, in its theory and practice, is the work of the exile who has experienced unsettlement at the existential, political and metaphysical levels. With this experience, he/she has unsettled the philosophical and aesthetic systems. The phenomenon of exile has emerged in our times due to uneven development within capitalism, and due to the movement forced by colonial powers. The uneven development has led to unprecedented migration of the Asians and Africans to the West ... . This movement has produced a new person whose mind works at least with two epistemologies.[3]

Naipaul's early fiction brought West Indian novel into the mainstream of contemporary English language fiction at a time when Derek Walcott was giving shape to West Indian poetry and drama to attract international attention. *The Mystic Masseur* (1957) is Naipaul's first full-length published novel though it was written after *Miguel Street* which could come out after *The Mystic Masseur* and *The Suffrage of Elvira*. Emigrant East-Indians and their Trinidadian locality form the background of the novel. Trinidad, an effervescent meeting place of different races and cultures, becomes a centre of neglect in *The Mystic Masseur*. The life-long journey of the protagonist of the novel symbolizes a common experience of the entire East-Indian community at Trinidad. Move of Ganesh from isolated rural existence to city life and creolization ultimately signifies a transformation of an expatriate Indian from an East Indian identity to the West Indian mixed identity. The acculturation of the East Indians and other migrants in Trinidad is the pivot of these novels. *The Mystic Masseur* is the testimony to his concern for these displaced people with a drifted consciousness. It is the heart-rending story of a man's deliberate negation of his origins in his material pursuits. It recounts the reverse tale of the process not of repossession, but of defeat—of how Ganesh Ramsumair, a Brahmin of Indian origin, turns into G. Ramsay Muir—a mimic man. The drifted Indian expatriates in Trinidad dominate Naipaul's early works and represent the people with torn-identies. He represents all those contradictory features of Trinidad life that Naipaul wishes to pen down. Ganesh in *The Mystic Masseur* is a representative of an expatriate lost in island's essential hybridity.

Besides, Ganesh represents the characteristic East-Indian emigrants' aspirations and ambitions in the cultural, economic, political, and social backdrop of Trinidad. He starts his career as a school teacher after successfully completing secondary school education and the basics of teacher training. He enriches his education with his flamboyancy as a pundit after inheriting the partial understanding of his uncle's Sanskrit texts in due course of time. He is a master trickster who can mould the state of affairs according to his own designs. Ganesh's career is shown as a tale of success as he begins as a struggling masseur and rises to occupy the highest position of the Member of British Empire, something which his fragmented society could not offer. For example, he applies psychological treatment and pretentious gestures of exorcism while treating the boy haunted by a black cloud. The narrator of *The Mystic Masseur* rightly affirms in his introductory remarks: "I myself believe that the history of Ganesh is, in a way, the history of our times … ."[4] The narrator announces the mock-heroic dimension of the novel's political fable through this statement.

Naipaul gives the name of a Hindu god to the protagonist of his first novel and then makes him speed up his conversion into

G. Ramsay Muir, Member of British Empire (MBE). It is a premeditated attempt of the novelist to project the conflicting pulls attracting Ganesh. His political and cultural creolization is caused by the conflation of contrasting tendencies of Hinduism, native culture, colonial education and imperial supremacy. It further results into the shift from native to Creole culture. He best represents Naipaul's concern with the colonial hybridity at the wake of large-scale emigration and displacement. The upward move of Ganesh is presented as a symbol of the rise of the first generation of colonial migrants who wickedly exploit the existing social, economic and political opportunities. The inherent expatriate tendency of mimicking among the colonized figures like Ganesh even makes them look down upon their native cultural norms. On his wedding ceremony, as the novelist puts it, "He didn't send the messenger around to give the saffron-dyed rice to friends and relations and announce the wedding. 'That old fashion,' he said. He wanted printed invitations on scalloped and gilt-edged cards". (*The Mystic Masseur*, p. 49)

The sense of inadequacy in Ganesh is unmistakably visible when he goes to the college in Port of Spain. He is subjected to too much embarrassment because of his Indian name leading him to spread a story that he is actually *Gareth*, and not Ganesh. Naipaul is benevolently aware of the pains of adjustment in an alien environment while presenting Ganesh's manoeuvre to hide behind the assumed name *Gareth*. Exploring the hurdles in the preservation of identity in an alien environment is a typical theme in Naipaul's fiction. Further, Ganesh experiences discomforting humiliation during his stay at Queen's Royal College where he puts on customary Indian clothes that give him the look of an East-Indian villager. The common practice among immigrant Indians at Trinidad to take on English names suggests that these displaced people find it easier said than done to preserve their cultural identity in the multicultural colonial society. However, their sacrifice of their original names does not help them in the long run and in their endeavour to identify with their borrowed setting they experience self-contempt and bitterness. One of the Calypsos composed by Doris and Dorothy rightly mocks the Indians as Indian Sumintras and Ganesh have turned into Emily, Jean and Gareth. When he takes to teaching at Port of Spain, he is humiliated by Miller who comments sarcastically: "… this teaching is a art, but it have all sort of people who think they could come up from the cane field and start teaching in Port of Spain" (*The Mystic Masseur*, p. 26). Ganesh feels happy to leave Port of Spain when he is forced to return to Fourways on his father's death as his sense of intense alienation and resentment in a creole world finds a sort of temporary relief. The narrator adds:

> He had spent five years there but he had never become used to it or felt part of it. It was too big, too noisy, too alien. It was better to be back in Fourways, where he was known and respected and had the double glamour of a college education and a father recently dead. They called him 'sahib'… . (*The Mystic Masseur*, p. 31)

Though his return gives him a sense of temporary relief, his interaction with Port of Spain life and his education induce a vague sense of estrangement in him. He feels very much at home when he is either called a *sahib* or *Teacher Ganesh*, but an unknown or undefined uncertainty starts tormenting him. Naipaul presents with full sympathy his deep sense of dislocation and his groping towards a tangible solution. He is trapped between ancient Indian past and a West Indian Creole present.

Finally, Ganesh's rise from teacher to masseur, masseur to mystic, mystic to Member of Legislative Council (MLC) and M.L.C. to Member of British Empire (MBE) is a sort of mockery of the existing social, political and economic scenario of Trinidad. He does not take his vocation of mystic lightly, he prepares seriously and dedicatedly for his first case as a mystic. Leela wonders: "Anybody would think you was a school child doing homework" (*The Mystic Masseur*, p. 128). When he observes the boy haunted by cloud, he notices his condition with genuine sympathy and concern. There is no indication of the fraud or cheat in his approach as a mystic. Ignoring all the commercial aspects, both Ganesh and Leela are by any means involved in their compassion for the troubled people. Leela shows her concern for the sufferers when she shares Ganesh's excitement saying: "Man I hope you could help the lady out. I feel too sorry for she. She just sit down quiet all the time, not saying anything, she face small with sadness" (*The Mystic Masseur*, p. 131). He takes up an effective psychosomatic approach by maintaining a compassionate identification with his clients. His excessive pretentiousness and pompousness can be noted when he wants to impress the suffering boy through self-praising idioms: "It just can't touch you with me around. I have power over these things, you know. Look around at all these books in this room, and look at all these writings on the wall and all the pictures and everything … So don't frighten". (*The Mystic Masseur*, pp. 129–30)

Though he has attained a remarkable reputation as a mystic, he falters while launching his fresh move towards the unfamiliar world of Port of Spain. On his visit to the Registrar General's office, he feels ashamed of getting clad in his traditional Indian attire and wears typical English clothes. Similarly he feels utter sense of unease while attending Governor's ceremonial dinner as an M.L.C. For him, the whole ritual is humiliating and according to narrator: "The meal was a torture to Ganesh. He felt alien and uncomfortable. He grew sulkier and sulkier and refused all the courses. He felt as if he were a boy again, going to the Queen's Royal College for the first time" (*The Mystic Masseur,* p. 209). Ganesh's in-betweenness and harassing experiences take the reader back to Naipaul's personal ambivalence as an expatriate. Dilemma of the protagonist suggests that though the creole culture is fascinating and tempting, it is never easy to severe one's links with the roots.

The ultimate move of Ganesh from Fuente Grove to Port of Spain after reaching the height of his achievements is a typical anticipated twist in his life. This is not merely a physical shift of an expatriate; it rather signifies the destined mental acceptance and assimilation with the urban poly-culture. It is an essential penultimate condition for a migrant before his much sought after transmigration into the metropolitan culture. The indispensable movement of the protagonist from the ghettos to the hub of economic and political centre is a recurrent theme in all the novels of his early phase. In *A House for Mr Biswas,* Mohun Biswas starts his journey from Parrot Trace that ends with Sikkim Street in Port of Spain. Anand's leaving Trinidad for London is the climax of emblematic colonial sojourn. Similarly, in *Miguel Street,* the residents of the street aspire to merge in the larger culture of London. They keep on mimicking the colonizers until they don't feel unnerved and disillusioned there also. In *The Mystic Masseur,* Ganesh bursts with tears while leaving Fuent Grove for Port of Spain. He seems to be sad not only on leaving Fuente Grove; he rather feels lost over leaving behind something of his past forever. He expresses his deep agony over his departure when he says: "I wish the whole thing did never happen … . I wish I did never become a mystic" (*The Mystic Masseur,* p. 210). He may have presumed to survive in the Creole world of Port of Spain; he will have to surrender his authentic self—a process which has already begun with his giving up *dhoti, koortah* and turban for English suits.

The economic gains make Ganesh compromise with his basic integrity and a cherished sense of the past. His conciliation with the material needs of the world goes on increasing and his austerity gives way to a more subtle and commercialized way of living. Gradually his resistance against the Creole culture grows weaker. It is apparent that while his own attitude undergoes subtle adaptation for the sake of material success, those close to him, Leela, Behary, Suraj Mooma and Ramlogan—almost induce him to use the means he does not endorse initially. The narrator emphatically considers the innocence of Ganesh when he blames Leela and others for their self-centred practices:

> He didn't have the business mind. In fact, he despised it. The Taxi-service was Leela's idea. So was the restaurant, and that could hardly be called a business idea ... and since Fuente Grove was so far from anywhere else, she had to charge a little extra. And then people made a lot of fuss about Beharry's shop. (*The Mystic Masseur*, pp. 152–53)

The attractive advertisement, Ganesh's acquiring of the fleet of taxis and a restaurant, and finally Beharry's rich-look shops all are consistent but unavoidable steps in the absolute commercialization of Ganesh's customs.

Throughout his career, Ganesh had never really lost the reader's sympathy owing to his warmth and humanity. Though following Ganesh's movement to Port of Spain, he reaches the pinnacle of his career by getting himself nominated as M.L.C. and the M.B.E., he loses a sense of affiliation and hearty attachment to any place in Trinidad. One can sense a sort of withdrawal in his attitude. As a political representative, he indulges in all corrupt practices. He takes recourse to walk-outs and other methods of protest to pose himself as a politician deeply concerned with the rights of the commoners. Ganesh and the walk-outs become synonymous to each other. But the narrator exposes his duality when he says: "He exposed scandal after scandal ... for such favours his fees were never high" (*The Mystic Masseur*, p. 213). The award of an M.B.E. by the English authorities in Britain is a gesture based entirely upon the British authorities' misinterpretation of Ganesh's vibrant role in a labour dispute. Mr Stewart, the wandering English-man is a transplanted, ahistorical, and apolitical Kashmiri Hindu manifesting extensive and ubiquitous cultural devaluation. He prompts Ganesh to write which further opens new horizons of brilliant career for the latter. He dedicates his autobiography to "LORD STEWART OF CHICHESTER Friend and Counsellor of Many Years" (*The Mystic Masseur*, p. 42) who died after six months of their fruitful meeting.

Naipaul's fictional story of one of Trinidad's candidates in its first ever elections under universal adult suffrage is, therefore, a mockery of the colonies not used to democratic practices. The healthy and much experimented political practices of England are transplanted in the colonies like Trinidad. Naipaul presents the typical mimicry of an established system in the novels of the early phase and more elaborately in *The Suffrage of Elvira* and *The Mystic Masseur*. He creatively brings together characteristics of various newly emerging mimicking political leaders. Ganesh's rise to political eminence occurs immediately after the Second World War when the British were voluntarily trying to dissociate themselves from their colonies. It was an intermediary phase when only ostentatious individuals rather than party organization and ideologies were projected at political fronts. It was remarkably a period when Trinidadian politics was notably corrupt and when some of the politicians were London returned educated people. Indarsingh represents such British returned smart politicians in the novel. Inefficient and ineffectual political figures like Indarsingh recur in Naipaul's early novels. They are hardly accepted by the Trinidadians back home and their illusive ideas do not appeal to the voters who have developed superficial apathy for everything that is English. His high profile political campaign is highlighted thus by the narrator:

> His speeches were long, carefully thought-out things—later published by the author in book form with the title *Colonialism: Four Essays*—about The Economics of Colonialism, Colonialism in Perspective, The Anatomy of Oppression, The Approach to Freedom ... . illustrating his arguments with diagrams ... . (*The Mystic Masseur*, p. 201)

The borrowed metropolitan practices do not make anything happen and Indarsingh's sophisticated canvassing ends in his defeat. British political culture in Trinidad in 1946, which was marked by absence of education, political ethics, nationhood and a common history, is ridiculed in the novel. Subsequently, the inference of the novelist's intention may be that the island was not yet ready for such Herculean political task. Naipaul's ambivalence about postcolonial political potential in Trinidadian context gets an explicit expression in the novel. It places him with a large group of other postcolonial writers who are preoccupied with this theme of indefinite and uncertain future of the just-liberated colonies.

George Lamming castigates Naipaul for his condemnation of colonial experiences and goes to the extent of saying that his early books can't move beyond a castrated satire. His criticism seems to rest on the claim that: "When such a writer is a colonial, ashamed of his cultural background and striving like mad to prove himself through promotion to the peaks of a 'superior' culture whose values are gravely in doubt, then satire, like the charge of philistinism, is for me nothing more than a refuge."[5] Lamming's accusation is that Naipaul's outlook is essentially Eurocentric and therefore cultural values, which provide the gist for satire, irony, or farce in the novels, are judged by a Westernized and antagonistic moral and civil code. In response to Lamming's charge that Naipaul's early novels are *castrated satire*, Gordon Rohlehr chooses to point out that:

> Lamming can see little that is visible in a society whose history is one of underprivileged. One appreciates his point. The early Naipaul is at times the irresponsible ironist, subtle, but lacking in a sensitive participation in the life he anatomises .... Satire is the sensitive measure of a society's departure from the norm inherent in itself. Since Naipaul starts with the conviction that such a norm is absent from his society, his task as satirist becomes doubly difficult .... [6]

The ambivalence that strikes the readers in Naipaul's early novels is owing to the essential oscillation between sympathy and antipathy in his treatment of the themes concerning postcolonial practices in Trinidad. In *The Mystic Masseur*, the use and misuse of the Indian Hindu tradition's prolonged existence and religious practices are subject to ruthless satire. The novelist stresses the elaborate use of ancient native cultural capital by Ganesh for material gains. The subsequent political dividends he is able to enjoy have nothing to do with any vision enriching native culture; rather, he performs elaborate rituals just for the sake of worldly gains. However, dual and binary inclinations of Ganesh ultimately make him self-reliant. The economic development within a colonial setting overrules the need for cultural struggle and its frequently associated nationalistic idiom. Ironically, the disclosure of fraud in the novel suggests the intrinsic repelling tendencies inherent among the colonized. Thus the novel institutes the foundation for Naipaul's subsequent notion of the opportunism of Trinidad's political milieu in *The Middle Pasage*, which also forms the basis for most of his later analyses of postcolonial circumstances. Thus Ganesh's story suggests that one individual's story is the nation's story too. To justify the commonality of diasporic sensibility, Cudjoe asserts: "What begins as a purely particular and parochial matter becomes a general and national matter, and in the process that is purely Hindu merges with the general and socio-political history of the country."[7]

The migrants keep on compromising Hinduism and the practices attached to it at every juncture. The crossing of the ocean by the indentured labourers from India is an assault upon essential Hindu dogma. Thus the profound contradictions inherent in the religion's fearful hierarchy of prohibitions discredit its relevance in a democratic polity. Naipaul's descriptions of the rituals practiced by the Indian expatriates, therefore, are almost always self-contradictory.

As a part of Ganesh's initiation ceremony, when he is symbolically asked to go to Benaras to study, he literally takes his staff and starts walking briskly from Fourways. The shopkeeper named Dookhie runs after him saying, "No, boy. No. Don't go away to Benares to study … . Cut out this non-sense, man. Stop behaving stupid. You think I have all day to run after you? You think you really going to Benares? That is in India, you know, and this is Trinidad". (*The Mystic Masseur,* p. 21)

Accordingly, the novel stresses the vital irreparable inconsistency between home culture and the borrowed culture. Ganesh tries to transplant the Indian practices in Trinidad when he believes that reading by any light other than daylight is harmful and according to the narrator, he goes to "sleep with the hens and woke before the cocks" (*The Mystic Masseur,* p. 21). The novel delineates colonial hybridity of the Hindu East Indian community in the larger Trinidadian political and sociological scenario. It is the first among many novels of Naipaul, which demonstrate his account of the varying concept of postcolonial nationalism. The relocated denizens resist the novelty of their acquired structure by imitating the cultural referents of irrevocable traditions. Therefore, the novel illustrates the first sketch of a colonial mimic man.

In *The Mystic Masseur,* Ganesh is the self-made hero of the typical nineteenth century novel treated in terms of a despoiled society which hardly offers any opportunity for innovation. Ganesh defies the conventional norms by refusing to marry the woman his father chooses and by quitting his teaching job. He has a strong sense of himself as destined for something larger than what exists in contemporary Trinidad. He endeavours to find a distinct role, first as a mystic masseur, and then as a shrewd politician. He enjoys the courtesy of Ramlogan and others for his survival until he can launch himself as a successful entrepreneur. Later, as a celebrated spiritualist, he maintains a fleet of taxis and a restaurants. Instinctively, he realizes that his friendship with books will facilitate him to realize his long cherished dreams. He uses client-psychology and expert salesmanship to restore the health of his patients. He not only reconstructs himself by continually rewriting his history and adopting new identities, but also brings together the codes of various cultures of Trinidad—Hindu, Moslem, Christian—modern and traditional. He even uses, according to circumstances, English, regional Fuente Grove dialect, Hindi and a bit of Spanish. He offers an ironic, Trinidadian version of a rags-to-riches story. He is the epitome of Trinidadians of the Indian diaspora, remaking themselves, in ways that are necessarily unsophisticated, unruly, and clownish. The novel portrays the jumbled attitudes of aversion, indulgence, gratification and acceptance along with hilarity. Ganesh Ramsumair's metamorphosis into G. Ramsay Muir M.B.E. suggests that his career signifies the protagonist's expedition towards *Whiteness*. It is a conceit that persists in all of Naipaul's works as if *Whiteness* is the predetermined end of all colonial cultural identity-formations. Lamming's and Rohlehr's views on the function of satire and irony in Naipaul's early works acknowledge the inherent ambivalence in the choice of referents Naipaul adopts. Naipaul's early works are most effective in the figurative consequences of the demonstration of love-hate relationship with the home culture and the borrowed culture and ultimate *self-hatred*. Though Naipaul's early novels have a capacity for joy, there has all along been an undercurrent of sadness beneath this jollity arising from the comic altercations of imperial arrogance and colonial aspiration. Like his other Trinidad stories, *The Mystic Masseur* is also about a miniature India on the margins of the British Empire, far removed from the original land. The scenes of the restricted life his immediate forefathers had experienced in their exile, have been reproduced. The Trinidad he portrays here is a slice of India. It is a very unhealthy, dwarfed, distorted version of India that has been transported across some thousands of nautical miles half a century before but it still smacks of its Indianness.

A casual reading of *The Mystic Masseur* may suggest it to be a pleasurable, entertaining parody about a wayward swindler's upward journey and ensuing deterioration in the constricted social framework of a secluded Caribbean island. But an analytical and insightful reading makes the reader observe the underlying twentieth century uncertainties and damaging effects of imperialism upon the people of the Third World. Cultural hostility, deracination indicative of life in exile, and the ultimate annihilation of the self mark the lives of the Indian expatriates in Trinidad. The apparently humorous story of Ganesh's quest for recognition and achievement is thus a reversed image for the distressing experience of insecurity, uncertainty, disappointment and fissure that is the lot of the marginalized man displaced from the familial soil and tossed away indifferently on some rocky shore with its unfamiliar geographical and cultural landscape, its inevitably imperfect fortunes and probabilities. Lillian Feder rightly notes:

> The comedy *The Mystic Masseur* ... is undercut by the reality that the characters are trapped by the poverty of their education, the lack of opportunities for intellectual and cultural development in their surroundings and, no doubt as a result, the shallowness of

their emotional lives. Yet some aspire to improve their lot by any means they can devise … . His [Ganesh's] struggle is both pathetic and comic.[8]

Underneath Ganesh's comedy runs a catastrophic awareness of an estranged, disjointed, expatriate Indian in exile, who is alienated not only from the ancestral surroundings but also from his very self. The realization of parting from the "homeland" i.e., India, and a longing for the retreat is unequivocally presented by the novelist. Naipaul cautiously confirms as to how both he and the society he depicts are haunted by ancestral memories through his projection of Trinidadian India. Nostalgic hangover of roots continuously poses a threat to the immediate environment. Artistic representation of the past in the novel is a parody of India, which fails to replace the real India, and remains an agonizing mockery of the authentic.

The narrator narrates the tale of a mystic masseur turned writer and politician by recollecting his childhood encounter with a masseur and from Ganesh's own autobiography. The narrator asks his mother on the eve of his first meeting with masseur about the identity of Ganesh. But his mother scolds him annoyingly for his ignorance about Ganesh whose popularity has already become the talk of the town. The same question reappears in Trinidad Sentinel in less than a year later. The persistent enquiries about his identity establish him as an extraordinary colonial. Actually it is the story of a typical Indian-born enthusiastic youth in Trinidad in early twentieth century. He fails to attain any genuine distinctiveness so he keeps on experimenting with various vocations. His contracted circumstances force him to adopt trickery and dishonesty, which eventually make him lose even the insubstantial identity of a displaced Indian and his emergence as the "mimic man"—Mr G. Ramsay Muir, M.B.E.

The history of Ganesh signifies the tale of the displaced émigrés who have been separated from their "roots" and are caught in an everlasting tension between present and past, reality and imagination, *self* and *other*. They fail to realize a sense of self-gratification or the security of an identity in the alien land. The ridiculousness of the dilemma is best reflected through the figure of Ganesh Ramsumair and his type by comical and ironical handling. The awkwardness of his situation preoccupies his mind since childhood when he feels ashamed of his Indian identity and burdens himself with a pseudo identity by declaring his name as *Gareth*. His manners are essentially coarse and unrefined: "He continued to dress badly, he didn't play games, and his accent remained too clearly that of the Indian from the country" (*The Mystic Masseur*, pp. 20–21). The initiation-ceremony episode is quite significant as people here are seen as being trapped between the two versions of India—the one remotely prevailing and directing the life and consciousness of the *mimic* here, and the other as reproduced in the creole world. This is at the root of much of the unusually traced comic taste of the book. The individual is represented in alien surroundings where he is actually conscious of his loss of connection with his native culture. He regrets the loss of nourishing native convention and lives provisional life in temporary homes which are devoid of warmth and vibrance. The landscape and geographical details constantly remind these expatriates that their new locale is not their true India; rather it is Trinidad—"full of crazy people" (*The Mystic Masseur*, p. 17). The panic underlying this awareness comes into view through the description of Fuent Grove which is quite small, remote, wretched, and practically insignificant.

Fuent Grove is a representative unproductive place devoid of vegetation and of delight. While living in London, the narrator brings to his mind the childhood memories of driving the long way to *waste landish* Fuente Grove, "There was no hint of a fountain anywhere, no hint even of water. For miles around the land was flat, treeless and hot … . It was a sad little village …" (*The Mystic Masseur*, p. 12). It is a sterile land overlooking settlers' hopeless endeavour to rebuild an Indian domain in exile. Though they are undermined all the time by the consciousness of the reality of exile, they keep on pipe-dreaming. A contemptible homesickness underlies their conscious and subconscious efforts thus enabling them to re-enact the customs and rituals. They stick to the superstitions and taboos of the lost homeland of the ancestors. They have been imitating typical Indian attitudes, norms and values. Family loyalty, predestination, Indian mythology and contemporary Indian heroes—both political and cinematic—govern their lives. Symbols and mascots of Indian politics, society and culture, Indian lifestyle of eating, washing, dressing, even the language of India continue to hold their sway on the people who are no more Indians. Their daily food, the cuisine and eating manners, including polishing the plate with one's fingers, drinking water in the *orthodox Hindu way*, the loud washing of hands and mouth, Ganesh's *dhoti* and Leela's *sari*, his morning *puja*, the picture of the goddess Laxmi on her lotus in Ganesh's room, all are signs of this life modelled on the norms of life lived by their forefather's generations back.

The names of the personae are obviously Indian. Through the inventory of names—*Ganesh*, *Ramlogan*, *Soomintra*, *Leela*, *Beharry*, *Suruj*, *Dookhy*, *Bisson*, *Basdeo*, *Pratap*, *Phulbassia*, *Sookram*,

Indarsingh and certain Indian gods and goddesses—these isolated and frail expatriates assert their Indianness on the unfamiliar landscape of the island. Ganesh's name also has a mythical overtone which is ironically suggestive of the Hindu god with an elephant face. He is believed to be the god of triumph, insight and learning. He is also believed to be the great scribbler who penned down the Hindu epic *Mahabharata* as uttered by Vyasa. Through this metaphor, the novelist seems to satirise Ganesh's aspirations. Ganesh, the protagonist is the mirror image of Ganesh, the god as he also characterizes double image like the namesake god whose human head is replaced by the head of an elephant. The god reminds one of the twin-identities like that of Ganesh who is divided between two identities, i.e., one native and other borrowed.

Stewart acquires a special implication in the Trinidadian framework dominated by the wretched Indians. Though he is English by birth, he claims that he is an Indian Kashmiri Hindu. He is also shown clad at times in a yellow cotton robe carrying a staff and bundle like a Budhist monk. The *here* and the *there* i.e., Trinidad and India are accordingly presented as counterpoints through Stewart. He even makes clay statuettes of Hindu gods and goddesses. He has also been working on a water colour for years portraying brown hands reaching out for a yellow light. He validates the brown colour adding: "Hindu hands. Only people really striving after the indefinite today" (*The Mystic Masseur,* p. 39). Paradoxically, in spite of all his day-dreaming about India, Stewart does not want to go back to India, as he does not want to get involved. Stewart's embracing of Hindu identity offers a parallel perspective to the central theme presenting ambivalence of a homeless nomad. Ganesh and Stewart are identical and their commonality is even pointed out by Ramlogan. Ganesh also does not betray the connection and he pays his homage to him by dedicating his autobiography to him. Stewart's significance lies in the meaninglessness of his search for an identity in some remote land with an alien and imagined religion which is not his heritage. The term "Hollywood Hindus" (*The Mystic Masseur,* p. 160) that Beharry gives to Americans showing their interest in Ganesh, the Hindu god and Ganesh, the mystic, somehow elaborate Stewart's ambivalence.

Stewart's search that ends up in failure can be taken as an explicit observation of Naipaul on the typical neurosis of his personae in their diasporic existence. This mental illness gets reflected in their outlook, their lifestyle, and in various niceties of their everyday life. Naipaul captures the agony of these displaced people incessantly looking for an inaccessible native soil in terms of comparison and contrast, and the balance always apparently inclining in favour of *there*. Rama Kundu rightly observes:

> The creative spectrum of Naipaul's works, from *The Mystic Masseur* (1957) to *Half a Life* (2001), repeatedly brings out Naipaul's inability to leave India behind him ... his inability to integrate his ancestral past with his diasporic present and and loving-fond-impassioned-embittered—deconstruction of the icon that is India.[9]

The success and failure of these *wretched of the earth* in Trinidad is measured in terms of the success and failure of Indian people. The narrator's mother makes the ailing boy understand the eminence and worth of the masseur saying: "But Ganesh ain't the fool you think he is. He is the sorta man who woulda be a rishi in India. The day go come when you go be proud to tell people that you did know Ganesh" (*The Mystic Masseur,* p. 17). India is, in their loving imagination, the paradise where only the good and pleasing things can come to pass. Justifiably, India and Indians become Ganesh's great love. While buying a book, he examines the index first to understand whether there are any references to India and Hinduism. He buys the book only if there are complimentary references.

Soon after, when Ganesh turns into a clever politician, he arouses the dormant Hindu consciousness of Indian migrant audience at Trinidad by passing complimentary remarks about their native religion to get applause and approving responses from them. These are the well-designed and politically motivated speeches to escalate the Indian sense of self. He addresses the political gatherings in the form of prayer meetings intermittently using Indian references in Hindi. For example, he says:

> ... I am a candidate for the elections next month. I can compromise nothing. In everything I shall consult God and my conscience, even at the risk of displeasing you ... . We were talking, you remember, about the transmigration of souls. Now, this theory was also put forward by a philosopher of Ancient Greece, but I have brought along some books tonight to show you that it is more than likely that the Greek got the idea from India. (*The Mystic Masseur,* p. 199)

He gives a ceremonial touch to his political meetings and sits below a statue of Hanuman, the Hindu god and recites a long Hindi prayer before supposedly sprinkling Ganga water over the assembled people. The week before polling day, Ganesh organizes a Bhagwat or prayer meeting which is a common sacrosanct practice still popular among devout Hindus in India. Even the rituals of funeral and marriage are not personal occasions; they rather take the shape of community events to be shared and celebrated by the whole family and the village. The Indian miniature community at Trinidad simply considers it their sole responsibility to get together to console Ganesh on his father's death. They take command of everything because they feel: "Oh Ganeshwa boy, at a time like this you want your own family around you" (*The Mystic Masseur,* p. 47). The rites are as authentically performed as possible in accordance with the standard norms of India. Similarly, the host of uninvited people gather at his house on the eve of his marriage ceremony. They usually refer both to the olden and the present-day India in their talks.

While discussing the repercussions of the world war, Ganesh shows his frustration when he wishes: "... Hitler would come over and start bombing up Trinidad" (*The Mystic Masseur,* p. 112). But Beharry stresses the insignificance of island in the world order when he comments: "But you forgetting that we is just a tiny little dot on some maps ... . I think Hitler ain't even know it have a place called Trinidad ..." (*The Mystic Masseur,* p. 112). During the turbulent times of world war, they seek a refuge in Indian memories and recollect the war of *Mahabharata*: "Beharry was full of quotations from the Gita, and Ganesh read again, with fuller appreciation, the dialogue between Arjuna and Krishna on the field of battle" (*The Mystic Masseur,* p. 113). Leela's evolving into a good Hindu wife and Ganesh's wearing his father's old *dhoti* and *koorta* to look like a devout Brahmin are other examples suggesting their adherence to native Indian culture. Beharry insists on wearing their original dress by more and more Indians. The taxi-drivers enjoy singing Hindi songs on the road to Fuente Grove and such taxi-drivers hang up "a framed picture, issued by the Gita Press of Gorakhpur in India, of the goddess Laxmi standing, as usual, on her lotus" (*The Mystic Masseur,* p. 147) instead of the display of tariff. Ganesh puts up on his drawing room wall a photograph of a simpering Indian film-actress. When Ganesh prospers and decides to get a temple built, an Indian architect from British Guiana is invited to build a temple in proper Hindu style. Their firm belief in fate, providence and omens characterizes the typical Indian approach that seem to preoccupy and oversee their lives at every turn. Again in their routine life they keep on referring to Indian icons like Gandhi or Jawaharlal. Soomintra, the daughter of Ramlogan feels proud in naming her son Jawaharlal "after the Indian leader; and her daughter was called Sarojini, after the Indian poetess" (*The Mystic Masseur,* p. 85). She reveals her plan for the baby in her womb saying, "... if he is a boy, I go call him Motilal; if she is a girl I go call she Kamala" (*The Mystic Masseur,* p. 85). When Ganesh feels disturbed over Narayan's incessant assaults, he asks Beharry as to what Mahatma Gandhi would do in a situation like this.

On the publication of Ganesh's *101 Questions and Answers on the Hindu Religion,* Ramlogan pompously reads out certain questions from his son-in-law's first book. There are questions like "Who is the greatest modern Hindu?" and "Who is the second greatest modern Hindu?" (*The Mystic Masseur,* p. 96) followed by their answers "Mahatama Gandhi" and "Pandit Jawaharlal Nehru" respectively. Ganesh even sends a copy of his first book to Mahatma Gandhi. The spare space of a local Trinidadian magazine is filled up with quotations from the Gita or the Upanishads. Similarly when Ganesh plans to launch his own paper his partner Pratap expresses his reverence for Gandhi. He declares: "If I did ever start up a paper, I would dedicate it to Mahatma Gandhi" (*The Mystic Masseur,* p. 174) but ironically Pratap devises unfair means to manage "a block with Gandhi picture from the Sentinel office" (*The Mystic Masseur,* p. 174). Narayan, the president of the Hindu Association of Trinidad feels proud while sitting wrapped with the saffron, white and green Indian tricolour. The boy who sees the ridiculousness of using Gandhi for vested interests presents the essential irony of the mimicry. He adds: "But I wonder what people go say when they see in one side the page dedication to Mahatma Gandhi and in the other side attack, attack". (*The Mystic Masseur,* p. 175)

Even in their local political bickering they try to reinforce their status by showing their association with someone important from India. On his election as the President of the Hindu Association of Trinidad, Narayan sends: "... cables to India, to Mahatma Gandhi, Pandit Nehru and the All-India Congress; in addition to anniversary cables of all sorts: he noted centenaries, bicentenaries, tercentenaries. And every time he sent a cable the news was reported in the *Trinidad Sentinel*". (*The Mystic Masseur,* p. 166)

Similarly, when Ganesh becomes the President of the same association after ousting Narayan with depraved means, what he does first is to send a cable to the All-India Congress. The telegram reads as: "KEEP MAHATMAJI IDEALS ALIVE STOP HINDU ASSOCIATION TRINIDAD WITH YOU INDEPENDENCE STRUGGLE STOP BEST WISHES" (*The Mystic Masseur,* p. 197). Even Indarsingh, the absurd *mimic man* finds it crucial to compromise his racial ideology by introducing the concept of "Socialinduism". (*The Mystic Masseur,* p. 217)

After a close scrutiny of episodes suggesting penetration of India and "Indian" in the lives of expatriates in Trinidad, *The Mystic*

Masseur seems to present the enigma of Naipaul himself. Lillian Feder also holds this view when he observes:

> Naipaul's contradictory ties to his ancestral heritage rooted in the Indian community in Trinidad, trapped in the poverty, the limited opportunities of amelioration ... yet sustained by a 'community identity' forged out of the 'independence movement, the India of the great names' and its past grandeur.[10]

Ganesh's progress in the desolate setting of Caribbean Colonial Island may be viewed as a caricatured description of the representative search for the recognition of self. The typical diasporic quest meets anticipated disappointment and bewilderment as the split self which is a necessary condition of life in exile, does not get nourishment from the unfamiliar soil. Sooner or later, the tormented self of the émigré is bound to decline into ludicrous poignant moral decadence. The cautious description of the sterility of the Fuente Grove where no plants, except sugarcanes strike roots is highly symbolic of its inhabitants' impotency and irrelevance.

The alternating use of correct "standard" English and the creolized vernacular dialect nevertheless suggests the continuing influence of Hindi on the speakers of the island. Though, now and then, Ganesh and the expatriates of his type prefer severing the linguistic bonds with Hindi to harness the benefits of colony and to enable themselves to be proficient in standard English, they find it extremely difficult. One day he asks Leela, "Leela, is high time, we realise that we living in British country and I think we shouldn't be shame to talk the people language good" (*The Mystic Masseur,* p. 76). Leela also shows her eagerness to start with pure English. But as soon as Ganesh starts with the first statement, he wobbles, uttering: "Good. Let me see now. Ah, yes. Leela, have you lighted the fire? No, just gimme a chance. Is "lighted" or "lit" girl?" (*The Mystic Masseur,* p. 77). When Leela takes her turn, she is also subjected to mockery. Beharry accepts this idea as "a master idea" but as Ganesh starts getting pace, he starts laughing over him with sarcastic comments: "Ganesh, you know you look damn funny". (*The Mystic Masseur,* p. 77)

However, creation of links between the ancestral home and the island of exile, and mimicking alteration of the former under the burden of imposing imperial history is a sort of personal craving for Naipaul. The informal interaction in the novel shows grafting of English words into the sentence structure of Hindi language and vice-versa. For example the expressions "prutty, prutty things," "he thinking, thinking all the time" (*The Mystic Masseur,* p. 27), and compressions like "two-three months" (*The Mystic Masseur,* p. 21) etc., point towards the out of order, distorted, silly language of a populace jerked away from their roots, and forced to take up the socio-linguistic habits of others. This vacillation between two languages actually brings out the author's personally experienced sense of absurdity of the exile life. Naipaul's endeavours to bring forth the mockery of these people by pointing out certain peculiarities in their lifestyle and language used by Ganesh and others is one of the most peculiar features underlining the typical predicament possessing their lives. Ashok Mitra furnishes a typical analysis of the Naipaulian state of mind when he says: "Naipaul had a precise ear for the nuances of English prose which he developed to capture the magic of West Indian living, its quirks and follies, its delights and sorrows, its lightness and pains."[11]

Indarsingh who comes to a Bhagwat in an Oxford blazer, is introduced in a typical Indianized English by Swami: "I got to talk English to introduce this man to you, because I don't think he could talk any Hindi. But I think all of all you go agree with me that he does talk English like a pukka Englishman ... Ladies and gentlemen—Mr Indar Singh, Bachelor of Arts of Oxford University, London, England". (*The Mystic Masseur,* p. 204)

He is such a snob that instead of sharing religious feelings at *Bhagwat,* he talks about politics, and so he has to face the joking remarks by Ganesh and also from the narrator for his being a typical mimic man. The irony lies in the fact that after switching from one role to another in swift progression, Ganesh himself proves to be another mimic man like Indarsingh. At the end when the narrator warmly calls out fashionably dressed Pundit Ganesh Ramsumair coming out of first-class carriage, he says "coldly", "G. Ramsay Muir" (*The Mystic Masseur,* p. 220). He has, of course, given a slight hint of the possibility of conversion earlier when, as a school boy he inadequately pretends that his name is "Gareth". It is a clownish conversion of a very serious nature that has haunted Naipaul all along during the early phase of his career. The novelist is preoccupied with the presentation of crisis of identity among Indians in exile.

Ganesh suits the design of Naipaul who intends to reproduce a contemplative, apprehensive, ambiguous and self-beguiling figure like his own through the novel. He keeps on discovering the enigma of his own position and the mysteries underlying the deeper consciousness of an émigré's life. It grabs the attention of an attentive reader that though Ganesh tries to fit himself somewhere in the colonial scheme of things, he fails to reach the state of self-gratification. He is a constant seeker with a mission to undo his anonymity first as a student, then as a teacher, masseur and a mystic. His long-cherished ambitions to be a self-taught scholar and a writer end up in the heterogeneous collection of books and the publication of bizarre booklets. As an apprentice politician in colonial set up, he goes on to reverse his role from the fierce anti-establishment M.L.C. to pro-establishment M.B.E. His continuous search for recognition and identity leads him to a pre-destined ambivalence and a comic failure. Ganesh represents the predetermined destiny of the displaced émigrés under an alien sky which ultimately leads him to seek alliance with the colonizer at the cost of his selfhood and individuality.

Naipaul's attachment with the consciousness of some misplaced "imaginary homeland" that he can not leave behind, gives impetus to his writings. His enduring association with diasporic literature has been taken as a fight back with his own fixation or homesickness. Naipaul's one constant and uninterrupted obsession throughout his career has been the colonial rootlessness forced by imperialism and its far reaching consequences on the psyche of these twice-torn individuals. It is his recollection of the past of the overpowered expatriate marginal men that offers the characteristic essence to his novels. His characters, from Ganesh to Willie Chandran in *Magic Seeds*, are predominantly individuals of Indian past, who are brought up in the British Caribbean islands. They seem to illustrate in concrete terms the exile syndrome which Said too perceptively sums up in his concluding observation in "Reflections on Exile":

> Exile is never the state of being satisfied, placid, or secure. Exile, in the words of Wallace Stevens, is 'a mind of winter' in which the pathos of summer and autumn as much as the potential of spring are nearly but unobtainable. Perhaps this is another way of saying that a life of exile moves according to a different calendar, and is less seasonal and settled than life at home. Exile is life led outside habitual order. It is nomadic, decentred, contrapuntal; but no sooner does one get accustomed to it than its unsettling force erupts anew.[12]

These postcolonial nomads waste their lives fighting against the agony of cultural dislocation and identity crisis. The timid, insecure, wavering, agitated, rootless, meaningless, fickle-minded and ambivalent characters like Ganesh, Harbans, Lorkhoor, Mohun Biswas, Ralph Singh, Bobby, James Ahmed, Salim and William Somerset occupy the centre stage in Naipaul's novels.

Similarly, *A House for Mr Biswas* traces the story of a man's struggle to claim his position in a confined and restricted environment. Although the novel primarily focuses on the community of Hindus from India, this society is seen as a part of the larger society of a colonial Caribbean island. The constant struggle to claim *a portion of the earth* in a colonial setting is a pertinent question linked with the question of survival. *A House for Mr Biswas* considers the world already delineated in the preceding books and develops further the themes already initiated in them. It depicts a social history of the community of indentured labourers from India who have replaced the emancipated Black slaves after the abolition of slavery by England in 1833. Their never-ending isolation, adherence to traditional culture and reverence for Hindu norms of life, form the pivot of the story. S.L. Sharma rightly puts the pathetic condition of the expatriate Indians abroad: "... overseas Indians tend to recreate Indian social structure wherever they go. The second is that they tend to hold fast to their native culture in their lands of adoption. The third is that their mode of adaptation is marked by a clear preference for economic integration more than cultural assimilation".[13]

Their constant search for a permanent foothold captures the attention of Naipaul in *A House for Mr Biswas*. The novel depicts *house* as the predominant metaphor signifying the universal diasporic disorder. The hero of the novel Mohun Biswas represents the psychology of every East-Indian colonial at Trinidad. He endeavours to create something significant and substantial out of the "unimportant, uncreative, cynical"[14] Trinidad.

Biswas is a more complex version of Ganesh as he also follows the same process of growing up from nothing. His sense of alienation and homelessness is perhaps derived from the characters of *Miguel Street*. The Creole multicultural society in which he grows up reminds the reader the crazily mixed-up world of *The Suffrage of Elvira*. His life is a complex tale of an expatriate Indian's ambivalence presenting the typical expatriate sensibility. Mr Biswas, whose life-long ambition is the ownership of a house, finds himself caught in an inescapable trap. The symbol of *house* embodies Naipaul's personal diasporic predicament.

However, Mr Biswas stands different from the protagonists of *The Mystic Masseur*, *Miguel Street* and *The Suffrage of Elvira* as his only concern is to occupy a house and that is also through creative and socially acceptable means. Chandra B. Joshi defends Biswas against Ganesh when he adds: "Without repudiating his name or his religion he concentrates on the task of making a place for himself in the creole world. His search ends with the shaky, jerry-built house he finds himself owner of at the end of his life."[15]

Biswas's dying *accommodated* at the age of forty-six is shown as the big question in the novel. His individual quest for selfhood, identity and coherence in his life terminates with the owning of a house of his own. Though the multiple defects and drawbacks of the house lessen his charm, he is excited because he has now found some meaning in his existence in the world. He exclaims: "How terrible it would have been ... to have lived and died as one had been born, unnecessary and unaccommodated."[16] The darkness, decay, death, horror and disasters recurrent in Biswas's life represent his nothingness and also the nothingness of his surroundings. The unsettled life of an expatriate poses a serious challenge before the nomads like Biswas. In the epilogue, Naipaul shows the depth of this inherent darkness: "This was a darkness that seemed to come from within, as though the skin was murky but transparent film and the flesh below it had been bruised and become diseased and its corruption was rising". (*A House for Mr Biswas*, pp. 587–88)

Mohun Biswas's continual acceptance and condemnation in his own family, in Tulsi family, Sentinel Office, Community Welfare Department and in Trinidadian society as a whole mark the typical dilemma of an unhoused and uprooted expatriate. His constant encounter with oddity, adversity and misfortune make the reader witness the outline history of Trinidad in the first half of the twentieth century. Through Biswas Naipaul presents the deep insight into economic, sociological and historical events responsible for the transformation of Trinidad. Certain economic changes, global wars, introduction of cinema and motor cars, brain-drain, arrival of Americans in bulk, urbanization, etc., have made an impact on the social scenario of Trinidad considerably. Naipaul's obsession however, as N. Ramadevi observes, primarily intends to unfold:

> The gradual Indian accommodation to what was originally a foreign land. The process involves a great deal of sacrifice—a sacrificing of traditions and self-respect leading to an acculturisation and mimicry. First of all the people have to be dispossessed of what is naturally and originally theirs ... a gradual decay of Hindu spirit in the New World which could be evidenced in the marriages of the Tulsi sons to Presbyterian Indians.[17]

Assimilation of immigrant Indians with other societies gives rise to a creole or hybrid culture. Naipaul here takes up the theme of the general history of three generations of East Indians and their struggles to survive and to be accommodated in Trinidad. Mr Biswas's aim in this world is to die as an accommodated individual after claiming his share of land on this earth, which, if viewed from a modern man's perspective, becomes or appears to be a universal problem, the problem of everyman in the modern world. Gordon Rohlehr in his article "The Ironic Approach: The Novels of V.S. Naipaul" comments that certain universal implications can be detected in Biswas's personal struggle:

> Biswas is everyman, wavering between identity and nonentity, and claiming his acquaintance with the rest of them ... if Biswas represents all the things, I feel he does, it is because he is fully presented as a person whose very quirk and idiosyncrasy we know, in a world whose every sight, sound and smell is recorded with fidelity and precision.[18]

The novel focuses on how East-Indian immigrants in Trinidad have been left with nothing but to seek refuge in fatalism. When Biswas's mother complains to her father about the ill-treatment meted out to her by her husband, Raghu, he consoles her uttering: "Fate. There is nothing we can do about it" (*A House for Mr Biswas*, p. 15). The plight of immigrant-indentured labourers from India is the pivot of the novel suggesting their unavoidable helplessness and alienation as they are left with no other option but to curse their destiny. The first generation of indentured labourers at Parrot Trace seems to have established a community life that is in no way different from an Indian village. Naipaul vividly describes the agony of such unwelcomed expatriates missing their past and native culture but now they feel entrapped and experience a common loss. The old Indian-born homesick people gather in the arcade of Tulsis in the evenings only to talk about their retreat to their homeland. Their pipe-dreaming tendency is portrayed by Naipaul when the narrator elaborates:

> They could not speak English and were not interested in the land where they lived; it was a place where they had come for a short time and stayed longer than they expected. They continually talked of going back to India, but when the opportunity came, many refused, afraid of the unknown, afraid to leave the familiar temporariness. (*A House for Mr Biswas*, p. 194)

Naipaul's diasporic ambivalence gets projected when on the one hand he finds these changes inevitable and, on the other hand, he regrets the loss of an ancient Indian way of life in a hybrid and alien world. The multicultural colonial society offers no stability in the present and no hope for the future. The Indians left there are left with no alternative except blind imitation of the imposing imperial culture. In his popular non-fiction *An Area of Darkness,* his ambivalence is more evident: "... we knew there had been change, gain, loss. We knew that something which was once whole had been washed away. What was whole was the idea of India."[19] According to Homi Bhabha: "... gatherings of exiles and émigrés and refugees, gathering on the edge of 'foreign' cultures, gathering at the frontiers; gathering in the ghettos or cafes of city centres"[20] is a sort of movement from nationhood to culture and from historicity to temporality and *hybridity* which may result from exclusion from origins and essences leading these immigrants to an essential creolization of identity. Comparing the expatriates to a banyan tree, Hugh Tinker observes:

> The banyan tree has thrust down roots in soil which is stony, sandy, marshy—and has somehow drawn sustenance from diverse unpromising conditions. Yet the banyan tree itself has changed; its similarity to the original growth is still there, but it has changed in response to its different environment.[21]

Bipti's father represents the first generation immigrants who opted to stay back in Trinidad for the reasons they could not even understand throughout their lives. The Indian emigrants like him form the majority in Trinidad as forty per cent against forty per cent of the blacks. Still, the Indian migrant society in Trinidad is a rootless, temporary and impoverished society. The Creole culture of Trinidad does not even leave the lives of these expatriates unaffected. Instead of cremating, Biswas's father is buried. Part One of the novel vividly presents the condition of the first generation Indians at Trinidad like Bipti's father: "No one paid him any attention. Fate had brought him from India to the sugar-estate, aged him quickly and left him to die in a crumbling mud hut in the swamplands; yet he spoke of Fate often and affectionately, as though, merely by surviving, he had been particularly favoured" (*A House for Mr Biswas*, p. 15). Born into a family of sugar-estate indentured workers at an inauspicious hour of midnight with an extra finger as indicator of ill-omen, the pundit predicted him to be a "lecher and a spendthrift, possibly a liar as well", further saying, "The only thing I can advise is to keep him away from trees and water. Particularly water" (*A House for Mr Biswas*, p. 16). The midwife also cautions the family: "Whatever you do, this boy will eat up his own mother and father" (*A House for Mr Biswas*, p. 16). Even his birth suggests certain imminent calamities and complications that stick to his psyche till his death. His innate aggression and self-willed nature make people blame him for the loss of Dhari's calf, for the death of his father by drowning in the village pond, for spoiling pundit Jairam, for stealing from Bhandat's rum-shop. He is constantly blamed for different reasons by different people. Pundit Jairam makes him to copy out Sanskrit verses that he can not understand. Series of unpleasant events occur after his father's death that make his mother leave their house at Parrot Trace to take shelter with her sister Tara at Pagotes. According to the narrator, the quest starts when:

> Mr Biswas came to leave the only house to which he had some right. For the next thirty-five years he was to be a wanderer with no place he could call his own, with no family except that which he was to attempt to create out of the engulfing world of the Tulsis ... it seemed to him that he was really quite alone. (*A House for Mr Biswas*, p. 40)

He resolves to get a job and a house of his own and promises not to let himself be victimized any more by the people after facing humiliation at Bhandat's rum-shop. He announces to his forlorn mother: "I am going to get a job on my own. And I am going to get my own house too. I am finished with this". (*A House for Mr Biswas*, p. 67)

His friend Alec helps him to choose a satisfying career in sign-painting, leading him to Hanuman House which turns to be the centre-stage not only of his own life but that of his children also. It represents a typical hegemonic colonial establishment providing security, shelter and subsistence but at the cost of individual identity and selfhood. Hanuman House is portrayed like a fortress providing protection as well as bondage. It demands ultimate submission of Biswas. The narrator describes it thus: "Mr Biswas had no money or position. He was expected to become a Tulsi. At once he rebelled" (*A House for Mr Biswas*, p. 97). He reacts to his society with defensive and often self-destructive designs. He has got a destiny to encounter numberless disasters beginning with his birth that may have occasioned the death of his father. His childish flirtation and casual approach to life lead him to marry Shama from Hanuman House governed by Tulsi, an epitome of a miniature predatory empire. The conservative Tulsi family sticks to all typical Indian racial and caste prejudices. It possesses Biswas not because of his individual merits but for the sake of his Brahmin status. But very soon: "He felt trapped ... he wanted nothing so much then as to be free of that house" (*A House for Mr Biswas*, pp. 91–92). With the end of the short-lived romance he finds that: "... it was he who had acted, and was unwilling to believe that he had acted foolishly ... . Against this he could set only his fear, and a regret he could explain to no one: he would be losing romance forever, since there could be no romance at Hanuman House". (*A House for Mr Biswas*, p. 93)

Biswas, being a picaresque figure who goes from pillar to post ascertaining his individual identity, condemns Hanuman House that provides him a false sense of security. No doubt, it provides him bread and butter but at the cost of his individuality. Nevertheless, he successfully overcomes the temptation by flinging all the norms of Tulsis to assert his freedom. This assertion of his authentic self motivates him to create something out of nothing. Perpetual humiliation, disgrace and insults aggravate his dilemma. He and his family are subjected to embarassment by the people like Seth, Ajodha and Mrs Tulsi. When Anand asks Ajodha, Tara's husband to contribute to a charity fund, he reacts sharply: "You are a funny sort of family. Father collecting money for destitutes. You collecting for Polish refugees. Who collecting for you?" (*A House for Mr Biswas*, p. 457). Mrs Tulsi is also fed up with Biswas and one day she bursts out saying: "Let him go to hell… Let him get out" (*A House for Mr Biswas*, p. 556). Even Anand, representative of the next generation, feels hurt and shows his open dissent against the life of his father more as a visitor and less as a dweller in the world. He says: "Pa. We must move … I can't bear to live here the another day" (*A House for Mr Biswas*, p. 551). He condemns the life style of Biswas commenting: "When I get to your age don't want to be like you" (*A House for Mr Biswas*, p. 465). In all, the story of Biswas is an exploration of the complex fate of a displaced person who finally emerges as a symbolic individual who dies with a sense of relief as he has anyhow claimed *a portion of the earth* to be his own.

Hanuman House being a symbol of imperialism in its miniature form, a mechanical hierarchy is maintained in the house with Tulsi at the top of the ladder to rule over the daughters and sons-in-law giving special priviliges to her sons Shekhar and Owad. Her treatment revives Orwell's popular dictum—*all are equal but some are more equal than others*. The organization of Hanuman House is a typical colonial one:

> The organization of the Tulsi House was simple. Mrs Tulsi had only one servant, a Negro woman … . The daughters and their children swept and washed and cooked and served in the store. The husbands, under Seth's supervision, worked on the Tulsi land, looked after Tulsi animals, and served in the store. In return they were given food, shelter and a little money; their children were looked after, and they were treated with respect by people outside because they were connected with the Tulsi family. Their names were forgotten; they became Tulsis. (*A House for Mr Biswas*, p. 97)

In such a circumscribing system, Biswas is bound to be condemned for his insistence upon his recognition as a unique member and not as a cog in the wheel. His marriage in Tulsi family compels him to be loyal to it but his real self keeps on asserting at regular intervals. He is provoked to challenge Tulsidom quite often. Feeling lost, Biswas, at times, appears to be quite ruthless and despicable in such instances as his kicking of Shama in the stomach while she is pregnant. Bruce King adds: "Biswas's situation is that of the colony, his own attempts at independence are limited by the condition of the society into which he is born; frustrated self-assertion turns into self-destructive rage, the tempest that temporarily disorders Biswas's mind."[22]

He starts naming Tulsi with certain nicknames like the *old queen*, *the old hen*, and *the old cow*. He does not even spare her sons and names them as the two gods. His intermittent acceptance and rejection of Hanuman House reflect his psychological dilemma and ambivalence. Whenever he feels that his individuality is questioned, he is once again set to face the chaotic colonial outside world. His choice to run a shop at Chase, to construct a house of his own at Green Vale and Shorthills, and ultimately owning of a house of his own at Sikkim Street, are the parts of his belief in the motto "paddle your own canoe" (*A House for Mr Biswas*, p. 140) that is at times ridiculed by Seth and other members of Tulsi House, as he does not have the ample means and methods to survive without essential support from Hanuman House. The idea of having a house fascinates Mr Biswas so much that he keeps on making the castles in the air and the outline map of the house drawn by Mr Maclean stirs up his deep-seated craving. King Bruce rightly comments on the protagonist's dilemma saying: "Biswas's fear of harm and death is also a fear of extinction, annihilation, the void. The void is in his mind, a kind of insanity in which his selfhood and individuality are lost."[23] After his breakdown at the Green Vale, his ambiguousness, which is a symptom of his meagerness, undergoes a change. The Green Vale episode reinforces his attachment to his never-ending ambition and also to Tulsis where he feels temporarily anchored. Still Biswas never gives up. N. Ramadevi adds that he:

> Constantly seeks to negotiate a free and own space for himself wherein he can overcome the degenerating and suppressing tendencies of the Tulsi environment. In this cruel, comic world, both crowded and solitary, bullying and servile, Mr Biswas keeps alive a mere glint of independence and self by refusing to be either a sauve or a mild victim.[24]

Defying the Hanuman House codes, he presents a doll house to Savi and associates himself with *Arya Samaj*. These are the deliberate actions undertaken by Biswas to provoke and challenge the colonial organization of Hanuman House. It also stands for a reproduction of typical Indian set up to remind the immigrant East-Indians at Trinidad about their roots, native culture, customs and rites, and Hindu institutions like marriage and family. The inherent sense of loneliness is imprinted in his psyche so deeply that even after his marriage and the birth of his children, he longs for a sterile, fruitless world where he can be alone. Hallucinations of "billowing black cloud" (*A House for Mr Biswas,* p. 266) and an uncertain fear of people haunt him while he is at Green Vale reminding the reader of the boy in *The Mystic Masseur* haunted by the same cloud. He is afraid of *people* for nothing as:

> No road was without them, no house. They were on the newspaper on the wall, in the photographs, in the simple drawings in advertisements. They were in the book he was holding. They were in all books. He tried to think of landscapes without people ... with himself safely alone, a speck in the centre. (*A House for Mr Biswas*, pp. 266–67)

He seeks solace and escape through reading and creative writing though it could not be his only obsession. Landeg White presents the mockery of Biswas's condition when he says: "He reads Samuel Smiles and tries to see himself as young and poor and struggling. But the romantic sagas of self-help make sense only in countries where ambitions are credible, where heroes can propel themselves up ladders already in existence."[25] Ultimately, the casual reader Biswas, under the dynamic guidance of Mr Burnett, attains a position in society through journalism. His open-ended stories represent the wavering and flickering nature of a homeless wanderer. About his creative writing the narrator comments: "The hero, trapped into marriage, burdened with a family, his youth gone, meets a young girl. She is slim, almost thin, and dressed in white. She is fresh, unkissed; and she is unable to bear children. Beyond the meeting the stories never went". (*A House for Mr Biswas*, pp. 344–45)

Throughout the novel, Mohun Biswas's search for a house of his own is an attempt to find both independence and a meaning for his life, and the often chaotic account of petty island life is marked with a deeper sense of the essential loneliness of the human state. His is a search for a sense of self and place. He identifies his highest achievement with the possession of a house of his own. In his campaign to possess a house, he is made to encounter a series of exhausting disasters. He struggles against the real dreadfulness of life, its insignificant authenticity and its unassailable world-weariness. In a mood of ultimate despair after every minor or major failure, Biswas realizes the inability of contemporary society to make life meaningful for the ordinary denizens. Stuti Khanna defends the hypothesis when she reacts: "Naipaul's position as a third generation Caribbean settled in England makes the idea of return (to an unsullied past, and thereby a complete, rooted identity) doubly problematic. What past does one return to? Whose? The aboriginal peoples of the Caribbean have long been extinct."[26] His sense of insecurity and lack of wholeness in life get exhibited when he talks to his dog: "You are an animal and think that because I have a head and hands and look as I did yesterday I am a man. I am deceiving you. I am not whole" (*A House for Mr Biswas*, p. 268). Similarly when asked by Anand about his relation to Mohun Biswas, he convinces him: "Wrong. I am not your father. God is your father ... I am just somebody. Nobody at all. I am just a man you know" (*A House for Mr Biswas*, p. 279). The colonial world leaves the common man lost in nothingness making him feel indecisive, disillusioned and disoriented.

Naipaul aims at presenting the frustration of Mohun Biswas by showing his ambiguous attitude to his past. Amitav Kumar does not condemn Mohun Biswas as a fractured and uprooted being. He finds a progressive positive metamorphosis through certain changes that mark Biswas's life. For him, the imposed disintegration leads the hero to certain assimilation in the main stream of Trinidad life. He puts it thus:

> The single line that comes to Biswas every time he wishes to test a new ribbon in the typewriter is the following one: 'At the age of thirty-three, when he was already the father of four children ... .' The half-finished sentence lights up momentarily a whole dark universe of desire and futility. And yet, despite the terrible isolation of his ambition, it is also true that Biswas's haphazard, incomplete actions carry him from the plantation to a life in writing. It is a supreme achievement.[27]

Autobiographical elements lie beneath all the writings of Naipaul without exception. While he was away in England, where he had moved out after earning a government scholarship, his father suffered a cardiac illness and died. The death utterly shocked the son. Naipaul's early years were very problematic and he was made to suffer and the early books were created with great nervousness and suffering. After his father's death, Naipaul wrote *A House for Mr Biswas*, which he described as very much his father's book. However, his father's death also liberated Naipaul from the liabilities that would not have permitted him to write about his father. The novel redeemed the failure that had haunted the elder Naipaul, who had dreamed of success as a writer. The personal failure of the novelist is underlined by Bruce King when he says:

> The unsettled period of Naipaul's own childhood, moving houses, living among relatives, is reflected in Biswas's story as, probably, are fears for the future of the Indians in Trinidad and the insecurities of his early period as a writer in London. Houses, gardens and family gatherings ... represent order, society, civilization ... .[28]

But, first and foremost, *A House for Mr Biswas* is a tribute to what Naipaul had been taught by his father. It derives its strength from the journalism and stories of his father. Naipaul finds himself portrayed in the character of Anand. The novel shows the bond between the: "Father and son, each saw the other as weak and vulnerable, and each felt a responsibility for the other ..." (*A House for Mr Biswas*, p. 374). The editor of The Sentinel, Mr Burnett has been drawn from someone whom Naipaul had known as a child—Gault MacGowan, a journalist from Fleet Street who was there at Trinidad to breathe life into the Guardian. It was he who trained Seepersad Naipaul to launch his career as a journalist and a writer. Father-son relationship in real life, according to Landeg White, provides the background for the novel. He asserts: "What Naipaul has done ... has been to abstract from his father's life not a sequence of events but a quality of experience which he has shaped in such a way as to project his own vision of its significance."[29] In the novel, Anand represents Naipaul's dilemma and just before leaving for London, Anand asserts: "So later, and very slowly, in securer times of different stresses, when the memories had lost the power to hurt with pain or joy, they would fall into place and give back the past" (*A House for Mr Biswas*, p. 581). Anand justifies his father's endeavours to carve out a place for himself in the modern nomadic world and create for his children prospects for a more resourceful and promising future.

The novelist highlights various intrinsic ambiguities in the observance of customs and rituals by East-Indian Trinidadians. In Hanuman House, the Hindu deities seem irreverent and Hindi books are hardly taken seriously. Shekhar and Owad worship Hindu gods wearing crucifixes while Chinta chants Hindu mantras handling a candle and wearing crucifix. Even Mrs Tulsi who considers herself an epitome of Hinduism, allows the celebration of the Christmas and Good Friday in Creole style, with English apples, cakes, ice-cream and Portuguese Cherry brandy. Tulsi sends her elder son to a Roman Catholic College. The marriage of Owad and Shekhar with Christian Presbyterian girls marks the acceptance of creolization by Indian Hindus at Trinidad. Tulsi's assimilation in western culture seems to be over after the death of Hari: "Since no pundit could please her as well as Hari. And, no pundit pleasing her, her faith yielded. She sent Sushila to burn candles in the Roman Catholic Church; she put a crucifix in her room; and she had pundit Tulsi's grave cleaned for All Saints' Day". (*A House for Mr Biswas*, p. 522)

Naipaul shows the predicament of those with a divided cultural heritage with excellence. William L. Sachs seems to be very much in tune with Naipaul when he observes:

> Fear of losing one's remembered culture breeds frustration. The West becomes an unwelcome interloper, which one can not escape but to which one can not adapt. Historical and social realities blur in a sense of dispossession; of being cut off from an imagined glorious past. Frustration mounts and engenders anger ... Indigenous forms of life must be reanimated.[30]

Biswas keeps on mocking at the Tulsis for their affiliations with Roman Catholics but at the time of deep agony at Green Vale he prepares beautiful placards showing his Hindu faith. Similarly in the horrifying stormy night, he starts remembering the names of Hindu gods chanting "Rama, Rama, Sita Rama" (*A House for Mr Biswas*, p. 283), asking his son to do the same. His Hinduism and Indianness is evidenced when he plans to name his first male child as—Krishandhar Haripratap Gokulnath Damodar Biswas. In addition to pointing out the fickleness of the expatriate Indians at Trinidad, Naipaul shows the perceptible ways in which the immigrants leave their native traditions and gradually assimilate into western-oriented Creole culture of Trinidad. The process of obvious creolization affects the traditions and mores, which ostensibly appear to be exclusively Indian but are sharply customized by the local environment. Anthony Boxill remarks: "Naipaul is like Biswas, who having no tradition to turn to, must create his own. And this tradition has its roots in the rootlessness of the West-Indian society rather than in the well-established European and Indian societies."[31]

Influential Indians like the Tulsis realize the insufficiency of the inherited Indian locale in the face of modern aspirations. Tulsi family's removal from Arwacas signals the gradual decay of the iron grip of Hanuman House which stands for deep-rooted Indianness. The crumbling and the fall of Hanuman House is almost complete by the end of the novel. It is something like the historic fall of Constantinople that dislocated the natives but for the good of generations to come. The members of Tulsi family in Port of Spain aspire to touch new horizons through material and intellectual gains for the next generation. Each and every member of Hanuman House aspires to have the house of his own. The narrator explains the rising instincts of the Hanuman House:

> The crowding became worse ... . The widows were now almost frantic to have their children educated. There was no longer a Hanuman House to protect them; everyone had to fight for himself in a new world, the world Owad and Shekhar had entered, where education was the only protection. As fast as the children graduated from the infant school at Shorthills they were sent to Port of Spain. (*A House for Mr Biswas*, pp. 433–36)

A sort of correlation may be established between Biswas's progress to selfhood and the divergence of Tulsi Empire that further symbolizes the ongoing loosening grip of empire on the colonies. Port of Spain has become the focal point of fast track life providing requisite coaching, schooling and competitive environment enabling the gen-next to win scholarships for their higher education in London which will further enable them to get rid of the sordid environment of Trinidad. The noticeable shift from the country to town, from Hindi to English, from reliance on fate to preoccupation with ambition, Biswas to Anand, native to Creole and from combined family to nuclear family, can be noticed by the end of the novel.

Subsequently, Biswas also moves to Port of Spain to establish his autonomy by taking up the job of a journalist and then that of an officer in the Community Welfare Department. Later he happens to be a journalist of the Trinidad Sentinel, which gives a kind of shape and form to his life for the first time. It is during this stage of his life that Biswas comes closer to his family. But the threat of losing his job starts haunting him at the same time. By the time he achieves his target, the emblematic goal of his search for independence and selfhood, his energies, both physical and mental, are almost exhausted. The house is the equivalent of the stories he never finishes and the paintings he never makes. Almost immediately after occupying the house of his own, Biswas falls seriously ill and is put on half-pay by the Sentinel only to dismiss him before long. In the last phase of his life, he learns to find contentment in an insecure house and the people around him. So it is appropriate to say that Biswas dies a contented death. In the end, his house becomes the place from which he urges Anand to believe in God and the home from which he can be carried for cremation. The novel ingeniously traces dominance of one's past, which shapes the present and conditions the future. Remembering, Bhabha writes, "… is never a quiet act of introspection or retrospection. It is a painful re-membering, a putting together of the dismembered past to make sense of the trauma of the present."[32]

Biswas's struggle to assert himself in the suffocating colonial world is unique. Being a destined "derelict man in a derelict land"[33] he has remained neglected for more than two-third of his lifetime. Indeed he is at times, insignificant, gutless, and disgraceful. But the triumph of *A House for Mr Biswas* lies in Naipaul's presentation of a hero "in all his littleness, and still preserves a sense of the man's inner dignity".[34] He represents the fate of an average man who can master the risks and dangers of cultural dereliction. He can overshadow the neglect ensuing from the inconsistencies in space, time, history, and personality with commonplace abilities but with a commitment to defend his identity. He stands for rootless colonial entrapped in an alien society. Ultimate realization of the long-cherished dream and Biswas's charm of a winning champion get eclipsed with his loss of position, his ageing, his bad health, and his inopportune death. His agony gets reflected through the description: "His complexion grew dark ... this was a darkness that seemed to come from within, as though the skin was a murky but transparent film and the flesh below it had been bruised and become diseased and corruption was rising". (*A House for Mr Biswas*, pp. 587–88)

One may suspect that the world of *A House for Mr Biswas* is modelled upon a society from which the author has himself wished to escape. He himself confesses: "These people [Trinidadians] live purely physical lives, which I find contemptible ... . It makes them only interesting to chaps in universities who want to do compassionate studies about brutes."[35] The world in which Mr Biswas lives is hostile to his overwhelming faith in life with which his author endows him is greater than his impulse to escape. Owning a house of his own by Biswas confirms the prospect of finding order amidst chaos. Biswas does not seek political or economic influence; rather he is engaged in a constant quest for a moral order and meaningful existence. By the end of the book Biswas's self-determination becomes his home.

Bruce King suggests that his is a journey from homelessness, reliance on others, paucity, lack of familiar place in the world to a landowner, chief of a family, a father with two children studying abroad. *A House for Mr Biswas* marks an important phase in Naipaul's literary career. Naipaul maintains that the novel "became the story of a man's search for a house and all that the possession of one's house implied."[36] The persistent panic that Biswas experiences as a homeless seeker is the typical characteristic of Trinidad, "a materialist immigrant society, continually growing and changing, never settling into any pattern, always retaining the atmosphere of the camp ... ."[37]

Expatriates are perhaps experiencing the fatal ambivalence because they are living in an interstitial luminal zone, on the margins of two worlds, belonging to neither. Chandra B. Joshi makes an interesting observation:

> Exile has been the spur as well as the subject of his writing. The early work is to a large extent an attempt at defining his own situation and seeking an answer to the problem that hampered him at the start—I didn't know who I was. With the epic *House* behind him he knew at last who he was and how he came to be on the tiny island of Trinidad.[38]

The Trinidadian comedies comprising *The Mystic Masseur*, *Miguel Street*, *The Suffrage of Elvira* and *A House for Mr Biswas* are the exploration of Naipaul's personal agony during his childhood and early youth but the symptoms of the imminent gloomy vision of the novelist in the later works are clearly visible in these comedies. The novel presents the detailed account of contradictions that make an Indian immigrant at Trinidad feel divided and ambivalent. The dilemma of these expatriates matches Hamlet's dilemma, i.e., *to be or not to be* and they are placed at an isthmus torn between dual identities. Hindi–English dichotomy is not less important to portray the inadvertent move of the immigrants from country to town. Hindi is the common language of communication among the first generation of expatriates but for the third generation expatriates it is an obsolete object. Ganesh and Biswas both use Hindi in their informal chat but when it comes to ceremonious use of language, they prefer English. Homi Bhabha's idea of "ambivalence" is justified when these ambivalent protagonists of fluid identities are shown moving forward while looking backward. Bhabha apprehends that: "… ambivalence is a seizure of cultural viscosity; it turns the dialectical *between* of culture's disciplinary structure—between unconscious and conscious motives, between little acts and grand traditions … . That sows confusion between opposites and sands between the oppositions at once."[39]

Naipaul's obsession in his early stage is to expose the colonial experiences of the diaspora using the device of comic irony. The decline of their native culture, along with the ruthless restrictions imposed on their life pattern in Trinidad, reduce them to a state of non-existence. In an interview with Ray Suerez, Naipaul admits:

> … although I come from the Caribbean—Trinidad—I'm of Indian origin, and the Indian experience has always been interesting to me and necessary for me to explore and to come to terms with. You see, my interest begins with my community and my place of birth. My community commits me to an exploration of India and the Islamic world. My place of birth commits me to an understanding of the new world, the Spanish invasion, slavery, revolution in the new world. It also commits me to an attempt to understand Africa. So from that starting point, I have looked at the world, or tried to look at the world, … .[40]

The niceties and nuances concerning the social and cultural framework of Hindu East Indians in Trinidad offer the novelist the reference material from which Naipaul's early fiction draws its substance. Trinidad, according to Caryl Phillips, is a "place for him of double exile, a place where he became a culturally inscribed migrant within a migrant world, which gave to him his great theme: loss."[41]

Early fiction of Naipaul is based on memories of Trinidadian culture and political life before he left for England in 1950. These novels are extraordinarily popular because of their strong comic element. These novels also deal with social history showing the beginning of protest politics during the late 1930s and how Trinidad began to change during and after the Second World War. The infusion of American money and the beginnings of local self-government created new possibilities where few existed before; but such social change is treated amusingly, without the more analytical perspective found in the later novels. Though the East Indian emigrants cautiously preserve and reconstruct Indian village life in the West Indian Island, these men and women are well aware that they are no more in India. They find a sea change in their way of life perhaps under the push and pulls of the alien environment, notwithstanding how much they adhere to their native customs and rituals. People like Ganesh and Ramlogan want to harness the fruits of their dual identities. Harish Trivedi suggests that though the location of his early novels is Trinidad, "the ambience is unmistakably Indian, with Indian characters, Indian social structures, Indian psychology, customs and practices forming the warp and woof of the whole fictional fabric."[42] The personal ambivalence of Naipaul that he shares with his sister Kamla becomes more evident when he says, "A feeling of emptiness is nearly always on me. I see myself struggling in a sort of tunnel blocked up at both ends. My past—Trinidad and the necessity of our parents—lies behind me and I am powerless to help anyone."[43]

The anguish and ambivalence of the creator becomes the basis of his early novels. While delivering the Nobel Lecture in the Nobel Prize Felicitation Ceremony at Stockholm, he stressed upon the essential oneness of his works. He said: "I said earlier that everything of value about me is in my books. I will go further now. I will say I am the sum of my books. Each book, intuitively worked out, stands on what has gone before, and grows out of it … it could have been said that the last book contained all the others."[44] But still he is against producing typical Naipaulian novels as Dickens came out with characteristic Dickensian novels. He feels that Dickens was led to an early literary death by the tag *Dickensian novel.* His novels are ever-evolving though with the very attempt to explore the many sides of his anxiety over his missing past. This nervousness has been elaborated by Akash Kapur when he remarks, "It is the anxiety of man twice robbed of history: by the ancestral migration from the homeland

... and by the trauma of his own migration at 18 to England, where, cut off from home and family, he suffered a nervous breakdown."[45] It is in this sense that Mohun Biswas in *A House for Mr Biswas* appears to be a man who is always on tenterhooks as the roots of the family and home are severed with callous brutality in the wake of the cultural chaos witnessed by the protagonist and the thousands of others like him during the period of cultural upheavels. Biswas emerges as the spokesperson for the multitude of the dispossessed and deprived who grope for a security both in the physical as well as in the metaphorical sense in the times of such cultural tumult. His magnum opus *A House for Mr Biswas* marks a remarkable paradigmatic shift in the treatment of the theme concerning diasporic ambivalence and loss. His comic irony is further replaced by a harsh presentation of colonial predicaments in the later novels *Guerillas* and *A Bend in the River*.

Notes

1. Nasser Mustapha, "The Influence of Indian Islam on Fundamentalist Trends in Trinidad and Tobago," *The Indian Diaspora: Dynamics of Migration*, ed. N. Jayaram (New Delhi: Sage Publications, 2004) pp. 133–34.
2. Jasbir Jain, *Writers of Indian Diaspora: Theory and Practice* (Jaipur: Rawat Publications, 1998) pp. 15–16.
3. Gurbhagat Singh, "Expatriate Writing and the Problematic of Centre: Edward Said and Homi Bhabha," *Writers of Indian Diaspora: Theory and Practice*, op. cit., p. 21.
4. V.S. Naipaul, *The Mystic Masseur* (London: Penguin, 1964) p. 18. (All subsequent references from this text are cited in parenthesis as *The Mystic Masseur*, p. no.)
5. Quoted by Chandra B. Joshi in *V.S. Naipaul: The Voice of Exile* (New Delhi: Sterling Publishers, 1994) p. 25.
6. Gordon Rohlehr, "The Ironic Approach: The Novels of V.S. Naipaul", *The Islands in Between: Essays in West Indian Literature*, ed. Louis James (London: Oxford University Press, 1968) p. 122.
7. Selwyn R. Cudjoe, *V.S. Naipaul: A Materialist Reading* (Amherst, Mass.: University of Massachusetts Press, 1988) p. 41.
8. Rama Kundu, "Naipaul: An Indian who is Not An Indian", *V.S. Naipaul: Critical Essays*,Vol. I, ed. Mohit K. Ray (New Delhi: Atlantic Publishers, 2002) p. 146.
9. Lillian Feder, *Naipaul's Truth* (New Delhi: Indialog, 2001) p. 13.

10. Ashok Mitra, "Not Such an Enigma", 26 October 2001, *The Telegraph*, 23 September 2007<http://www.telegraphindia.com/1011027/editoria.htm#head3.
11. Edward Said, Reflections on Exile (London: Granta Books, 2001) p. 186.
12. V.S. Naipaul, The *Middle Passage* (Harmondsworth: Penguin, 1969) p. 43.
13. S.L. Sharma, "Perspectives on Indians Abroad," *The Indian Diaspora: Dynamics of Migration*, op. cit., p. 47.
14. Chandra B. Joshi, *V.S. Naipaul: The Voice of Exile* (New Delhi: Sterling Publishers, 1994) p. 124
15. V.S. Naipaul, *A House for Mr Biswas* (Harmondsworth: Penguin, 1961) pp.13 14. (All the subsequent references for *A House for Mr Biswas* have been taken from the same edition of the novel, cited hereafter, in the text with the corresponding page number(s) in parenthesis.)
16. N. Ramadevi, *The Novels of V.S. Naipaul* (New Delhi: Prestige Books, 1996) p. 54.
17. Gordon Rohlehr, Quoted by N. Ramadevi in *The Novels of V.S. Naipaul* (New Delhi: Prestige Books, 1996) p. 56.
18. V.S. Naipaul, *An Area of Darkness* (Harmondsworth: Penguin, 1964) pp. 187–188.
19. Jasbir Jain, *Writers of Indian Diaspora: Theory and Practice*, op. cit., p. 13.
20. Bruce King, *V.S. Naipaul* (London: Macmillan, 1993) p. 46.
21. Hugh Tinker, *The Banyan Tree: Overseas Emigrants from India, Pakistan and Bangladesh* (Oxford: Oxford University Press, 1977) p. 19.
22. Bruce King, *V.S. Naipaul*, op. cit., p. 37.
23. N. Ramadevi, *The Novels of V.S. Naipaul*, op. cit., p. 60.
24. Landeg White, *V.S. Naipaul* (London: Macmillan, 1975) p. 103.
25. Stuti Khanna, "The Novel of Migration", *V.S. Naipaul: Fiction and Travel Writing*, ed. Rajeshwar Mittapalli, Michael Hensen (New Delhi: Atlantic Publishers, 2002) p. 13.
26. Amitav Kumar, "Amitava Kumar on V.S. Naipaul", 3 September 2001, *The New Statesman*, 25 July 2007<http://www.amitavakumar.com/articles/notebook.html.
27. Bruce King, *V.S. Naipaul*, op. cit., p. 38.
28. Landeg White, *V.S. Naipaul*, op. cit., p. 96.
29. William L. Sachs, "V.S. Naipaul and the Plight of the Dispossessed," 17 November 1982, Religion Online, 7 August 2006<http://www.religion-online.org/cgi-bin/research.dll/showarticle?item id,1354, 4.

30. Landeg White, *V.S. Naipaul,* op. cit., p. 109.
31. Anthony Boxill, *V.S. Naipaul's Fiction: In Quest of the Enemy* (Fredericton, New Brunswick: York Press, 1983) p. 24.
32. Homi K. Bhabha, *The Location of Culture* (London: Routledge, 1997) p. 63.
33. V.S. Naipaul, *The Middle Passage,* op. cit., p. 200.
34. Gordon Rohlehr, "The Ironic Approach: The Novels of V.S. Naipaul," *Critical Perspectives on V.S. Naipaul,* ed. Robert D. Hamner (Washington D.C.: Three Continents Press, 1977) pp. 137–138.
35. Caryl Phillips, "Reluctant Hero," *The Humour and the Pity,* ed. Amitava Kumar, (New Delhi: Buffalo Books, 2002) pp. 133–134.
36. V.S. Naipaul, "Writing a House for Mr Biswas," *The New York Review of Books,* 24 November 1983, p. 22.
37. V.S. Naipaul, *The Middle Passage,* op. cit., pp. 57–58.
38. Chandra B. Joshi, *V.S. Naipaul: The Voice of Exile,* op. Cit., p.xi.
39. Tapas K. Roy Chaudhary, "Ambivalence, Colonial Text and Tagore", Summerhill *IIAS Review,* Shimla, Vol.XII. No. 2, 2006, p. 25.
40. Ray Suarez, "V.S. Naipaul", *Online News Hour,* 3 March, 2000< pbs. org/newshour/gergen/jan-june00/naipaul_3–3.html.
41. Caryl Phillips, "Reluctant Hero", *The Humour and the Pity,* op. cit., p. 137.
42. Harish Trivedi, "The Nobel Savage? India and Naipaul", op. cit., p. 148.
43. Pankaj Mishra, "The House of Mr Naipaul", *The Humour and the Pity,* ed. Amitava Kumar (New Delhi: Buffalo Books, 2002) p. 26.
44. V.S. Naipaul, "Two Worlds: Nobel Lecture", *V.S. Naipaul: Critical Essays,* ed. Mohit K.Ray, op. cit., pp. 2–3.
45. Akash Kapur, "A Million Neuroses", *The Humour and the Pity,* op. cit., p. 76.

2

Rediscovering Disillusionment

In the early novels of Naipaul, England has been presented as the dreamland for the Trinidadians who find their own world to be incomplete, unreal and devoid of opportunity. Ganesh in *The Mystic Masseur*, Bryant in *Miguel Street* and Anand in *A House for Mr Biswas* escape to London to realize their cherished dreams. Their departure from the colonial land marks the end of these books. The narrator does not go beyond this point and a suggestive silence is maintained about the aftermaths of their escape to the "Promised Land". It is only from *Mr Stone and the Knight's Companion*, a novel without even a single non-English character that an indirect study tracing the lives of the displaced subjectivities is taken up by the novelist. In the second phase of his literary career, Naipaul follows the expatriates' piquant tragedies by placing them in alien territories in the far-off lands and brings to the fore their intensified sense of ambivalence, loneliness, fear, a sense of futility, disappointment and mimicry in England as well as in Trinidad.

The fictional works—*The Mimic Men*, a novel, and *A Flag on the Island*, a collection of short stories appear thus to mark a departure from the novels of the early phase as these make use of the island stuff of the Caribbean as much as of England. If *The Mystic Masseur* and *A House for Mr Biswas* are the novels preoccupied with the monotonous island life of Trinidadians, *The Mimic Men* and *A Flag on the Island* present a more complex dilemma—the predicament of a colonial expatriate from an outsider's point of view. In *The Mimic Men*, Naipaul depicts a newly independent country in the Caribbean, the island of Isabella. In spite of the long-cherished achievement of the independence, it appears that the previously colonized people of the island are unable to establish order and administer their country. The feelings of dislocation, placelessness, fragmentation and loss of identity haunt their psyche and thus they are reduced to the status of "mimic" men who imitate and reflect the colonizer's lifestyle, values and views. In the words of Bill Ashcroft, Gareth Griffins and Helen Tiffin, *The Mimic Men* is a novel:

> ... which incorporates an extreme version of the opposition between center and margin ... . The book contrasts the metropolitan center, which is the location not only of the power which comes from the control of language but also of order itself, with the periphery of colonial world, in which only the illusion of power exists and in which disorder always predominates.[1]

Like *The Mimic Men*, *A Flag on the Island* is also a first-person account of an American narrator who deftly unfolds the story by interweaving his past recollections with his present observations. The writing of *A Flag on the Island* fairly covers the period that of *The Mimic Men* which accounts for its appearing to be a shadow of the later works of Naipaul. Here too, Naipaul limits himself to the idea that though the island has attained political independence, as is evident in the display of its own flag, its residents are filled with a sense of their own insignificance, unreality and remoteness. They desperately try to live up to the *tourist* image of themselves. Both the works demonstrate Naipaul's consummate interest in history, in the relations between the past and present, and in finding an answer to certain questions concerning the untold history of the West Indian futility. For him, history is a record of achievements and creation but unfortunately he finds no creativity in the West Indies.

A Flag on the Island (1967), Naipaul's second volume of short stories, after *Miguel Street* (1957), brings together short fiction written between 1950 and 1962. *A Flag on the Island* addresses the variety of themes that bind Naipaul's philosophical arbitration on the postcolonial journey of the self—a haphazard self, subjected to prevailing threatening powers of historical transformation. It is a collection of stories with the title story "A Flag on the Island" as the only *new* piece. Most of the stories of *A Flag on the Island* have their background in Trinidad and deal with the common theme of obvious clash of values among local Trinidadians of Indian descent who endeavour to construct their lives around a distant culture that is now dimly remembered, but of no avail. Some of the stories deal with the underlying panic in the everyday lives of émigré in London. The cluster of stories from an earlier stage of his career offers something of a respite from the grim new realism that his publication since *A House for Mr Biswas* increasingly delved into. While this collection also uses comic effect to strengthen the themes of alienation, failure, and racial bias, and the wide-ranging tone of the collection is much more harsh and gloomy than that in *Miguel Street*, another collection of stories by Naipaul.

The stories in *A Flag on the Island* range from visual rendering of Trinidad street life to the metropolitan setting of London. "My Aunt Gold Teeth", dated 1954, the earliest of Naipaul's collected writings, is set in the Hindu heartland of rural Trinidad. It presents the entertaining picture of the community that was transforming through its interaction with other cultures. It further exposes the antipathy in diverse social relations underlining the social comedy resulting from the temptation leading them to adopt the ways of others. In this story, an orthodox Hindu's wife Gold Teeth resorts to Roman Catholic prayers to overcome her barrenness. Later on, her prayers are said to have caused the death of her husband, an orthodox pundit. She is blamed and tortured with harsh words for her divided faith in two religions. Being considered a sinner, she is reminded that she will have no child to care for her in old age. The Aunt Gold Teeth's unawareness of the implications of the Hindu and Catholic rituals she practices, as well as the ethnic hostility within the community, take us closer to the title story "A Flag on the Island". The two stories are in part about communal antagonism and the cultural confusion and mimicry of cultural behaviour that occur when different groups are brought together and society is facing a phase of transmutation. The title story also emphasizes the obligation and the hazards involved in this Americanization of the West Indians. The confluence of heterogeneous cultures adds to the ambivalence of the figures like Aunt Gold Teeth.

The title story "A Flag on the Island" shows the difference in an East Caribbean island before and after independence. The wartime American soldiers and rum shops have been replaced by tourists and modern American buildings respectively. It could be said that there is no valid divergence between an island depending on soldiers and one relying on tourists—so a new form of "mimicry" has replaced the old. The narrator, Frank, is a former American serviceman whose ambivalence about his unintentional return is characterized by his drunken and apparently unpredictable behaviour among an anomalous group of passengers. In the middle of the story, when Frank is lying in drunken stupor and surveys the transformed familiar sights of his earlier stay, he remarks on the presence of American War: "… we brought the topics to the island. Yet to the islanders it must have seemed that we had brought America to them."[2] This identification allows the narrator a long recollection of the conditions of his past and that of the island. While presenting the dichotomy between a sense of the past and the present, Naipaul creates a narrative frame to contrast varied pictures of island culture. His idea of "culture" seems to be a derivation of Edward Said's definition: "... all cultures are involved in one another; none is single and pure, all are hybrid, heterogeneous, extraordinarily differentiated, and unmonolithic."[3]

Naipaul shows that despite their resulting prosperity, the obvious transformations reveal their corresponding nothingness. Among Frank's former friends on the island is an aspiring novelist of English romances, Mr Blackwhite. Humiliated by English civilization, he takes refuge in writing. His imitation of English fiction, language and style brings to light the contrast between foreign daydreaming and the reality of the West Indian artist. He insists upon having his own language. Influenced by the model of African decolonization, he is trapped into a forged cultural chauvinism. He displays a signboard outside his house containing the additional information: "PATOIS TAUGHT HERE" (*A Flag on the Island*, p. 183). Subsequently, mimicking Black Americans, he writes a book *I Hate You*, subtitled *One Man's Search for Identity*. Landeg White comments, "Mr Blackwhite becomes H.J.B. White, writing stories called 'I Hate You' with the help of money from American foundations producing versions not of the life he lives but of the myths the Americans require."[4] Similarly, Frank in "A Flag on the Island" says: "I hate the poor and the humble. I think poverty is something we should all conceal" (*A Flag on the Island*, p. 177). Considering him the preferred West Indian writer of American foundations, the book is purchased by tourists until he wants to write a matter-of-fact novel. He deliberately avoids writing the stories about a "black man rescued from a bad white woman" or a "black woman rescued from a bad white man". (*A Flag on the Island*, p. 198)

The narrator of the story is an American who decides to leave after realizing that he cannot act without getting involved in the society. He also ridicules Blackwhite's earlier attempt at historical romances set in Georgian English setting. The change in Blackwhite's novelistic style allows Frank to ironically mock the abusive use of distorted island themes such as miscegenation and interracial sexual relations. At this time of his literary career Naipaul was also concerned with questions of legitimacy, commitment and creativity.

Similarly, Leonard, one of Frank's fellow American passengers on the ship, is eventually exposed to be an unreliable philanthropist. He represents the new generation of moderate humanists who under the guise of seeking native authenticity simply continue to feed their self-indulgent absorption with a notion of the exotic. Similarly Henry's place and its conversion into a privileged tourist cultural nightclub, and the priest's metamorphoses from preacher to insurance salesman, to radio announcer and advertiser, all confirm the unfounded "mimic" position that each has achieved. All of them tend to live half a life characterized by the colonial ambivalence.

The narrator hero, Frank is an American salesman of the books who, during the war, had been a soldier in an American base on an unnamed Caribbean island. Now, some years later, his ship is forced to dock in this island because of an impending hurricane. Unenthusiastically, he visits the familiar places in a kind of mental haze. In his surrealistic misadventures, he moves through the island in a drunken haze and begins to recall the past when he had been a soldier stationed in the American base on the island. It recreates the time when the island did not have its own flag. Frank now remembers a sexual encounter: "Above me a foolish face; the poor body offering its charms that were no charms. Poor body; poor flesh; poor man" (*A Flag on the Island*, p. 34). Naipaul's narrator, Frank, with his aversion on his return, suggests that he is conscious of his own connivance in helping to create caricatures of his island friends, as their present situation is portrayed as apathetic. They, in turn, also display an awareness of their synthetic status, so that the cumulative effect of mood of the story is an abnormal nostalgia for something that never was. The "flag", therefore, is the easy symbol for the fabricated and pretentious nature of the island's autonomous identity. The island has attained political independence, which it proclaims with a flag of its own. It represents the multiracial fusion of its inhabitants, rather than a culturally genuine mix of its locally bred hybrid traditions. Unwilling to revisit the island, Frank says: "All landscapes are in the end only in the imagination; to be faced with the reality is to start again" (*A Flag on the Island*, p. 149). As his ship approaches the familiar island, Frank is "jumpy, irritated, unsatisfied, suddenly incomplete" on seeing "channels and islets which I had never hoped or wished to see again" (*A Flag on the Island*, pp. 149–50). To underline the essential ambivalence among the expatriates, Fawzia Mustafa adds: "The localized moment of *Miguel Street* (1959) and the early stories of *A Flag on the Island* (1967) depict scenes of the transitory and static tension of urban migrations … ."[5]

The characters in *A Flag on the Island* demonstrate the common disorder of Naipaul's West Indians. They are filled with a sense of their own insignificance, unreality and remoteness. In spite of their identity—as the "flag" denotes—the lives of the people have become more fantastic because they are still living up to a tourist image of themselves. In an article published only three months before this story, Naipaul underlines the same fact when he says of Trinidad: "… we felt we existed only when we were known by others. We were truly dependent. To know ourselves, to get a necessary self-esteem, we did not need writers. We required tourists … ."[6] The statement made with respect to India's post-independence confusion of identity in *An Area of Darkness* suits the context: "Indians floundered about in a new world whose forms they could see but whose spirit eluded them. In the acquiring of an identity in their own land they became displaced."[7]

Most of the features of the story are obviously determined by Naipaul's personal preoccupations. Typical Caribbean setting and familiar Naipaulian themes reappear in this story. Various details, ideas, and phrases from his earlier works reappear in "A Flag on the Island". The basis of many of the subsidiary details of the story can be found in *The Middle Passage*. In the very opening paragraph of the story Frank decides not to go ashore with the others. This statement straightaway carries the reader back to *An Area of Darkness* and *The Mimic Men*. It demonstrates Naipaul's method of reproducing his personal experience into his fiction. The protagonists of different novels bear a resemblance to their creator in disposition and responsiveness as they all echo the familiar ambivalence. The narrator of the story is an American and there are no East Indian characters, but it hardly makes any difference to Naipaulian image of Caribbean life.

Moreover, the characteristic nostalgia of an expatriate may be observed in the story when Chinese Ma-Ho is always shown dreaming of his return to China. His shop walls are covered with charming calendars of Chinese beauties and picturesque birds and waterfalls, which appear odd in a Caribbean island. For him, "these pictures were like a longing for another world, and, indeed Ma-Ho did not plan to stay on the island" (*A Flag on the Island*, pp. 190–91). It reminds the reader of comforting fantasy of the first generation Indians in *A House for Mr Biswas* who always talk of returning to India. Similarly, in the story, Blackwhite even questions the existence of the island. He reminds Frank: "This place, I tell you, is nowhere. It doesn't exist. People are just born here. They all want to go away … ." (*A Flag on the Island*, p. 187). Naipaul here projects his personal displacement from his Trinidadian past onto an American soldier Frank, who realizes that the past cannot be reclaimed. The displaced expatriate consciousness, in its desperate hunt for stability, is reproduced through Frank. He feels that the whole world is being washed away and he is being washed away with it. The castle in the air nurtured carefully in the expatriate imagination is contaminated by the present reality when he comes to understand: "All landscapes are in the end only in the imagination; to be faced with the reality is to start again". (*A Flag on the Island*, p. 124)

In the story "My Aunt Gold Teeth", Naipaul deals with the credulous nature of his hybrid society through the character of Gold Teeth, a barren lady from an orthodox Hindu family who indulges in irrational Christian practices. By chance, her husband falls ill and everyone believes that her simultaneous belief in Christianity is responsible for her husband's suffering. In the meantime, Pundit Ganesh poses as rational and finds nothing objectionable in Gold Teeth's dual faith, and one day her husband dies unexpectedly. This story narrates the adventures of the narrator's aunt Gold Teeth who is childless, plump and gullible. Aunt Gold Teeth's internal reservations about crossing the religious limits of Hinduism do not dissuade her from taking refuge in Christianity, a more influential curative faith for her sterlity. Paradoxically, her husband pundit Ramprasad falls ill during her Christian ordeal. Later on, her affection to divergent spiritual practices allegedly causes her husband's death. It makes Aunt Gold Teeth resent her acts of unorthodoxy. The clash here is symbolic of a larger conflict, i.e., between the West and the East. The superstitious Gold Teeth confronts the boy narrator who is annoyed at the melodrama performed by his aunt when the spirits control her: "I was rather ashamed at the exhibition, and annoyed with Gold Teeth for putting me into a fright". (*A Flag on the Island*, p. 17)

Aunt Gold Teeth wants instant results through superficial faith and her divided loyalty, but ironically her faith turns her into a childless widow. Now, she is tormented by the idea that her secret Christian practices might be responsible for the tragedy. Sometimes she feels that her husband's death may be the result of the consecrated ash he was fed in enormous quantity. This episode certainly takes the reader back to Ganesh's temple in *The Mystic Masseur* where the idols of Hindu gods are put with the cross. Naipaul seems to suggest that a person of dual faith and identity may be suicidal. Tulsi's diversion towards Christian practices in *A House for Mr Biswas* after the death of the family priest is another example worth mentioning here to demonstrate Naipaul's typical hypothesis. Ganesh, the proficient spiritualist, has become very much like a pathfinder to resolve the predicament of a hybrid colonial life. Recurrence of Ganesh in Naipaul's fiction *The Mystic Masseur*, *Miguel Street* and *A Flag on the Island* establishes a philosophy of convenience rather than ideology in colonial set up. He is one of the most prevailing characters in Naipaul's stories who believes in practical means to avoid exploitation. The narrator adds: "In his professional capacity Ganesh was consulted by people of many faiths, and with the license of the mystic he had exploited the commodiousness of Hinduism and made room for all beliefs. In this way he had made many clients, as he called them, many satisfied clients". (*A Flag on the Island*, p. 13)

As the story, "My Aunt Gold Teeth", is narrated from a Hindu insider's point of view, it underlines the cultural changes observed in orthodox Hindu families in Trinidad. Ganesh in *The Mystic Masseur* insists his wife Leela upon using pure English instead of dialect. When tried, they perform badly resulting in humiliation and embarrassment. Similarly, this story also illustrates the Indian expatriates' mimicking tendency. Gold Teeth initiates a dialogue with her husband saying:

> "Man", she said.
>
> Ramprasad continued to eat.
>
> "Man," she said in English. "I thinking about going to the church to pray. You never know, and it better to be on the safe side. After all, the house ain't tied."
>
> "'I don't want you to pray in no church," he whispered, in English too. (*A Flag on the Island*, pp. 18–19)

Naipaul skilfully dwells on the absurdity of a situation where Aunt Gold Teeth enters a church for the first time but she is unaware of the mannerism of the church. The narrator captures the essential ambivalence among the displaced expatriates like Gold Teeth and ridiculousness of their situation in the following words:

> ... carried herself into the churchyard ... feeling like an explorer in a land of cannibals ... . In the gilt and images and the resplendent cloths she found much that reminded her of her Hindu temple ... picked up a candle and muttered a prayer in Hindustani. A brief moment of elation gave way to a sense of guilt, and she was suddenly anxious to get away from the church as fast as her weight would let her. (*A Flag on the Island*, pp. 14–15)

Further, Ganesh's astrological prediction about the seven spirits haunting Ramprasad is the testimony of the black cloud haunting the narrator boy in *The Mystic Masseur* and then tormenting Mohun Biswas in *A House for Mr Biswas*. His professional and mature statement after performing certain rites for Gold Teeth: "There is nothing more I can do. God will do all the rest" (*A Flag on the Island*, p. 16) gets hold of the tormented psyche of the clients. There are many instances in the story where the traditional Hindu culture clashes with the Christian faith. Aunt Gold Teeth's tragedy is shown to be the result of this obvious conflict between the native and the borrowed faith. Again the story shows that Indian way of life prevails among the Indian expatriates at Trinidad. Their nostalgia adds to their feeling of alienation and rootlessness. While introducing the protagonist of this story, the narrator says:

> She ate little and prayed much. Her family being Hindu, and her husband being a pundit, she, too, was an orthodox Hindu. Of Hinduism she knew little apart from the ceremonies and the taboos, and this was enough for her. Gold Teeth saw God as a Power, and religious ritual as a means of harnessing that power for great practical good, her good. (*A Flag on the Island*, p. 13)

It is evident here that the obvious clash between different cultures in multicultural landscapes gets due representation in the story. The irony here is more agonizing, as the story satirizes Christianity, as much as Hinduism. The narrator of the story "Aunt Gold Teeth" presents the dilemma and ambivalence of the postcolonial expatriates when he says:

> She was living at the time in a country village called Cunupia, in County Caroni. Here the Canadian mission had long waged war against the Indian heathen, and saved many … . At no time was Gold Teeth persuaded even to think about being converted. The idea horrified her. Her father had been in his day one of the best-known Hindu pundits, and even now her husband's fame as a pundit, as a man who could read and write Sanskrit, had spread far beyond Cunupia. She was in no doubt whatsoever that Hindus were the best people in the world, and Hinduism was a superior religion. She was willing to select, modify and incorporate alien eccentricities into her worship; but to abjure her own faith—never! (*A Flag on the Island*, p. 14)

Naipaul hence satirizes the orthodoxy among the expatriates in a mock-heroic style. The story is the mockery of the multicultural society with confused loyalty. Aunt Gold Teeth's gradual inclination towards Christianity is a typical diasporic phenomenon indicating acculturation. She acknowledges that her assimilation in Christianity is not instinctive. The narrator observes her confusion aptly: "She carried herself into the churchyard, awed by her own temerity, feeling like an explorer in a land of cannibals" (*A Flag on the Island*, p. 14). Naipaul portrays the displaced society for which religion implies rituals only and the values attached to it are hardly revered. *A Flag on the Island* does not adhere to one period and place only; rather, it refers to the late 60s also when the Indian communities were at the verge of losing their identity due to Presbyterianism and its impact on the second or third generation expatriates.

Another story that illustrates the diluting Hinduism and Indianness in Caribbean islands is "A Christmas Story". Once again, history seems to repeat itself when Choonilal buries his traditional name under the influence of Western practices. Like Ganesh in *The Mystic Masseur*, Choonilal-turned-Randolph is very much proud of his acquired identity. The in-betweenness of the colonial by products like Randolph has always overshadowed Naipaul's fiction throughout his career. Randolph never develops any sense of belongingness with the religion of his grandparents. He is always uneasy like Mohun Biswas in *A House for Mr Biswas* who could hardly make any sense of Hindu prayers and rites. This episode reminds the reader of Ganesh's movement towards assimilation in the creole society of Trinidad in the novel *The Mystic Masseur*. In "A Christmas Story", the narrator hero of the story finds his Hindu identity outworn, old-fashioned and irrelevant as he admits:

> I continued a Hindu, though of that religion I saw and knew little save meaninglessness and shameful rites, until I was nearly eighteen … . Perhaps it was the inertia with which that religion deadens its devotees … was a religion little fitted for the modern world. I had only to contrast the position of the Hindus with that of the Christians. (*A Flag on the Island*, p. 33)

To assert his identity, Randolph accepts the faith of the dominating class but ironically his conversion leads him to utter failure and worldly success always eludes him. Repeatedly, he describes progress as an attitude of mind rather than a superficial demonstration. He champions the Presbyterianism flouting all inherent Hindu norms just to get himself identified and to get rid off backwardness. The love-hate relationship of Mohun Biswas, Ganesh and Choonilal towards the native and alien culture, in *A House for Mr Biswas, The Mystic Masseur* and *A Flag on the Island* respectively, adds to their absurdity and ambivalence. Choonilal's artificial sense of pride on his conversion gets reflected in the following lines:

> It was a pleasure to hear myself called Randolph, a name of rich historical associations, a name I feel, thoroughly attuned to the times in which we live and to the society in which I found myself, and to forget that once—I still remember it with shame—I answered, with simple instinct, to the name of Choonilal … . I have buried it. (*A Flag on the Island*, p. 34)

In the story, Naipaul demonstrates the perils of hybridity in the colonial situation. The story traces the events in the life of Randolph [Choonilal] who notwithstanding his dedication to the vocation of teaching is incapable of managing the ultimate triumph. He measures his success in proportion to that of Hari whom he hates for his conservative orthodoxy. His catch-22 situation can be observed when he starts practicing the English ways of eating and wearing. As in *The Mystic Masseur,* Naipaul ridicules Ganesh's awkwardness at the Governor's Dinner; here also Randolph's uneasiness while handling the knife, fork and spoon is highly absurd. Moreover he has developed his taste for beef that is prohibited among the Hindus. His love-hate relationship with his roots gets reflected in his remarks:

> But that was not the end of my trials. I had up to that time eaten with my fingers, a manner of eating which is now so repulsive to me, so ugly, so unhygienic, that I wonder how I managed to do it until my eighteenth year. Yet I must now confess that at that time food never tasted as sweet as when eaten with the fingers, and that my first attempts to eat with the proper implements of knife and fork and spoon were almost in the nature of shameful experiments, furtively carried out; and even when I was by myself I could not get rid of the feeling of self-consciousness. It was easier to get used to the name of Randolph than to knife and fork. (*A Flag on the Island*, p. 36)

Cosequently, at the marriage of Hori's son, he realizes the gap between his wretchedness and Hori's prosperity. Nothing is in store for him except failure, frustration and dismissal after his severance from established Hindu family bond. It is a satire on the double standards and snobbish attitude of the people like Randolph, who jeopordizes his own identity in the process of acquiring a new image as a converted Presbyterian of Indian origin and a teacher by profession. He mocks at his Indian counterparts, Hindu religion and all that belong to the Hindus. He even condemns cow as a "filthy animal, far filthier than the pig, which they abhor" (*A Flag on the Island,* p. 37). Surprisingly, he relishes beef, but feels scared while eating it in Hori's presence. He says, "I was eating beef with knife and fork—to be found thus by Hori was a trifle embarrassing. I must have looked the picture of over-zealous convert" (*A Flag on the Island,* p. 37). Randolph considers Hinduism unfit for the modern world as it stands for subservience. Like Ganesh in *The Mystic Masseur* who starts adopting Western sense of dressing, Choonilal turned Randolph scorns *dhoti* worn by Hindus, as for him, they expose the legs. Paradoxically, he has all praise for the Christian girls who wear short-frocks, leaving their legs totally bare. He admires the missionaries who work amongst the backward people but he himself does not like the idea of backwardness. He delays his marriage to get a wife unlike the Hindu wives whom he hates for their lack of refinement and education. He says, "I wished to marry a Presbyterian lady who was intelligent, well brought up and educated, and wished to marry me. This last condition, alas, I could find few willing to fulfil" (*A Flag on the Island*, p. 40). But, his condemnation of Hindus is always baseless and ultimately he gets married to a lady of ordinary substance. His wife is unscrupulous as she silently approves her husband's misappropriation of school funds. Unlike a typical Hindu wife, she devises the melodramatic plot to burn off the school building just to save her husband from public shame. Randolph's personal absurdity gets intensified with his repeated sardonic remarks against the Hindus. Somewhere he seems to have understood the insignificance of his conversion, as his divided-self never allows him to relish his existence. Futility of his bold decision to severe the ties with his native culture just to soar high in the realm of colonial mimicking dream, gets vivid expression at the end when he contemplates confession at the moment when he is facing an enquiry for the corruption charges against him. Again the story is stuffed with the portrayal of Hindu and Indian way of life in contrast to the dominant Western norms. Choonilal turned Randolph is the typical Naipaulian figure characterizing the ambivalence and absurdity among the colonized who mimic the colonizers.

Indian names like Choonilal, Hori, Kedar; Hindu practices like abstinence from beef, cow-worship, austerity and theism; typical Indian customs like dowry, wearing *dhoti-kurtah*, community life, use of banana leaves for plates, eating with fingers, etc., stand sharply contrasted with the borrowed culture of the Western world. Naipaul suggests that the East–West dichotomy is the obvious phenomenon of the colonial landscapes. Mimicking the Western is common among the expatriates, émigrés and nomads of the colonial world. This mimicry can not provide them the enduring sense of fulfilment; rather, it intensifies their sense of instability and consequent ambivalence.

Similarly, "The Enemy", a story that figures in *A Flag on the Island* presents the dilemma of the boy narrator. His uncomfortable relationship with his parents, their separation, eventual death of his father, and the narrator's shift from the country to the city, construct the story. The story once more offers a colonial background that makes the narrator's family undergo traumatic experiences. His father's tyrannical attitude towards the cane workers is an index of the mindset bred by the colonial system of plantation. Intermittent fear haunting the narrator and his father presents the evident scepticism and ambivalence about his father's reputation as an authoritarian supervisor. In this way, the story explains the divergent forms of rural as well as urban life in Trinidad. This episode takes the reader back to "Green Vale" chapter in *A House for Mr Biswas*.

The narrator's dilemma bears a strong resemblance to the ambivalence of Anand in *A House for Mr Biswas*, who is in a fix whether to give company to his father on the plantation farm Green Vale or to return to the city with his mother, Shama. Like Shama, the mother of this boy also cannot stand the fright of intimidating plantation workers any more. Just like Mohun Biswas, the father tempts the son with a favourite inducement. The narrator adds: "My father was ill, and in bed. Besides, he had promised that if I stayed with him I was to have a whole box of crayons" (*A Flag on the Island*, p. 77). Like Anand, he chooses to remain with his father: "I chose the crayons and my father" (*A Flag on the Island*, p. 77). The replication of these Naipaulian episodes in "The Enemy", however, bears more intricate implications, as the preference of the boy is suggestive of his assertion against hegemony and traditional colonial social order. The son supports the father at the time of crisis when workers of the Cunupia estates intimidate his father. However he loses his father who dies of anxiety on one such terror-ridden night. His self-gratification can be ascertained only by his dismissal of the feudal structure of the houses like Hanuman House.

Besides, the opening of the story carries a note of heart-rending intensity. The narrator passes the shocking remarks: "I had always considered this woman, my mother as the enemy. She was sure to misunderstand anything I did ..." (*A Flag on the Island*, p. 77). The story seems to be the echo of "Green Vale" chapter of *A House for Mr Biswas* where Mohun is obsessed with the idea of a house of his own away from the tyranny of Tulsi House and it leads him to Green Vale where like the narrator boy in this story, Anand accompanies his father. Mohun makes Anand understand that at the time of crisis, only Hindu gods and goddesses may come to his rescue. He asks him, "Say Rama Rama Sita Ram, and nothing will happen to you."[8] Similarly, in this story, the boy remembers the advice of his father at Cunupia, when he remarks: "I went to another room and walked about saying, "Rama! Rama! Sita Ram! This was what my father had told me to say when I was in danger of any sort" (*A Flag on the Island*, p. 78). Killing of their pet dog, Tarzan, and father's "hanging up words of hope on the walls of the house, things from the Gita and the Bible" (*A Flag on the Island*, p. 80) in the story takes the reader back to *A House for Mr Biswas*. But, the most important resemblance between the accounts of Mohun's life and that of this boy narrator's life becomes evident when in this story also the father and the son indulge in a dialogue questioning their mutual relationship. The narrator puts it thus:

> "Boy," my father asked, "Who is your father?"
>
> I said, "You is my father."
>
> "Wrong."
>
> "How that wrong?"
>
> My father said, "You want to know who your father really is? God is your father."
>
> "And what you is, then?"
>
> "Me, what I is? I is—let me see, well, I is just a second sort of father, not your real father." (*A Flag on the Island*, p. 80)

Though the dialogue differs from the one in *A House for Mr Biswas* where Mohun says that he is someone Anand knows only. This detachment develops in the father's mind first because of his Hindu faith, and secondly for the reason that he himself is unaware of his established identity in a colonial background. It is an explicit reference to the author's childhood. In the story, the parents always indulge in bickering and leave the child unattended. The boy also receives a lot of beating and thrashing everyday. All his pains to win his mother's heart fail. It is only when he gets wounded and falls ill, that his mother shows the signs of her concern. He innocently reacts: "I wished I were a Hindu god at that moment, with two hundred arms, so that all two hundred could be broken, just to enjoy that moment, and to see again my mother's tears" (*A Flag on the Island*, p. 87). The story expands the matrimonial clash of Naipaul's own parents. The differences between the two stem from the culturally induced split between his mother's parents and that of his father. The conflict described by Naipaul here is developed as a continuance of family theme in his masterpiece *A House for Mr Biswas*. Here, Naipaul intermingles his personal experiences with his fictional characters, and the awkwardness and disorder projected in the tales is mainly due to the ambivalence rooted in the psyche of the novelist himself.

The comic stories "The Perfect Tenants" and "Greenie and Yellow" are set in boarding house owned by the landlady Mrs Cooksey in England. The first story gives us an entertaining portrait of the hostilities between the once-favoured tenants, the Dakins and the landlady with whom they develop enmity within no time. The narrator is a dispassionate tenant and observer, but well aware of his pathetic condition. "Greenie and Yellow" is a figurative story narrated in a fable like manner. It is a narrative of three birds—Bluey, Yellow and Greenie. Bluey, a favoured bird that has been Mrs Cooksey's pet, fights back to supplant two other birds Greenie and Yellow—those which have briefly replaced Bluey in the affections of the landlady. Bluey is a cage bird, constantly joyful and energetic while playing with its toys. With the entry of another intimidating, snobbish and ear-splitting bird Greenie, Bluey finds itself at a complete loss. Bluey is unable to resist Greenie, so it remains submissive and resigned in the cage. Another bird, Yellow, is brought as a companion for Greenie but Yellow dislocates it. Yellow plays with Greenie and does not let it take rest, but Greenie takes no notice of Yellow's light-heartedness. Yellow disturbs Greenie to the extent that it falls seriously ill and then dies. Greenie's death brings frustration for Yellow so it is put with Bluey which takes interest in it, but of no avail. Eventually, Yellow also dies like Greenie. After the death of two rivals, Bluey again feels revitalized as it used to be in the past. Through this tale, Naipaul conveys the truth that the enclosed life has made Bluey incompetent of living in a free mood. The cage symbolizes the world devoid of prospect for creativity. After their death, the skeleton skulls of Greenie and Yellow could hardly be identified, thereby suggesting the fact that the two birds are essentially identical. The story has its background in England, and Naipaul here attempts to recount slavery, disappointment, desperation and the ridiculousness of creative work in the world where every creature is indulged in a never-ending quest for recognition.

Likewise, the stories "My Heart", "The Mourners", "The Raffle" and "The Enemy" bring to light the world of childhood which is constantly threatened by the grown-ups. The vision of attachment with a dog is the central idea of the story "My Heart". It is an emotional study of the growth of a sub-standard child Hari who is born to affluent parents. He assaults his pet dog as if to avenge against other figures of power such as his schoolmates who intimidate him, or the violent Alsatian dogs he encounters on his way to school. The story elaborates the theme of the undesirable interference of parents in the life of an only child who wishes to assert his own identity. Naipaul presents the correlation between Hari's weak heart that doesn't allow him to be a normal child, and the Bleeding Heart Vine in the courtyard of his family home. The ethical point stressed in the story is that the daydreaming can be dangerous both for the child and the parents.

In "The Mourners", the protagonist Romesh pays a condolence visit to share the grief of Sheila and her husband, who have lost their only son, Ravi. He fails to deliver any compassion towards the aggrieved parents. The cold sentiments of the narrator fail to console the bereaved parents. He is repeatedly asked to view the photographs in the leather-bound album but ironically Romesh is preoccupied with his own priority, i.e., preparation for the scholarship exams, which will enable him to get out of the backwardness of his country. Thus, the formal relations are subjected to ridicule and humiliation in the story.

In "The Raffle", the schoolboy Vidiadhar, slowly but surely realizes the hazards of being a favourite student of his teacher, Mr Hinds. The hilarious episode in the story is the gifting of Mr Hinds's goat to Vidiadhar in a raffle. It is a premeditated plan by Mr Hinds to get rid of the barren goat. The maltreatment of the children by the tyrannical teachers especially within the colonial education system produces the more serious propositions in the story. Vidiadhar is lashed for the first time by Mr Hinds because his mother has arranged to sell the goat. It makes the boy leave the school once for all.

Naipaul's keenness and concern for the traditional norms of racial discrimination are documented in "The Baker's Story". Here, the black narrator puts great effort to launch himself as a baker in Port of Spain. He is introduced as black as the Ace of Spades. Once again Naipaul sets the stage to present the enigma of multicultural society. The obvious clash between different races is vivified in the story. He exposes the altercations between the Indians, the Chinese and the Blacks over unimportant issues. The crisis of the "bastard" narrator cast off by his mother is further aggravated by his poverty.

In the course of time, he starts his mission to establish his identity as a "behind the scene worker" in a small Chinese bakery. He has no doubts about his lowest position in the racial hierarchy. Racial discrimination consequent upon essential clash of cultures is accompanied by the gap between the rich and the poor. The narrator cautiously respects this gap when he mentions the difference between the dough from which bread is baked: "But as I was saying this bakery used to bake ordinary bread for the poorer classes. For the richer classes they used to bake too. But what they would do would be to collect the dough from those people house, bake it, and send it back as bread, hot and sweet". (*A Flag on the Island*, p. 114)

As a business tactic, ironically, the black proprietor of the bakery deliberately hides his racial identity while naming his shop. He names his shop "Young Man" baker, imitating the Chinese way of spelling and writing. He appoints a Chinese boy to serve in the shop while he remains behind the curtain baking the bread. Gradually he turns out to be the richest men in Port of Spain but his awareness of the colonial ambivalence jeopardizes his position and social status.

He admits: "… as I say I only going in the shops from the back" (*A Flag on the Island*, p. 146). The baker has earlier experienced the inevitability of these racial prejudices in the Creole society of Trinidad. He says: "And then I see that though Trinidad have every race and every colour, every race have to do special things". (*A Flag on the Island*, p. 120)

Therefore, the stifling of the narrator's aspirations due to racial discrimination represents the agony of the colonized who accept subjugation and slavery as their destiny. He always fails to realize his individuality and self-esteem. With the passage of time, he comes to establish himself in a respectable livelihood but with the acceptance of his inferiority that gets reflected when he says:

> You know, it never cross my minds in those days that I could open a shop of my own. Is how it is with black people. They get so used to working for other people that they get to believe that because they black they can't do nothing else but work for other people. And I must tell you that when I start praying and God tell me to go out and open a shop for myself I feel that perhaps God did mistake or that I hadn't hear Him good. (*A Flag on the Island*, p. 140)

Consequently, the narrator here is doubly condemned due to the apathetic attitude of the Trinidadians towards the Grenadian Blacks. He insists upon making a place of his own through the hard-earned money and obviously he succeeds in prospering. But his riches are unable to give him social gratification as the sense of insecurity and alienation keeps on haunting his psyche. About his financial position, he admits: "Sometimes I find it hard to believe it myself … Grenada, where I come from – and that is one thing these Trinidad black people don't forgive a man for being …" (*A Flag on the Island*, p. 135). Economic security somehow lessens the misery of the colonial figures like the narrator. Money surmounts all other requirements in a typical colonial setting chracterized by all common racial, communal and social biases. The narrator could establish his identity in the multicultural society only through his proprietorship. He is devoid of any individual recognition but he shows his resolute determination to become a well-off man, though he pays the price for it.

Though Naipaul has always been sensitive towards the community, race and caste-based issues in colonial countries like Trinidad and India, he has no sympathy for the colonized Indians as he, "does not say anything useful about colonialism; in fact he blames the colonized for their failure to become postcolonial."[9] In "A Baker's Story", the narrator prefers the back door entry in his shop to hide the identity of the proprietor of the bakery. He deliberately avoids writing his name on the signboard of his bakery and keeps himself in the background. The socially disadvantaged émigrés understand that only the back entrance is meant for them. He observes:

> I was worrying to hell about the name I should give the place ... and I get a proper sign painter to copy a few letters from the Chinee newspaper. Below that, in big letters, I make him write:
>
> YOUNG MAN
> BAKER
>
> I never show my face in the front of the shop again ... was hard in the beginning to get real Chinee people to work for a black man. But money have it own way of talking, and when today you pass any of the Young Man establishments all you seeing behind the counter is Chinee. Some of them ain't even know they working for a black man. My wife handling that side of the business, and the wife is Chinee .... As I say, I only going in the shops from the back. (*A Flag on the Island*, p. 146)

The colonial expatriates like the baker can very well understand the worth of money as the only medium of assertion. In *The Mystic Masseur*, Ganesh could realise his partial selfhood only through monetary gains. Here also, the Black Grenadian baker comes to terms with the alien environment by the means of worldly gains. The story establishes the point that caste, class, as well as race determine the nature of social networking in Trinidad.

In the story "The Night Watchman's Occurrence Book" the narrative is carried out through a set of daily entries maintained in a register by the Night Watchman, who records the activities in the hotel. The comedy is caused by the gap in awareness and expectations between the Manager of the hotel and Night Watchman, Hillyard. Thus, the stories are insightful penetration into the psychological uncertainties, ambivalence, anxieties, disgrace, vacillating mindsets and a flinching sense of self. Essentially displaced identity and uprootedness of expatriates leave no scope for optimism and day-dreaming. Naipaul's reflection hangs around all the postcolonial stories included in this collection. These are the tales concerning the questions of survival, disguise, withdrawal or escape. The central characters of the stories lack self-expression and self-esteem; they are indulged in a constant combat with the dominating forces. The issues raised in these stories are varied—the humiliation due to poverty, the anxiety of childhood enslavement, the racial and religious conflicts, emptiness of exile, and the torn-identities. The stories again reproduce small island colonies with inadequate opportunities. They sensationalize the prevalent threat of existence among the expatriates in an alien land where they are bound to compromise with their native religious faith.

To all intents and purposes, the stories in this collection extend to three stages—Trinidad, emigrant life in England, and Trinidad re-visited. They span Naipaul's boyhood, the first phase of his search for a postcolonial identity through conscious recall of the formative years. The stories bring about troubled aspects of the author's personality in the displaced orthodox family, the colonial education, and expatriate rehabilitation in England. The eleven stories demonstrate the growth of Naipaul's personal postcolonial mission. There is a growing tendency in his fiction for his protagonists to pose like his alter ego resulting into the repetition of themes that have preoccupied him. His recurrent issues emanate from the isolation of an expatriate writer. In an interview with Adrian Rowe Evans in 1971, he said: "By the nature of one's situation one is really writing in a vacuum … . Writing is essentially local … . One does need the response. One needs to have the exchange; otherwise it becomes such a private activity. I've got to accept this now, that it's totally private … ."[10]

By and large, the dichotomy of the multicultural colonial societies is the recurrent theme of his fictional works. His own "expatriate status makes his work 'interstitial' in that they capture the texture of the lives of the people of both the cultures at the very crack between culture."[11] Like the novels of the first phase, the dilemma of the second and third generation immigrants seeking to rebuild their lives preoccupies *A Flag on the Island*. The confused pulls of the colonial experience are nicely intertwined in the collection by presenting the characters who feel the pain arising out of their dislocation from their native culture.

Generally, the stories come out with the poverty stricken depressing survivors and the few exceptional assertive figures that ironically repeat an ancestral pursuit to improve their destiny in the alien land. Reflecting the oppressive colonial locale, the stories present the postcolonial journey of the self. The linear handling of the phases of the narrator's development of perception, from boyhood to adulthood and expatriation, unifies the collection. In his stories, he imbibes the reliable experiences of a writer and the voices of the immigrant population in the Caribbean colonies. The obvious modification in the way of life, psyche and language of the insecure colonials provoked by European colonialism, becomes the heart of the matter for the perturbed diasporic writer V.S. Naipaul. The stories portray the predicament of a colonial population whose long-established structures are withering away. The writer shows steady urbanization of the island. The characters are shown fighting for their identity and recognition. The tales are typically the narration of "the assertion of cultural nationalism, or the voice of the people who unheard so long, the voice of people who were formerly underdogs."[12]

In his fictional works, V.S. Naipaul portrays the people living on the Caribbean island equally prone to the vices of the contemporary world. They suffer from common human colonial weaknesses such as egotism, superstition, narrow-mindedness, corruption, double standards, and a tendency for exploitation. Hence the common occurrence in the stories is ambivalence. The characters are multifaceted in nature. The writer does not pay much attention to the outwardly noticeable social realities of life but with the inner, psychosomatic condition of the minds. There is no common narrator in the book rather the narrator changes from story to story. In the title story, Frankie and Henry assert their roots when they argue: "What we want is our own language. I intend to write in our own language ... 'Yes,' Henry said. 'We must defend our culture.' And sadly regarding his new customers, he added: 'We must go back to the old days" (*A Flag on the Island*, p. 205). The degeneration of the Hindu families in Trinidad is another favourite theme of Naipaul who himself has been the victim of "double-exile".[13]

In *A Flag on the Island*, the stories present a sardonic analysis of the lives of the colonials, young and old, men and women caught in conventional family situations. They represent the life in the colonial school, a life of insufficient opportunities, and the life deprived of anything meaningful that may prevent the distortion of their identities. Paucity of resources frustrates the aspirations of most of the characters in this selection of stories and it is only in the title story "A Flag on the Island", that Trinidad is shown benefitting from its expansion as a tourist paradise. Adopting a comic vision, Naipaul correlates the sketches of his family's history to his fictional account.

In the same way, *The Mimic Men* is a popular novel of Naipaul written in the early stage of decolonization and the disintegration of empire. The novel is an attempt to highlight the sense of futility regarding mimicking of the colonizer by the colonized. However, the novel can also be read and interpreted in the light of Bhabha's sense of "mimicry" as empowerment. Bhabha remarks:

> Mimicry is, then, the sign of a double articulation; a complex strategy of reform, regulation and discipline, which 'appropriates' the Other as it visualizes power. Mimicry is also the sign of the inappropriate ... function of colonial power, intensifies

surveillance, and poses an immanent threat to both 'normalized' knowledges and disciplinary powers.[14]

This mimicking ambivalence is the result of the effects of advancement on the colonial émigrés. Further Bhabha seems to discredit this mimicking tendency put forth by Naipaul in his novels when he says: "The menace of mimicry is its double vision which in disclosing the ambivalence of colonial discourse also disrupts its authority. And it is a double vision that is a result of what I've described as the partial representation/recognition of the colonial object."[15] The colonial "mimic" man resists modernity through his dissimilarity but he/she also desires it. *The Mimic Men,* a fictional autobiography, is a sort of retreat to the world of the first four novels—but it is a retreat with a difference. While Trinidad is the locale of the first four novels, in this novel Naipaul chooses the fictitious island of Isabella, a representative Caribbean island. The protagonist of the novel shows that the typical colonial happenings of Isabella do not only represent West Indies but also the remaining colonies worldwide. Ralph Kripalsingh asserts: "It has happened in twenty places, twenty countries, islands, colonies, territories."[16] In *A House for Mr Biswas*, Anand, Naipaul's voice, leaves Trinidad for England after winning a scholarship. The signs of the neurosis, which preoccupies Kripalsingh in *The Mimic Men*, are noticeable in Anand's letter to Mr Biswas also. He writes: "They [the letters] were gloomy, self-pitying; then they were tinged with a hysteria which Mr Biswas immediately understood."[17] *The Mimic Men* is an addendum to the earlier works of Naipaul answering the question of the consequences of much hyped escape of the colonials like Ralph Kripalsingh.

The narrator of the novel is Ranjit Kripalsingh or Ralph Ranjit Kripal Singh [R.R.K. Singh], as he desires to be known. He is the only son of a Hindu family on the illusory Caribbean island of Isabella. He is a man with a troubled psyche owing to his disturbed childhood and youth, a severed marriage and an abortive political career. With the harrowing experiences of a colonial, he writes the account of his life in a suburban London hotel. He makes himself known as a man with a poignant psychological injury that makes him ineffective in love and friendship. Being self-absorbed, he is unable to form consequential or long-lasting relationships. He is obsessed with the idea of consistency in life that results into his abounding interest in history. This obsession further forces him to reproduce the history of his own. He seeks refuge in writing while encountering obvious disorder in his life. Kripalsingh runs off from the Caribbean island for England with the usual expectations of the colonial people. Considering himself as deserted on this island, he never feels settled. Seeking fulfilment and a sense of affiliation to a well-established order, he flees from the essentially mimicking culture of the colonial society. Yashoda Bhat observes an expatriate's common preoccupations: "... incessant travel, displacement and homelessness. At the heart of an expatriate is a growing restlessness that makes him launch on 'temporary journeys'. 'Flights' and 'escapes' are common features in expatriate life."[18] But here also he finds a more severe remoteness, a more heightened sense of being aimless, and a keen sense of being *shipwrecked* in London. He takes refuge in sexual promiscuity to fight the awesome sense of isolation and the shock of disillusionment. On the realization of the futility of his escape, he marries a London girl Sandra in a distressed proposal for reviving assurance. He is attracted towards her strength, boldness and volatile nature. For him, she represents vivacity that he lacks.

Ralph Singh tells the story of a middle class Indian West Indian of Naipaul's generation who, after a colonial education that includes a British university degree, returns with an English wife to the island of Isabella. After his eventual disappointment in politics, he turns back to England at the age of forty. There he writes the memoirs of his active life from his room in a suburban hotel, ignoring all of his former friends, lovers, and acquaintances. The confidence of Ralph Singh while reproducing the circumstances and events of his life provides a tone of dispassionate analysis to the novel. Although he takes himself as the subject, he comes out to trace the surfacing of a historical phenomenon. While writing *The Mimic Men* Naipaul has been wise enough to introduce a narrative technique that is, according to William Walsh, "dissolving and non-linear, in correspondence with the starts and swerves of the recovering memory, his instrument of self-examination".[19] Kripalsingh attempts to review his own experiences in perspective. He indulges in introspection while looking back at his past. He recollects his past and struggles to order his life in a meaningful pattern.

The narrator here tells his own story of 'shipwreck' without isolating himself and without proposing any choices. Ralph Ranjit Kripalsingh is a failed politician in a postcolonial political environment. When he could make nothing happen, he decides to take off from the island he ruled over some time ago. Kripalsingh is the narrator who at last honestly acknowledges that he too is a victim of that restlessness which has been his subject. The pensive mood of Kripalsingh while writing his memoirs enables him to touch upon the comprehensive themes. Chandra B. Joshi rightly points out his colonial predicaments when he observes:

> The violation inflicted by the colonial educational system, the taint of the slave past, the loneliness of the big city, the futility of chasing ideal landscapes, racial wounds and fantasies, the trauma of placelessness, politics and power and the far-reaching consequences of childhood experiences ... these are held together by the embracing theme of the reconstruction of an individual life and the attempt to understand the hidden workings of personality.[20]

Kripalsingh gets hold of each experience revived by reminiscence and observes it in the framework of the situation at hand.

The characters—Ganesh, Mohun Biswas and Kripalsingh in *The Mystic Masseur, A House for Mr Biswas* and *The Mimic Men* respectively—fail to enjoy the bliss of marriage. The marital discord between husband and wife has been a prevailing theme in the novels of V.S. Naipaul. In *The Mimic Men*, the schoolboys talk about "marriage and the absurdity of the institution that would turn all the foolish boys ... into husbands, lords and masters to girls who, poor things, could not at that moment guess their maturing fate" (*The Mimic Men*, p. 163). The ultimate failure in marriage is not only because of poverty, ugliness or sullen nature of husbands or wives rather the root cause behind their dissatisfaction in marriage lies somewhere in their colonial milieu. After inheriting a 120 acre block of land from his grandfather, Ralph is prosperous enough to live a graceful life. His rare farsightedness makes him develop this land into a residential area. He admits: "I was one of those who foresaw the post-war spread of cities, the destruction of the open spaces between settlements; and on Isabella I was the first". (*The Mimic Men*, pp. 59–60)

After the completion of his studies in London, he comes back to the island he had resolved never to visit again with his English wife, Sandra. Sandra is taken as a talisman to fight against his deep-rooted inhibitions of his native place, Isabella. Paradoxically, he fails to understand that Sandra, his wife, has accepted him as a husband out of the same need. He is so engrossed in his own psychological distress that he fails in his marital relationship. He can never assess the depth of Sandra's expectations who wants to escape a future of lackluster triviality. In the alien island of Isabella, she needs his constant emotional support and guidance but he fails to get rid of his personal uncertainty. His mother never accepts Sandra as her daughter-in-law. But all faults lie with Ralph who did not let his mother know of his marriage. Moreover, he did not feel like informing Sandra of the expected inhospitable welcome at his home. He claims that theirs, "were an intermediate race, the genes passive, capable of disappearing in two generations into any of the three races of men .... My mother's sanctions were a pretence, no doubt; but they were also an act of piety towards the past, towards ancient unknown wanderings in another continent" (*The Mimic Men*, pp. 58–59). Kripalsingh undermines the insulting behaviour of his mother towards Sandra. But Sandra is unable to overlook the indifference. Obviously, the marriage never recovers from the unpleasant start.

Consequently, the incongruous match breaks with the ultimate departure of Sandra. Ralph is deserted at a time when he is an affluent man with the status of a "playboy". Consequently, a former schoolmate, Browne, a Negro, draws him towards politics. Their fantasy turns grave when their party prevails in the elections and Browne becomes the Prime Minister and Kripalsingh is nominated a cabinet minister. His essentially wavering and indecisive nature reasserts itself very soon when he starts withdrawing himself from political life. Being frustrated over his failure to bring about a nationalization of the sugar estates and managing the race riots, he absconds from Isabella for the second time. As a displaced colonial ex-politician at forty, he withdraws from the dynamic life and settles down in a suburban London hotel. His urge to write his memoirs takes over his mind within the first eighteen months of his exile.

Initially, Kripalsingh decides to conclude the memoirs within three or four weeks but it takes him fourteen months. These recollections help him not only to understand himself but also to interpret the dilemma of every colonial in the postcolonial world. Like Mohun Biswas, Ganesh and many other protagonists of Naipaul, Ralph also takes the process of writing as a medium to bring about a desired harmony in life at a time when he is feeling *shipwrecked*. The narrator protagonist himself asserts:

> By this recreation the event became historical and manageable ... it will no longer disturb me. And this became my aim: from the central fact of this setting, my presence in this city which I have known as student, politician and now as refugee-immigrant, to impose order on my own history .... (*The Mimic Men*, p. 266)

It gives him an opportunity to shape his outlook in a proper direction. From looking on writers as "incomplete people, to whom writing was a substitute for what it then pleased me to call life" (*The Mimic Men*, p. 266) he comes to see that "the recording of a life might become an extension of that life" (*The Mimic Men*, p. 267). He has shed some of his illusions: "It does not worry me now, as it worried me when I began this book, that at the age of forty I should find myself at the end of my active life. I do not now think this is even true. I no longer yearn for ideal landscapes and no longer wish to know the god of the city". (*The Mimic Men*, p. 273)

Finally, he feels that he has, through setting his memories in order, achieved a sort of catharsis, and has freed himself from the burden of the past. He shows his enthusiasm for a fresh start when he says: "... I have cleared the decks, as it were, and prepared myself for fresh action. It will be the action of a free man" (*The Mimic Men*, p. 274). He has given up an expatriate colonial's futile search for a homeland and his dreams of flight to some idyllic land. He behaves like a genuine spokesperson of Naipaul himself who has realized that he carries his alienation within himself irrespective of the place. Naipaulian acceptance of his homelessness is evident in Ralph Kripalsingh at the end of the novel also. He does not feel like having any affiliation to anything or anybody outside himself. His loneliness empowers his psyche after he has resolved not to attach himself to a particular setting. Chandra B. Joshi compares his situation with that of Biblical figures when he says: "Like the exiled Adam and Eve, he too, as a permanent exile, has the entire world before him."[21]

Though V.S. Naipaul is often accused of being the spokesperson of the imperial power because he underestimates the creative possibilities of the Caribbean in the colonial past and in postcolonial present, the close reading of *The Mimic Men* suggests that these charges are unjustified and uncalled for. Fawzia Mustafa defends Naipaul when he refutes the charges levelled against him:

> By choosing to open the novel at the point in his life when as a student in England he faced the uncertainties of where and how he could fit in the unfamiliar milieu, Naipaul foregrounds the central ambivalence of his protagonist. An early allusion to the Jewish experience of the Holocaust in Europe subtly evokes both the tenor of a colonial experience and the vagaries of the diasporic condition. The second indicator of ambivalence occurs with the troping of snow, the image of which is synecdochal of the colonial desire for the metropole.[22]

His description of expatriation is persistently hopeless when he finds the multifarious outcome of the encounter with colonial situation quite harmful for the growth of the individual identity. In *The Mimic Men*, the "shipwrecked" personality of the protagonist makes it impossible for him to achieve a sense of authenticity of the self. His submission is that the migration and the displacement can only aggravate the ambivalence as the new landscapes can not help him in forgetting his agonizing past. Naipaul writes in *A Way in the World*: "Most of us know the parents or grandparents we come from. But we go back and back, forever; we go back all of us to the very beginning; in our blood and bone and brain we carry the memories of thousands of beings ... sometimes we can be strangers to ourselves."[23]

Obviously, in the novels of Naipaul, colonial subjects always enjoy the status of insignificant emigrants even if they do not share the distress of their parents. The colonial émigrés suffer from a cultural, temporal and spatial exile simultaneously. *The Mimic Men* is an account of Ralph Kripalsingh's alienation, rootlessness and homelessness. He represents the victimized colonial subjects facing the binaries of past and present with an obvious sense of frustration. Like the other protagonists of early novels, he too encounters certain challenges confronting his self and individual identity. Kavita Nandan observes that, "*The Mimic Men* narrates the condition of exile through semantics of loss. The semantics of loss is not seen as desirable, and that is partly why Naipaul is seen as a colonialist and typecast as a mimic man."[24]

The Mimic Men hence underscores the fact that the colonial subject's separation from his/her original home and the resultant strain of exile can not be reduced or compensated by his borrowed location and culture. Though "multiculturalism" is generally defined as a means of winning control of that knowledge which enables one to fight racism and promote postcolonial interests, hybridity, creolization and multiculturalism do not offer any vital reassuring choices. The much-debated term "multiculturalism" came in vogue in Canada during 1960s when it emerged as world's main immigrant receiving country. By 1971, the term was officially adopted by the Federal Government of Canada. As per the official records, the government used the term to: "... refer to a society that is characterised by ethnic or cultural heterogeneity; to refer to an ideal of equality and mutual respect among a population's ethnic or cultural groups; and to refer to the policy proclaimed by the Federal Government in 1971 and subsequently by a number of provinces."[25]

In the beginning, Ralph is enchanted by snow in London; he performs tricks with the famous street names; he observes with a painter's eyes the spectacle of light in a pleasant zone, the soft cloudiness revealing colour everywhere, and the slow progression of dusk. Yet he is ultimately lost in oblivion and subjected to misrepresentation. He is a refugee living with other immigrants in rooms rented out by an expatriate Jew. The city's enchanting sights cannot hide the absurdity of the naming ceremony, the quickness of a London death, or stop him from surrendering himself to one unknown woman after another. No doubt, he is prevented from committing suicide by his trust in Sandra. As he has started relying on her candidness, her gift for phrases, her ostensible ability to handle situations, he returns to Isabella. Gradually, he realises that she too is lost, that in spite of her perceptible confidence, she depends on him to protect herself from insignificance in England. The raucous housewarming party is a symbolic failure, suggesting the duplicity of their marriage ceremony. Ralph is trapped in a catch-22 position, as he never feels at home as a native or an expatriate in a multicultural society of London. He admits:

> The restlessness, the deep disorder, which the great explorations, the overthrow in three continents of established social organizations, the unnatural bringing together of peoples who could achieve fulfilment only within the security of their own societies and the landscapes hymned by their ancestors … . The empires of our time were short-lived, but they have altered the world forever; their passing away is their least significant feature. (*The Mimic Men*, p. 32)

It is in this way that the picture of the colonial world portrayed by Naipaul through this novel is repressive and dehumanizing. Ralph is led to a sense of ruination in London, initially through his sexual encounters that seem associated with the crucial experience of violation in colonial conditions. The colonialism is shown to be a source of defiance in the novel. Stanford Encyclopaedia of Philosophy rightly defines "Colonialism":

> Colonialism is a practice of domination, which involves the subjugation of one people to another … . The term colony comes from the Latin word *colonus*, meaning farmer. This root reminds us that the practice of colonialism usually involved the transfer of population to a new territory, where the new arrivals lived as permanent settlers while maintaining political allegiance to their country of origin.[26]

The violent colonial images of being offended, disfigured and spoilt are perceptible in the novel. Colonialism is a violation because the colonial subject is dehumanized and reduced to his economic value. Naipaul's perception of colonialism is on familiar terms with the historical consequences that the imperial centre had on the colonial periphery. Molly Maureen Mahmood in his *The Colonial Encounter: A Reading of Six Novels,* interprets *The Mimic Men*:

> The primal, wrongness of Caribbean colonialism in all its phases—the creation of a slave society and economy, the prolongation through indentured labour of a form of serfdom long after black slavery ended, and the relegation of the islands for many decades to the status of slums of empire … . This was the

> violation the novel never lets us forget, as it traces out the pattern of rejection, impairment, alienation, in individual lives as well as in the groups that compose this heterogeneous society.[27]

A highly political author George Lamming is credited, along with Wilson Harris, V.S. Naipaul and Derek Walcott, with making the emergence of a Caribbean identity possible through his writings. Lamming makes powerful narratives about the island's competence to create history and to ensure political emancipation. His statement—"to be colonial is to be in a state of exile"[28] bears upon Naipaul's novels to a great extent. But this state of exile is much more depressing for Naipaul than it is for Lamming. Exile and the subsequent despair are persistent in Naipaul's fiction from first to last. He could hardly ever celebrate transculturation and hybrid identities unless he gave up his search for a home. In *The Mimic Men* Naipaul doesn't succumb to hybrid and interrelated forms of identity because he views the split-identity in terms of loss only.

Going a step ahead, V.S. Naipaul stands in sharp contrast with Lamming here as he fails to restore any self confidence among his Caribbean narrators. In *The Mimic Men*, Ralph Singh acquires the hybrid or mixed character of the island, but he envisions himself as an intruder at the same time. He feels misled by a history that has alienated him from the colonial relationship. He regrets over his sense of loss when he says: "The descendant of the slave-owner could soothe the descendant of the slave with a private patois. I was the late intruder, the picturesque Asiatic, linked to neither" (*The Mimic Men*, p. 78). Naipaul's novel confirms the importance of history in the lives of émigrés. Similar sentiments may be observed while reading A *Way in the World*, where the narrator proclaims that with every visit he had made to Trinidad he found, he was more and more cut off from the past.

Fawzia Mustafa construes *The Mimic Men* as a novel underlining insufficiency in postcolonial empowerment. She could only notice the apparently transient worth of postcolonial solidity as the main argument of the novel. Obviously Naipaul underlines the idea of postcolonial solidarity as imbalanced and unreal because the imaginary island of Isabella in which a heterogeneous group of people are forced to live together, is a mimicking society ready to harness the gains of colonial profit. The island society cannot be made powerful until and unless it comes closer to the power relations. Naipaul always feels sad to present the dismal picture of powerless Caribbean colonial society. The narrator puts the inherent hopelessness when he says: "... the bigger truth came: that in a society like ours, fragmented, inorganic, no link between man and the landscape, a society not held together by common interests, there was no true internal source of power". (*The Mimic Men*, p. 206)

It is so because the reticence of this newly emerged postcolonial society of the Caribbean is reproduced in the mimicry of the colonized. The fundamental conflict between the West, which signifies dependability, and the Caribbean, which suggests mimicry and nonexistence, can be observed in the *The Mimic Men* where the narrator observes:

> We, here on our islands, handling books printed in this world and using its goods, had been abandoned and forgotten. We pretended to be real, to be learning, to be preparing ourselves for life, we mimic men of the New World, one unknown corner of it, with all its reminders of the corruption that came so quickly to the new. (*The Mimic Men*, p. 146)

This account of the island by Ralph presents it not as an integrated and unitary whole, but, according to Chris Bongie, as "a fragment, a part of some greater whole from which it is in exile and to which it must be related—in an act of completion that is always also, as it were, an exile, a loss of the particular".[29] Ralph's description of Isabella as an island being enveloped by a tainted sea further adds to the bleakness of the image of Isabella.

More often than not, Naipaul himself has been condemned as a partial spokesperson of the West, an imperialist in dark robes, a colonial traitor and even a racially prejudiced mimic man. According to Selwyn R.Cudjoe, both Naipaul and the protagonist of *The Mimic Men*, Ralph, are "colonial people [who] are doomed forever to be pale reflectors of the dominant power."[30] Homi Bhabha's discussion of insubordinate ambivalence of mimicry seems to get reflected here in *The Mimic Men*. In his essay, "Of Mimicry and Man", Bhabha refers to the character of Ralph Singh, along with other prominent figures like Decoud in Conrad's *Nostromo* as the parodists of history. He further argues that despite their motivated and deliberate efforts, they mark the colonial text randomly in such an order that their narrative can hardly be taken as representative. Their desire to emerge as authentic through mimicry and through a process of writing and reproduction is the final irony of partial representation. According to Bhabha:

> Colonial mimicry is the desire for a reformed, recognisable other, as a subject of a difference that is almost the same, but not quite. This is to say, that the discourse of mimicry is constructed around an ambivalence; in order to be effective, mimicry must continually produce its slippage, its excess, its difference.[31]

Ralph and his English wife Sandra belong to a peculiar group on the island of Isabella. The group consists of the Indian men like Ralph and their expatriate wives. They are indulged in mimicking memoirs, tales, autobiographies and landscapes that they do not possess individually. Their alienation from their native cultures and island landscapes is a product of colonialism that further results in a certain kind of defencelessness and disintegration. The colonial expatriates like Ralph try to redefine the Caribbean and remakes *home* through a tradition of Englishness. He inherited his name from Indian tradition of his ancestors that he always prefers to hide: "Ranjit is my secret name … it is a custom among Hindus of certain castes. This secret name is my real name but it ought not to be used in public" (*The Mimic Men*, p. 100). He feels embarrassed over his Indian origin and it makes Ralph to alter his real name—Ranjit Kripalsingh—to an anglicized adaptation, R.R.K. Singh adding Ralph as the prefix. He narrates the account of this change: "I broke Kripalsingh into two, correctly reviving an ancient fracture, as I felt; gave myself the further name of Ralph; and signed myself R.R.K. Singh … . From the age of eight till the age of twelve this was one of my heavy secrets. I feared discovery at school and at home". (*The Mimic Men*, p. 100)

The anglicized names of Indian expatriates in Trinidad—Gareth, Randolph and R.R.K Singh in *The Mystic Masseur*, *A Flag on the Island* and *The Mimic Men* respectively, bring to the fore the deep-rooted ambivalence among the colonials. Mimicry is at its height when the reader observes the replication of a Midland landscape by the alienated figures of Isabella. While recollecting his endeavours of past to anglicize his name, culture and traditions, he finds that it was never truly a genuine experience. Colonialism is a shattering experience for this particular homogeneous group because they have severed their ties from the native experience and identity. But Ralph's awakening does not represent the general experience of the colonized individuals in the postcolonial setting.

Ironically, if Ralph is ensnared in colonial tradition, his mother's generation is nostalgic about the Indian cultural background. Mimicry in relation to his mother's Indian tradition is not commanding or imposing but it holds him back. The performance of Hindu religious rites by Ralph's mother on his return to Isabella with his English wife Sandra is symbolic of the significance of past in the awareness of present. Ralph is aware of the absurdity of this display of Indian rites on the island. However, he also appreciates the requirement of pretentious display to get reconnected with an exiled past. He affirms: "'Oh, look, there's my mother'—might easily be imagined. Yet not easily: we are a melodramatic race and don't let pass occasions for public display. Picture, then, Sandra in her carefully chosen disembarkation outfit coming face to face with a conventionally attired Hindu widow" (*The Mimic Men*, p. 54). He considers his mother's sustaining the association with the past as an effort to gain better stability and totality. He further elaborates the relevance of the rites when he adds: "My mother's sanctions were a pretence, no doubt; but they were also an act of piety towards the past, towards ancient unknown wanderings in another continent. It was a piety I shared" (*The Mimic Men*, p. 59). He frankly concedes that the display of linkage with the past is incoherent with the instant truth. He admits the irrelevance of the scene when he engages himself in his routine assignments and reacts: "I paid no attention to my mother's interjections … . I was calm because I felt that the situation was not important" (*The Mimic Men*, pp. 54–55). Like Frank in "A Flag on the Island", Kripalsingh also returns to the island he had never expected to revisit. His return too is touched with an uncertain fear. For him, the "return so soon to a landscape which I thought I had put out of my life for good was a failure and a humiliation". (*The Mimic Men*, p. 52)

Ultimately, the suppression of his own history while acquiring the fascinating imperial tradition causes instability, inauthenticity and mimicry in the life of Ralph. This realization of his expatriate status haunts him persistently. It is something that is common among all other migrants too:

> Each person concealed his own darkness … . Not the panic of being lost or lonely; the panic of ceasing to feel myself as a whole person. The threat of other people's lives, the remembered private landscapes, the relationships, the order which was not mine. I had longed for largeness. How, in the city, could largeness come to me? How could I fashion order out of all these unrelated adventures … . (*The Mimic Men*, p. 27)

The novel hence is a testimony to the idea that the "mimic men" like Ralph always vainly seek order and coherence in their lives after having escaped from their native culture. To ensure their acceptance in the city, they are even ready to deny their pasts. *The Mimic Men* stands unique among other novels by the Nobel Laureate because he observes the similar restlessness among the English women who have resolved to find order in the disordered milieu of the colonialism. Ralph agreed to marry Sandra, an English woman, thinking that she was a confident, ambitious and an assertive lady. But Ralph very soon notices that Sandra has carried her own gloom with her and she has accepted him as a life partner to protect herself from her inner vacuity. After ascertaining her uncertainty and sense of placelessness, his love for her begins to liquefy. He comments: "She had begun to get some of my geographical sense, that feeling of having been flung off the world ... she told me she had awakened in the night with a feeling of fear, a simple fear of place, of the absent world .... The very things I had once admired in her ... were what I now pitied her for". (*The Mimic Men*, p. 69)

Ralph, the disillusioned politician of Isabella, again migrates to England. But while narrating his account, he comes to the realization that his colonial daydream of arrival is illusory. His arrival deepens his pre-existing sense of *shipwreck* and expatriation. Ralph's vision that the lasting reality resides in the English identity and tradition, is constantly overshadowed by the experience of *otherness* haunting the migrants. His vision comes to be challenged when he finds Sandra and other English people tormented by the fragmented identities. The perceptible conflict between the colonial desire and reality depicts the limits of colonial aspiration for both the colonized and the colonizer.

However, *The Mimic Men* advocates the hypothesis that colonial ambition does not only preoccupy the colonized, but it lingers among the colonizers like Sandra also. The character of Sandra best reflects the mimicking tendency among the English themselves. What and whom they mimic is the pertinent question that troubles the reader. Theirs is an awkward position as they are fed up with the complacency of England. Naipaul's interpretation of the colonial dichotomy and conflict is quite evident here: "To be a colonial is to be a little ridiculous and unlikely, especially in the eyes of someone from the metropolitan country. All immigrants and their descendants are colonials of one sort or another, and between the colonial and ... the metropolitan there always exists a muted mutual distrust."[32]

By some means, the marriage of Ralph and Sandra is an alternative to bring about harmony in the lives of both the colonized and the colonizer. The effort to synthesise the cultures of colonizer and the colonized, in fact, is futile, as the colonial complex does not allow the two to enjoy the mutual respect for one another. The mimicry of the colonizer's way of life highlights vacuum in the life of the colonized. Homi K. Bhabha's supposition suits Ralph's description of exile and contradiction, as the novel presents an "awareness that the epistemological 'limits' of ethnocentric ideas are also the enunciative boundaries of a range of other dissonant ... histories and voices".[33] Ralph's "partial presence ... incomplete, virtual"[34] stands in contrast to what he himself narrates: "... the too solid three-dimensional city in which I could never feel myself as anything but spectral, disintegrating, pointless, fluid .... The city made by man but passed out of his control ... becomes a source of pain". (*The Mimic Men*, p. 53)

Primarily Ralph considers England as "the promised land", which will provide him with the order, firmness and security, which he so desperately needs and he strongly believes that Isabella is not able to offer. For him, London is a place of enthusiasm, legends, enchantment and greater refinement at the time when he finds Isabella to be a substandard place. This deceptive assumption might have emerged from his colonial education that ensnared him in a well-designed colonial plot. This education propagates the colonial myth that London can deliver something significant to the escaped colonized emigrants. But London does not offer an escape from colonial mess; it reinforces that disorder more deeply than ever before. In *The Mimic Men*, Naipaul has created an imaginary tale that presents the tragedy of the displaced and disoriented. It suggests that Isabella is a representative country; a typical ex-colony whose history is, in a larger sense, the history of postcolonial times. Ralph generalizes the colonial predicament of the colonies like Isabella where the model of disorder has been common with no substantial variation:

> It has happened in twenty places, twenty countries, islands, colonies, territories ... these words with which we play, thinking they are interchangeable and that the use of a particular one alters the truth. I cannot see our predicament as unique. The newspapers even today spell out situations, which, changing faces and landscapes, I can think myself into. (*The Mimic Men*, p. 230)

Naipaul presents Isabella as the representative colonial island to mark the extensive dislocation and the widespread feeling of personal loss. Ralph is not the only character to feel neglected, to crave for far-off cities and legendary landscapes. Ralph's maternal uncle Cecil, for example, the enviable beneficiary to the Bella Bella wealth, wants to mark his name on the sand of a deserted beach. There is another character Hok, a boy of Chinese ancestry who weeps over the disclosure of that private hemisphere of fantasy where lay his true life. Eden, the blackest boy in the whole school is daily reminded of his peasant background and slave parentage. It makes Eden wish for the Negro race to be abolished. His complementary wish is to rule as a lonely Negro in a secluded land. Brown, the comedian and the singer, warns Ralph that the island's splendour is artificial and humiliating. He reaches to dismal fulfilment in the discovery of the past, but he is unable to bring any order in his life. Eventually, he prefers the company of other races, among whom his anguish is at least unique.

Browne convinces Ralph to pose himself as the successor of his father Gurudeva whose name has been acknowledged in the island myth. People will then certainly assume him to be the new champion of the poor.

Even Deschampsneufs family, apparently satisfied, is part of the whole colonial pattern. They are the architects of the man-made slave island of Isabella with their own whims and eccentricities. The glory they associate with the island, is still *shipwreck* for others in the island. In *The Mimic Men*, there is only this family that asserts its claim in Isabella. Shortly before leaving for the school in London, Kripalsingh visits this family that puts forward an idea of the island which contrasts enormously with everything he has seen before: "You know, you are born in a place and you grow up there. You get to know the trees and the plants. You will never know any other trees and plants like that … . But you will come back. Where you born, man, you born. And this island is a paradise, you will discover". (*The Mimic Men*, pp. 204–05)

Ralph's condition is all the more pitiable as he has been denied recognition everywhere he tried to settle down. He comes to the awareness that he had been betrayed by the concocted account of England:

> So quickly had London gone sour on me. The great city, centre of the world, in which, fleeing disorder, I had hoped to find the beginning of order. So much had been promised by the physical aspect … there is no light like that of the temperate zone. It was a light that gave solidity to everything and drew colour out from the heart of objects. To me … dusk was new and enchanting. (*The Mimic Men*, p. 17)

Ralph and other colonial immigrants keep their otherness undisclosed in the metropolitan centre as they did in the homeland also. Ralph affirms, "We have converted our island into one big secret" (*The Mimic Men*, p. 95). Though Ralph's sense of triumph is incomplete, his narration of the history of his own world is encouraging. As Bhabha notes: "This act of writing the world, of taking the measure of its dwelling, is magically caught in Morrison's description of her house of fiction—art as 'the fully realised presence of a haunting' of history."[35] Ralph's colonial fantasy is restricted, as his ambivalence does not allow him to resolve his differences with the imperialistic centre. Ralph says: "Here was the city, the world. I waited for the flowering to come to me … Its heart must have lain somewhere. But the god of the city was elusive. The tram was filled with individuals, each man returning to his own cell. But the god was veiled ... in this solid city life was two-dimensional" (*The Mimic Men*, p. 18). That is why home is always a matter of delay for Ralph and others like him. He finds solace when he notices the typical colonial insecurity in a young English student also who, according to Ralph, "out of his own insecurity, had attached himself to me, an outsider". (*The Mimic Men*, p. 18)

As a student in London and afterwards, Ralph Singh's steady interaction with cosmopolitanism makes him indulge in sexual encounters with neighbours, prostitutes, and Sandra, his English wife. Ralph's associations with the fair sex never results from any sentimentality towards the woman, rather these casual encounters are directed by his desire to assert his worth by subjugating the weak and vulnerable. He finds the English women as a starting point of escape from the anxiety of his past and through his contact with them he dreams that he can ally himself with a settled tradition. However, he views these relationships and his marriage in terms of their inability to offer security and coherence that he so keenly desires. He adds:

> How right our Aryan ancestors were to create gods? We seek sex, and are left with two private bodies on a stained bed. The larger erotic dream, the god, has eluded us. It is so whenever, moving out of ourselves, we look for extensions of ourselves. It is with cities as it is with sex. We seek the physical city and find only a conglomeration of private cells. In the city as nowhere else we are reminded that we are individuals, units. (*The Mimic Men*, p. 17)

Ralph's feeling of alienation in the metropolitan contre leads him destructively to indulge in sexual experiences. He takes refuge in these activities which he mentions as: "... encounters less with individual bodies than with anonymous flesh. Each occasion pressed me deeper down into emptiness" (*The Mimic Men*, p. 28). But ultimately he feels a greater sense of meaninglessness and repulsion. He ends up viewing sexual activity in terms of "violation and self-violation" (*The Mimic Men*, p. 25). The frustrated people like Ralph assemble in London after being exiled from their colonies because they could not fit into the postcolonial scheme of things. The arrival of Ralph in London or expatriates on the island like Sandra, according to John McLaren, "have become detached from their native systems of culture, production and nationality."[36] A colonial's life deteriorates into an uninspiring cosmopolitanism and a craze for English women as can be observed in Ralph's sexual affairs in London. Nevertheless the constant fluidity and emigration add to the maturity of the colonial exile.

After escaping to England, Ralph withdraws from uproarious life of suburbs to a London hotel. It provides him the essential force and perception to recollect and reproduce the history of colonialism with special reference to his own ancestry. His agonizing sense of turmoil and misrepresentation, of being disjointed and troubled, start rejuvenating to health through writing. Subsequently, he achieves some sense of order through the process of writing the history of Isabella and his individual and political understanding of exile with the consciousness of the devastating legacies of colonialism. Ralph's getting hold of self-enlightenment in relation to the superficiality of his political status is demonstrated in his expression:

> There was my sense of wrongness, beginning with the stillness of that morning of return when I looked out on the slave island and tried to pretend it was mine. There was my sense of intrusion which deepened as I felt my power to be more and more a matter of words. So defiantly, in my mind, I asserted my character as intruder, the picturesque Asiatic born for other landscapes. (*The Mimic Men*, p. 207)

Ralph represents an Indian Caribbean colonial subject but his escape from the Caribbean island makes him doubly displaced. His twice-torn background awakens in him the consciousness of the predicament. Alienation of Ralph can best be captured on the morning of his arrival to the island. He describes: "I have spoken of the mood of celebration with which I left London and which for the next ten years I sought to maintain … . I saw through each porthole the blue, green and gold of the tropical island. So pure and fresh! And I knew it to be, horribly man made; to be exhausted, fraudulent, cruel and above all, not mine". (*The Mimic Men*, p. 52)

But his mood of ecstasy gets mixed with certain apprehensions immediately. He counters his early submission regarding his arrival with the ambivalent expression: "I linger now on this moment of arrival more than I did at the time. This return so soon to a landscape which I thought I had put out of my life for good was a failure and humiliation" (*The Mimic Men*, p. 52). *The Mimic Men* registers a flight of self-exploration in which the stigmatic effects of colonization on the colonized are documented with live details of its protagonist's life as an inborn expatriate. Ralph concludes: "It is only during the climb back up that we can see how far, for all the continuing consciousness of wholeness and sanity, we had become distorted". (*The Mimic Men*, p. 26)

Nonetheless, the symbolic imagery used in the novel has been widely contemplated by numerous critics and researchers. The central dilemma of bringing about a concord between the binaries has been presented through the corresponding words and images. Kavita Nandan remarks:

> The frequent use of the words 'violation' and 'taint' in the novel suggests that Naipaul subscribes to a discourse of purity which is related to his idea that colonialism resulted in the violation of colonies like Trinidad ... . For Ralph, Aryan purity has been violated by history—by his exiled father's actions in an unknown island. He is not the only one on the island who attaches himself to an alien tradition in order to imagine his identity as authentic.[37]

Ralph's expatriate ambivalence is temporarily pacified when he observes the people like him wandering aimlessly in a colonial world devoid of protection and order. He sadistically mentions his Chinese friend with the Afro-Caribbean mother: "Hok had dreams like mine, was probably also marked, and lived in imagination far from us, far from the island on which he, like my father, like myself, had been shipwrecked". (*The Mimic Men*, p. 104)

Paradoxically, the colonials enjoy their secretiveness about their personal trauma and they feel all the more depressed when their true picture gets exposed. Like *A House for Mr Biswas*, the lingering pang of history is associated in Ralph's psyche with his father and not his mother. He admits his secret association with his father when he says, "I cherished my mother's family and their Bella Bella Bottling Works. But in my secret life I was the son of my father and a Singh" (*The Mimic Men*, p. 97). The inexplicable secretive bond between son and father is an important one in the book, and is, to a certain extent, based on Naipaul's personal relationship with his father. His hysteria and nervousness gets represented in his father's state of mind. His father falls down into a kind of frenzy which Ralph observes: "His face was drawn; the pouches under his eyes went dark; and the unusual mood of the day now showed itself to have been a type of hysteria" (*The Mimic Men*, p. 123). Ralph is saddened over the realization that his father's eccentricity has become his own. He sees a permanent relation between his present and past through his inseparable bond with his father. It brings him to a greater perceptive understanding of the consequences of the colonial experience. Through the legacy of his father's passion, he is able to discern how that neurosis is revived in his own personality. He concludes that history can never be restrained in total; rather, it deserves to be respected and preserved for the inherent 'pastness of the past'.

Mohun Biswas in *A House for Mr Biswas* feels alienated at his birthplace and he dreams of his own extinction. His vulnerability and sense of insecurity attract his son Anand. Similarly, Ralph is attracted towards his father owing to his susceptibility. William H. Gass elaborates the condition of Mohun Biswas and Ralph's father in terms of the premonitions of exile. He says: "Exile involves rejection by a loved one, as if the face in your mirror grimaced when it looked out and saw you looking in. It is a narcissistic wound."[38] Naipaul is always obsessed with the conception of that lost figure who envisions his own extinction. In *The Mimic Men*, Ralph inherits this fear of being a nonentity like his father, but this feeling haunts him equally in Isabella as well as in London. He could change his geographical setting but he fails to get rid of "the panic of ceasing to feel [him] self as a whole person". (*The Mimic Men*, p. 27)

Disclosure of identity results into shame and humiliation among the colonial expatriates. Ralph's friend, Hok starts crying over the disclosure of his personal life before his classmates. The narrator puts it thus: "It wasn't only that the mother was black and of the people, though that was a point; it was that he had been expelled from that private hemisphere of fantasy where lay his true life" (*The Mimic Men*, p. 102). Ralph and Hok pretend to deny the realities of their biculturalness by posing to be what they are not. Their rejection of their present state of ruination is sustained by the dreams of purity, which enable them to hold back their difference. But they are unaware of the fact that their pretensions further alienate them from their present setting. Likewise, in addition to the longing for the ancient homeland, makes them fly the colonial expatriate sensibility from the colony to England. Ralph finds his extended self in another character Browne about whom he says, "Here was a longing, like my own, for freedom and what we considered the truth of our personalities" (*The Mimic Men*, p. 212). The total absurdity of their situation is that racial or cultural dissimilarity makes the people cling to tradition of purity even more.

Like other fictional characters of Naipaul, Ralph also realizes that running off from the past results only in a greater sense of *shipwreck*. The restless expatriates who had left Trinidad for the West in the novels of V.S. Naipaul are never shown to flourish. In *The Mimic Men*, arriving in London only strengthens the protagonist's sense of not having arrived anywhere. Ralph admits that his departure from his native land did not contribute to his sense of belongingness. Nor does he feel that his escape will affect the island political scenario at all. He is well aware of his insignificance as a colonial expatriate and as a newly emerged colonial politician. He affirms:

> I knew that my own journey, scarcely begun, had ended in the shipwreck which all my life I had sought to avoid .... The pace of colonial events is quick, the turnover of leaders rapid. I have already been forgotten; and I know that the people who supplanted me are themselves about to be supplanted. My career is by no means unusual ... . We lack order. Above all, we lack

power, and we don't understand that we lack power. (*The Mimic Men*, p. 6)

Ralph is educated and brought up in the borrowed urban culture of London. He feels rooted neither in the island culture of Isabella nor in the Western culture. This borrowed mimicking reality only gives him confidence to discard the monotony of his island life and to seek refuge in the golden landscapes portrayed in English books taught in the colonial schools. Earlier he had found the life in the island very chaotic:

> To be born on an island like Isabella, an obscure New World transplantation, second-hand and barbarous, was to be born to disorder .... Now I was to discover that disorder has its own logic and permanence: the Greek was wise. Even as I was formulating my resolve to escape, there began that series of events which, while sharpening my desire to get away, yet rooted me more firmly to the locality where accident had placed me. (*The Mimic Men*, p. 118)

But at a later stage, he indignantly articulates the mimic nature of his ambivalent island life. The deep sense of restlessness that Ralph experiences after his flight to the hub of imperialism is a sort of *the enigma of arrival*. England does not offer him as much as he might have expected.

Shipwreck is used as a recurrent metaphor of homelessness or exile in *The Mimic Men*. He elaborates the term *shipwreck* in the words: "I have used this word before. With my island background, it was the word that always came to me. And this was what I had encountered again in the great city: this feeling of being adrift" (*The Mimic Men*, p. 26). The metaphor of *shipwreck* that he offers at the beginning of his story implies that all has ended before anything can begin. The *shipwreck* image is elucidated later in the story when Ralph Singh recalls the embarrassment he felt for his partially Chinese school friend, Hok, when they encounter Hok's black mother all at once. The ambivalence of the boys of mixed parentage is striking as, on the one hand, they cherish the ambition to get modern education and on the other hand they escape the world to avoid disclosure of their secrets of racial origins. Ralph Singh wants to hide his *Aryan* or Indian ancestry and Hok does not want the people to know about his Negro mother. Their fantasies encounter self-denigration that each has developed towards their island hybridity embodied by their oddly diverse identities. The consequential hostility of Ralph and Hok manifest itself in the sense of humiliation on the disclosure of their identity.

The protagonist's change of name at school and the subsequent naming of his real estate project as *Crippleville*, all such acts symbolize this essential mimicking predisposition. It expresses his feeling of uprootedness and of having been tossed away from the world. It demonstrates itself as a simple fear of place and the unaccommodating world. Ralph's desire for the imaginary home in England is threatened by his dull anonymous life in London. The term *shipwreck* is presented in terms of enclosed space and limited prospects. Ralph's first temporary residence in England, Shylock's Boarding House, is a place where the boarders live, narrowly in their private cells and their life is devoid of any perceptible aim.

The chain of short-term houses that Ralph occupies in England suggests the homelessness in *The Mimic Men*. He stays at Shylock's Boarding House, the expatriate bourgeois house in Isabella, and the London hotel room in which he writes his life narrative for the limited period. Ralph and Sandra are incapable of providing permanence to their home in Isabella rather he comes out with unusual remarks: "It had never seemed important to us to have a house of our own. I had no feelings for the house as home, as personal creation" (*The Mimic Men*, p. 74). It was so because of their neurosis that never allowed them to respect the house as home. He asserts:

> But to me as well as to Sandra our house was something to go out of whenever we could. Into that most inferior place in the world. Where could we go? ... We were at our happiest outside; it was outside (away from home), in a crowd, late at night, the champagne working, that we commune. (*The Mimic Men*, pp. 72–73)

The ambivalence of dispossessed Ralph Ranjit Kripalsingh is characteristically Naipaulian. Like Mohun Biswas, Ralph too is unable to create a home, for all recollections of home have proved futile for him. Shashi Kamra interprets his condition in the following words:

> His childhood home was a boarding house, so emotionally unsatisfactory was his life in it. His home with Sandra remained childless and the marriage broke up. He sees the Roman House, an unreal order he has imposed on his society and himself, as the cause of his political failure. His final retreat into the faceless boarding house in London also permits him his maximum freedom, committed only to himself and the moment.[39]

From Biswas's obsession to claim the "portion of earth" as his own home to Ralph's state of mind in *The Mimic Men*, Naipaul is deeply concerned with the typical obsession among the colonial exiles. Ralph continuously suffers on account of his homelessness in England as well as in Isabella. Before getting accommodation in the London Hotel, he had to meander from "small town to small town, seeking shelter with my sixty-six pounds of luggage, always aware in the late afternoon of my imminent homelessness" (*The Mimic Men*, p. 249). His condition gets reflected in the comment of Edward Said: "The exile knows that in a secular and contingent world, homes are always provisional."[40]

The sense of homelessness prevalent in Naipaul's protagonists makes the metaphor of journey quite common in the understanding of a colonial expatriate's dilemma. Landeg White remarks:

> Now, in *The Mimic Men*, there is a series of houses—Kripal Singh's childhood house whose collapse he anticipates daily; Browne's house, a racial prison; the boarding house in Kensington High Street, packed with immigrants and owned by an exiled Jew; the roman house, the Beach house, the Scandinavian house in the hills, expressions of expatriate taste. None of them are homes, islands of order, centres of light and beauty and achievement. They are the temporary residences of shipwrecked people ... the 'final emptiness'.[41]

Ralph's expatriate status torments his physique as well as psyche. During his stay in London, he reacts: "... but I felt I was bleeding, with that second intimation of the forlornness of the city on which twice, I had fixed so important a hope" (*The Mimic Men*, p. 251). Certain episodes in the novel suggest a chasm, gap and incoherence in the lives of the colonials. When the narrator happens to visit the proposed site of the Kripalville (later Crippleville) Housing Scheme in Isabella, the foreman, according to the narrator, "told me that they had run into the stump and roots of a giant tree; three charges of dynamite had been necessary to get rid of it. He showed me the crater: a monstrous wound in the red earth .... I would have liked to preserve it" (*The Mimic Men*, p. 63). The episode reminds the reader that the progress and advancement always try to annihilate the past but the past can not be obliterated.

Naipaul continually presents the Caribbean as devoid of history. His novels undertake the mission to penetrate deeper to find out the reasons behind that void. He develops his stories out of his own experience of colonialism during his stay in Trinidad. He does not restrict himself to his understanding of the present scenario; rather he rebuilds the native countryside in connection with its historical past. He succeeds in establishing a chronology in order to gain a sense of entirety and correlation with the world. Nonetheless, he acknowledges the limits of this re-ordering when he observes: "it was hard to hold on to the idea of the aboriginal and fabulous. What was familiar, the small-island colonial geography one had grown up in, was stronger."[42] Besides, he rewrites the colonial plots which hold the colonial expatriates responsible for the escape of the natives of the island: "We, who had come in a variety of ways from many continents, were made to stand in for the aborigines and were held responsible for the nullity which had been created long before we had been transported to it."[43]

Ralph Singh, the hero of the autobiography *The Mimic Men*, never enjoys certain social privileges like marriage, home, stability, money, status, leadership or children. His ambivalence is further problematized by the political gain he is able to harness because of his father's reputation as a popular, proletarian and saintly political figure. His political failure is a sign of the failure of Trinidad as an independent nation. His colonial background reminds the reader of other unsuccessful political figures like Harbans in *The Suffrage of the Elvira* and Ganesh in *The Mystic Masseur*. However, political failure and embarrassment at home and abroad confirming Ralph's sense of non-existence, becomes a force to recon with.

R.R.K. Singh turns to unfolding his past as a means of the ultimate draining out of his deserted self so that he might accept the challenge of the West with a new vision. But, his disillusionment comes to surface when he says: "It never occurred to me that the writing of this book might have become an end in itself, that the recording of a life might become an extension of that life" (*The Mimic Men*, p. 244). Writing for Naipaul's characters acquires cathartic significance as tormented by the implications of dual identities stemming from their East Indian and West Indian association, they wish to bridge the gap through creativity. The modern sensibility of these expatriates in Isabella is characterized by agony resulting from hostility, homelessness and rootlessness. They are no longer restricted to their narrow landscape and vision; rather, they dream of fleeing to the imaginary landscapes of the West. He takes up writing the memoirs to assert his coherent existence. During his final exile in London he comes across other exiled leaders of other colonial uprisings placed in similar circumstances. Ralph now condemns politics as an unrelenting fantasy, a set of borrowed phrases through which the new leaders conceal the inherent disorder they have created: "What did we talk about? ... Borrowed phrases! .... But we used borrowed phrases which were part of the escape from thought, from that reality we wanted people to see but could ourselves now scarcely face" (*The Mimic Men*, p. 237). Ralph recollects his visit as a colonial minister leading the government delegation to London. His egotistical condemnation by his counterpart in London hurts him all the more as he is considered a low-grade politician:

> It was a brief, humiliating meeting ... his manner indicated clearly that ... he had other things to do than to assist the public relations of colonial politicians. In about forty-five seconds he painted so lively a picture of the consequences of any intemperate action by the government of Isabella that I felt personally rebuked. (*The Mimic Men*, p. 244)

The noticeable pomposity and sophisticated diplomatic impertinence in Lord Stockwell's attitude reminds him of his association with Trinidad and its colonial past. Here he realises that there is no escape from his past and history in spite of the fact that he always wished to shed off his memory. This inconsistency between the significance he attaches to his mission and its informal dismissal by these representatives of power makes Ralph Singh ill at ease and it prompts him to indulge in further sadistic activities. His successive dream is evocative:

> I had not slept well ... As I slept and awakened, waiting for the light to come to the fantasy city, known and unknown, memory and the dream flowed together. When the light came I was weak and ill. The stopover was at an end. It was necessary to rise and prepare for another departure. (*The Mimic Men*, pp. 237–238)

He always prefers his existential sincerity to materialistc superiority. Shashi Kamra rightly observes the significance of his colonial background: "Trinidad, always the antagonist, the measure of his failure in life, becomes the measure of his success as an individual and as a writer."[44] Ganesh, Harbans and Ralph in *The Mystic Masseur*, *The Suffrage of Elvira* and *The Mimic Men* respectively, are trapped in the state of personal ambiguity where an individual is incapable of making a distinction between his individuality and that of the society. The three novels demonstrate the ridiculousness of democratic system as a form of government that has been transplanted in Caribbean island only to show the piety to England. The political system and the elections thereof did not develop out of the needs of the native people. The democratic practices in Trinidad are a troubled combination between capitalism and democracy where the interests of the aristocrats reign. The newly emerged political scenario in Trinidad has given a free rein to the voracious nature of the people who are already picaroon. In the novels of Naipaul, politics is shown as a threat to the colonial consciousness of

Trinidad. Fawzia Mustafa who interprets the narrator's alienation in terms of the experiences of an expatriate captures the colonial mimicry and subsequent ambivalence of Ralph. She observes: "Ralph's colonial experience, sexual encounters, the class affiliations, and the attitude of fatalism that characterise his adulthood are the scrambled responses of ambivalence."[45]

Naipaul explains the active life of Ralph in *parenthesis* as he excludes the identical disposition of pessimism between his first stopover in London and his later exile there. Ralph feels relaxed and contemplative only when he is away from the monotonous life of England or Isabella. It is during this period of *parenthesis* that he thinks about recapitulating his colonial experiences. Ralph likes to give precedence to his period of exile in London over his days as a colonial politician and an émigré in the island of Isabella: "This present residence in London, which I suppose can be called exile, has turned out to be the most fruitful" (*The Mimic Men*, p. 248). Ralph confesses that the lack of involvement that exile offers, led him to a privileged state of awareness: "I no longer yearn for ideal landscapes and no longer wish to know the god of the city. This does not strike me as loss. I feel, instead, I have lived through attachment and freed myself from one cycle of events" (*The Mimic Men*, p. 250). Naipaul refers to the parenthetical situation of Ralph in these words:

> It was during this time [of parethesis], I have said, that I thought of writing. It was my hope to give expression to the restlessness, the deep disorder, which the great explorations, the overthrow in three continents of established social organisations, the unnatural bringing together of peoples who could achieve fulfilment only within the security of their own societies and the landscapes hymned by their ancestors, it was my hope to give partial expression to the restlessness which this great upheavel has brought about ... I am too much a victim of that restlessness which was to have been my subject .... (*The Mimic Men*, p. 32)

However, Ralph does not realize his complete *mimic* status, until he enters politics. The assumption of Bhabha in connection with this issue is that "colonial mimicry is the desire for the reformed, recognisable *Other*, as a subject of a difference that is almost the same, but not quite."[46] The protagonist's self-understanding towards genuineness is discernible in the illustrious assertion in *The Mimic Men*, "We pretended to be real, to be learning, to be preparing ourselves for life, we mimic men of the new world, one unknown corner of it, with all its reminders of the corruption that came so quickly to the new" (*The Mimic Men*, p. 146). As a result, his chronicle of life emphasizing his non-conformity fails to identify: "What emerges between mimesis and mimicry is a writing, a mode of representation, that marginalizes the monumentality of history, quite simply mocks its power to be a model, that power which supposedly makes it imitable."[47]

Exhibiting essential paradigmatic shift in his fiction, he himself claims that:

> Each book took me to deeper understanding and deeper feeling, and that led to a different way of writing. Every book was a stage in a process of finding out; it couldn't be repeated. My material—my past, separated from me by place as well—was fixed and, like childhood itself, complete; it couldn't be added to.[48]

In spite of this proclamation by the author, the typical colonial issues predominate all of his fiction, though with a slight difference in focus and maturity. If Mr Biswas is displaced on a particular island, Kripalsingh bears the sense of loneliness to the centre of the world. *A House for Mr Biswas* is a novel looking hopefully about the issue of flight, but *The Mimic Men* highlights Kripalsingh's experience that London has betrayed him by not offering him any security, order or identity. Kripalsingh's aim behind his escape is revealed in his statement: "And this became my aim: from the central fact of this setting, my presence in this city which I have known as student, politician and now as refugee-immigrant, to impose order on my own history, to abolish that disturbance which is what a narrative in sequence might have led me to" (*The Mimic Men*, p. 292). Ralph could understand the ways of the colonial world fully only when his memoirs started taking shape. Now he comes to know that the fundamental truth of political life in colonies like Isabella is that the common feeling of personal insignificance leading to escape to fantastic landscapes can never be completely eliminated. With every possibility of escape barred and every promise denied, he faces his homelessness as never before. He recalls the suggestion of Deschampneufs family and returns to Isabella and involuntarily inflames a cultural war. Being utterly disillusioned, he flies back to England. His quest for order does not lessen until he takes to the recording of his memoirs.

His subject is not Empire, but his own short-lived career and the image of his homelessness. Now he realizes that his much-hyped marriage and his political career were the real acts of withdrawal, and that his autobiography has ultimately released him from the unproductive endeavour to fight his homelessness. He finds a deep sense of comfort and solace in writing. It becomes the source of extracting order from what has seemed disordered. Once the unification of "this man, this room, this city: this language, this form," (*The Mimic Men*, p. 85) is observed, the experiences fall obviously into their position. Ralph is able to find consistency in the series of trials that has left him desolate in his London hotel.

The significance of the *The Mimic Men* in terms of V.S. Naipaul's personal development lies in the fact that it evokes the climax of the earlier open-ended novels that do not follow a colonized escaping to the English landscapes. It takes him to discover not only their colonial ambivalences in Trinidad, but also their sense of dislocation beyond the colonies. The newly discovered perspective liberates the novelist from the phase begun in *Miguel Street* and sustained through *Mr Stone and the Knights Companion*. That is why, by the concluding pages of *The Mimic Men*, Kripalsingh is seen as an individual whose amateurish tryst with the adopted land and culture has come a full circle and he seems to be anticipating with fervid intensity—a life of equanimity and repose in an alien territory. Thereon starts the action of a free man. N. Rama Devi perceives a remarkable growth in Naipaul as a novelist after the publication of *The Mimic Men*: "It would not be incorrect to say that it is in this novel that Naipaul achieves, for the first time, that rare quality, total detachment or non-attachment—the mark of his maturity as a writer … ."[49]

Thus, the maturity perceived in the characters evolved can be easily alluded to the developed sensibility of the author himself. In fact, having read Naipaul's fiction from the beginning, the reader can hardly ever distinguish the author from his works. His personal ambivalence underlined in *An Area of Darkness* gets reflected when he puts:

> I came to London. It had become the centre of my world and I had worked hard to come to it. And I was lost. London was the centre of my world. I had been misled; but there was nowhere else to go. It was a good place for getting lost in, a city no one ever knew … . Here I became no more than an inhabitant of a big city, robbed of loyalties, time passing, taking me away from what I was, thrown more and more in myself, fighting to keep my balance and to keep alive … . All mythical land faded, and in the big city I was confined to a smaller world than I had ever known.[50]

This description of Naipaul in *An Area of Darkness* is identical to the observations of Ralph in *The Mimic Men*. There is a sort of reconciliation of identity between Naipaul and Kripalsingh. Fawzia Mustafa beautifully sums up Naipaul's treatment of the themes of mimicry, diasporic ambivalence and colonial disillusionment in the novel: "Mimicry and repetition, therefore, are the two narrative forms that Naipaul locks the colonial and the postcolonial characters he creates and their respective situations into. Fiction in the Caribbean, then, apparently originates in self-deception, not self-invention."[51] *The Mimic Men*, therefore, studies the essential sense of loss that characterizes the fragmented societies in the colony of Isabella. The writer explores through Ralph Singh the universal predicament of the confrontation between the *self* and the *other*, and the mimicry and originality. Perceived with acute anguish, the style and structure of the novel emphatically highlight such endless dualities that sum up the beleaguered identities of the expatriate and the displaced. Not only this, but Naipaul also finds the torn identities of the expatriates to be responsible for all the disorder, instability, anxiety and a sense of futility prevalent in their world. Besides, the narrator's endeavour to determine his individuality provides a remarkable postcolonial account. It investigates how colonization has hampered the knowledge of the colonized about their identity. The novel thus brings out the ambivalence among the colonials regarding the issue of their self-assertion.

Unlike *The Mimic Men*, Naipaul's *A Flag on the Island* explores the lives of torn subjectivities in kaleidoscopic spectrums. Instead of providing to the reader a perusal of a designated protagonist, Ralph Singh; the collection of short stories entitled *A Flag on the Island* delineates the anguish of fractured lives lived in multitude within and beyond the frontiers of the norm. Therefore, we find Ralph's life and his subsequent sense of inadequacy, bewilderment and incertitude getting cloned in many like him. Frank, Randolph, Aunt Gold Teeth and Hari are to be seen as the shadow images of Ralph himself for all these characters grope for their moorings in the turbulence of their *shipwrecked* life. Both *The Mimic Men* and *A Flag on the Island* mark a distinct beginning in the author's creative voyage as the parochialism of the sphere is deftly transcended and a spontaneous fusion of thematic and stylistics patterns is effortlessly achieved. Both of the books are first-person narratives narrated through an exciting intermingling of reminiscences of past and analysis of present. It is in this way that these fictional works stand for the felicity of the author's expressions as Naipaul creates a mesmerizing human drama by capturing the intensity of quintessential ambivalences in the life of a colonial expatriate.

Notes

1. Bill Ashcroft, Gareth Griffiths and Helen Tiffin, eds., *The Empire Writes Back* (London: Routledge, 1989) pp. 88–89.
2. V.S. Naipaul, *A Flag on the Island* (London: Andre Deutsch, 1967) p. 169. (All the subsequent references for *A Flag on the Island* been

have taken from the same edition of the novel, cited hereafter, in the text with the corresponding page number(s) in parenthesis.)

3. Edward Said, *Culture and Imperialism* (London: Vintage, 1993) p. xxix.
4. Landeg White, *V.S. Naipaul: A Critical Introduction* (London: Macmillan, 1975) p. 146.
5. Fawzia Mustafa, *V.S. Naipaul* (Cambridge: Cambridge University Press, 1995) p. 32.
6. Quoted in Landeg White, *V.S. Naipaul: A Critical Introduction,* op. cit., p. 144.
7. V.S. Naipaul, *An Area of Darkness* (London: Andre Deutsch, 1964) p. 212.
8. V.S. Naipaul, *A House for Mr Biswas* (London: Andre Deutsch, 1962) p. 283.
9. Kavita Nandan, "Exile in The Mimic Men", *V.S. Naipaul,* ed. Purabi Panwar (Delhi: Pencraft International, 2003) p. 126.
10. Adrian Rowe Evans, "Interview with V.S. Naipaul," December 1971. *A Transition Interview,* 5 November 2006<http://links.jstor.org.
11. N. Rama Devi, *The Novels of V.S. Naipaul: Quest for Order and Identity* (New Delhi: Prestige, 1996) p. 132.
12. Rama Kundu, "A Transcltural Voyage: The Agony and the Ecstasy," ed. Amar Nath Prasad (New Delhi: Sarup, 2000) p. 26.
13. Quoted by Sudha Rai, "V.S. Naipaul's A Flag on the Island", *V.S. Naipaul,* ed. Purabi Panwar, op. cit., p. 117.
14. Homi K. Bhabha, "Of Mimicry and Man", *The Location of Culture* (New York: Routledge, 1994) p. 86.
15. Ibid., p. 88.
16. V.S. Naipaul, *The Mimic Men* (London: Andre Deutsch, 1967) p. 230. (All the subsequent references for *The Mimic Men* have been taken from the same edition of the novel, cited hereafter, in the text with the corresponding page number(s) in parenthesis.)
17. V.S. Naipaul, *A House for Mr Biswas* (London: Andre Deutsch, 1962) p. 586.
18. Yashoda Bhat, *V.S. Naipaul: An Introduction* (New Delhi: B.R. Publications, 2000) p. 57.
19. William Walsh, *V.S. Naipaul* (Edinburgh: Oliver and Boyd, 1973) p. 146.
20. Chandra B. Joshi, *V.S. Naipaul: The Voice of Exile* (Delhi: Sterling Publishers, 1994) p. 165.
21. Ibid., p. 168.

22. Fawzia Mustafa, *V.S. Naipaul* (Cambridge: Cambridge University Press, 1995) p. 101.
23. V.S. Naipaul, *A Way in the World* (London: Heinemann, 1994) p. 9.
24. Kavita Nandan, "Exile in the Mimic Men," *V.S. Naipaul*, ed. Purabi Panwar, op. cit., p. 128.
25. Jean Burnet, "Multiculturalism", *The Canadian Encyclopaedia Vol. II* ed. James H. Marsh (Edmonton: Hurtig Publishers Ltd., 1985) p. 1174.
26. "Colonialism", *Stanford Encyclopedia of Philosophy*, ed. Edward N. Zalta, Fall 2002, 30 September 2007<http://plato.stanford.edu/entries/colonialism/http://plato.stanford.edu/entries/colonialism/p. 1.
27. Quoted by Kavita Nandan, "Exile in the Mimic Men", *V.S. Naipaul*, ed. Purabi Panwar, op. cit., p. 130.
28. George Lamming, *The Pleasures of Exile* (Ann Arbor: The University of Michigan, 1992) p. 60.
29. Quoted by Kavita Nandan, "Exile in the Mimic Men", *V.S. Naipaul*, ed. Purabi Panwar, op. cit., p. 132.
30. Selwyn R. Cudjoe, *V.S. Naipaul: A Materialist Reading* (Amherst: University of Massachusetts Press, 1988) p. 102.
31. Homi K. Bhabha, *The Location of Culture* (London: Routledge, 1994) p. 86.
32. V.S. Naipaul, *Literary Occasions: Essays* (London: Picador, 2003) p. 38.
33. Homi K. Bhabha, *The Location of Culture* (London: Routledge, 1994) pp. 4–5.
34. Ibid., p. 86.
35. Ibid., p. 12.
36. John McLaren, "The Power of the Word: Salman Rushdie and The Satanic Verses", *Westerly*, 1 March 1990: 61–65, p. 64.
37. Kavita Nandan, "Exile in the Mimic Men", *V.S. Naipaul*, ed. Purabi Panwar, op. cit., pp. 138–39.
38. Kavita Nandan, p. 142.
39. Shashi Kamra, *The Novels of V.S. Naipaul* (New Delhi: Prestige Books, 1990) p. 76.
40. Edward W. Said, "Reflections on Exile", *Out There: Marginalisation and Contemporary Cultures*, eds., Russell Ferguson et al. (New York: New Museum of Contemporary Art, 1990) p. 365.
41. Landeg White, *V.S. Naipaul: A Critical Introduction*, op. cit., p. 153.
42. V.S. Naipaul, *A Way in the World*, op. cit., p. 211.
43. Ibid., p. 77.

44. Shashi Kamra, *The Novels of V.S. Naipaul* (New Delhi: Prestige Books, 1990) p. 77.
45. Fawzia Mustafa, *V.S. Naipaul*, op. cit., pp. 101–02.
46. Homi K. Bhabha, *The Location of Culture*, op. cit., p. 86.
47. Ibid., p. 87.
48. V.S. Naipaul, *Literary Occasions: Essays*, op. cit., p. 15.
49. N. Rama Devi, *V.S. Naipaul: Critical Essays*, ed. Mohit K. Ray (New Delhi: Atlantic Publishers, 2002) p. 32.
50. V.S. Naipaul, *An Area of Darkness*, op. cit., p. 45.
51. Fawzia Mustafa, *V.S. Naipaul*, op. cit., p. 106.

3

Confounding the Confusions

In the "Trinidadian-tetralogy", V.S. Naipaul feels very much concerned about the portrayal of ambivalence among the natives and expatriates inhabiting Trinidad. The half-ness and in-betweenness of the Caribbean world is the focus of the novelist in his first four novels. Frustration and disappointment mark the lives of the denizens of the island resulting into their mimicking of western ways of life. Ganesh, Mohun Biswas, Bryant and Harbans in *The Mystic Masseur*, *A House for Mr Biswas*, *Miguel Street* and *The Suffrage of Elvira* respectively represent the essential dilemma haunting the minds of the so-called "wretched of the earth", more specifically those who have been displaced from their roots. In the next phase of his career, Naipaul comes out with *A Flag on the Island*, a collection of stories, and *The Mimic Men*, a novel. Both of these works complete the unfinished tales of his earlier novels, as now, he follows his protagonists to other territories of the world also. Ralph Singh's escape to London and his returning back to the colony is the symbolic futile journey of a failed colonial politician to the metropolitan centre in search of wholeness. Similarly, *A Flag on the Island* presents the bits of colonial life in confronting the "other". Obviously, Naipaul's canvas has enlarged with his discovery of the wider world order.

Departing from his earlier obsession, in his novels published in the third phase of his literary career, Naipaul focuses on the problem of colonial-imperial conflict in Caribbean as well as African settings. He creates the world of subjective reality through the omniscient, impersonal narrator in *Guerrillas* and *A Bend in the River*. In these novels, the characters, aware of a peripheral world from which they are separated, form a typical population of the scared and the lost. The omniscient narrator of *Guerrillas* and the first person autobiographical narrator of *A Bend in the River* present the identical image both objectively and subjectively. Underneath the apparent contradictions, oppositions and conflicts between the society and the individual, there are no two realities, but one, i.e., the disillusionment. In the racially and culturally complex societies portrayed in these two novels, Naipaul enables the narrator to present the essential dilemma of a fluid world. The objective reality of the displaced, mingled with the past and the present, with aspiration and fantasy, is completely distorted. Freedom is shown in disagreement with security and both the novels end in a depressing note. A characteristically telling snippet from *A Bend in the River* helps one to observe the author's viewpoint unmistakably:

> Life in our town was arbitrary enough. Yvette seeing me as settled, with everything waiting for me somewhere, had seen her own life as fluid. She felt she wasn't prepared as the rest of us … . That was how we all felt, though: we saw our own lives as fluid, we saw the other man or person as soldier. But in the town, where all was arbitrary and the law was what it was, all our lives were fluid. We none of us had certainties of any kind … . In the end we couldn't say where we stood.[1]

With all possibilities of self-realization fully exhausted, the characters realize limited authenticity in their understanding of their lives. The destined sense of failure lingers in their psyche and this awareness finally destroys their will to live. The frustration and annoyance mark the life of the island. They reorganize a remembered blurring past to appear acceptable to themselves and others.

The background of both the novels is as frenzied, anarchic, sadistic and almost chaotic, as the mental landscapes of the characters are. Both the novels underline the emotional and obsessive reality of anguish and panic-stricken fear that characterize the contemporary human situation. The natives are ignored, dismissed or suppressed by the widespread optimism generated by immense wealth and power that filters in the recently independent colonies. Naipaul reveals the limitations of a world that has dissipated its potential—a concern that finds an uneasy observation from the protagonist of *A Bend in the River* as he finds himself victimized by his environment:

> You mustn't think it's bad just for you. It's bad for everybody. That's the terrible thing. It's bad for Prosper, bad for the man they gave your shop to, bad for everybody. Nobody's going anywhere … . Nothing has any meaning. That is why everyone is frantic …. The bush runs itself. But there is no place to go to … nowhere is safe. (*A Bend in the River*, p. 291)

Likewise, *Guerrillas* holds a unique place for its meticulous depiction of imitative culture and the aftermaths of the confluence of the representative colonizer and the colonized beings. Here Naipaul returns to a fantasized Caribbean island that bears similarities to Trinidad, his birth-place. The most salient aspect of the novel is the willed exteriorization of the picture of Trinidad, the place which Naipaul knows personally. The island is seen entirely from the point of view of the white tourists. *Guerrillas* is an interesting staging of Naipaul's recurring themes—the failure of miniature underdeveloped nations to be truly independent, mimicry, the relationship between the Whites and the Blacks, and the clash between the natives and the emigrants. In this novel Naipaul is particularly critical of liberal whites who show their concern for the third world distress. They are taken as suspected heirs of the colonial whites, who are now frustrated with their own emaciated societies. They carry their emotional needs to the former colonies in search of drama, sexual fulfillment and access to power. Roche, a White South African ex-revolutionary, wants to be the anchor of his race, but incompetent as an activist and a reformer, he expects the Third World to entertain him as a substantial person. The narrator captures the disappointment of Jane and Roche when they confront Jimmy, another byproduct of colonial turmoil:

> Roche smiled at Jane. His irritation was like her own; but his smile depressed her. That smile of his, which had once seemed so full of melancholy and irony, issuing out of the largest vision of the world, now seemed to hold only a fixed, meaningless irony. And less than that: it had sarcasm, frustration, pettishness.[2]

Moreover, the vegetation is further suggestive of barrenness and fruitlessness. Instead of the growth of flowery plants, there grow weeds: "The vegetable garden was knee-deep in weeds … deformed, pale aubergines, stunted ochroes" (*Guerrillas,* p. 14). The pungent, reeking smell of gas fumes and the dust from the bauxite plant intensifies the sardonic effect of the novel. The setting of the novel is suggestive of decay, deterioration, confusion and perpetual ambivalence. The description of the island evokes the general fear of in-betweenness and uncertainty among the islanders. Even the symbolic description of the locale is awesome for the reader:

> The sea smelled of swamp … and the heat seemed trapped … the rubbish dump burning in the remnant of mangrove swamp, with black carrion corbeaux squatting hunched on fence-posts … rows of unpainted boxes of concrete and corrugated iron already returning to the shanty towns that had been knocked down for

> this redevelopment; after the naked children playing in the red dust of the straight new avenues, the clothes hanging like rags from backward lines … . (*Guerrillas*, p. 1)

In *Guerillas*, depressing, fake and derelict characters people the desolate landscape. Naipaul has chosen drought as an appropriate setting. The drive from the Ridge—the elitist residential area to Jimmy's Thrushcross Grange and back is accompanied each time by a description of the drought-ridden land, the haze of bauxite, the smoking hills, the acrid smell of the burning rubbish dump, the black carrion corbeaux, the abandoned industrial estates and the dismal shanty towns seen along the road. This picture of a hellish landscape is intensified by the mention of pariah dogs, either sharp faced or diseased. At the Grange, trees and vegetation present a dispiriting sight, filling Jane with desolation and the strong urge to get away. It is at this distressing period, that the chaotic population sheltered by disorderly army occupies the island. Earlier a pimp and Black-power leader, Jimmy Ahmed asserts himself as a guerrilla; Roche, the skeptical white liberal and escapist; and Jane, who uses the jargon of sympathy effortlessly, herself awaits genuine sympathy. Jane plays with the words that she may use at any time, as easily as she has picked them up, and forgets that she has ever spoken them. The narrator describes:

> She was without memory … She was without consistency or even coherence. She knew only what she was and what she had been born to; to this knowledge she was tethered; it was her stability, enabling her to adventure in security. Adventuring, she was indifferent, perhaps blind … and this indifference or blindness, this absence of the sense of the absurd, was part of her unassailability. (*Guerrillas*, p. 18)

Guerrillas portrays the intricate political and psychological aspects concerning the truth of experience during a period of racial conflict on an unidentified Caribbean island that bears a strong resemblance to Trinidad. Jimmy is one of the three leading characters in the novel. The novel is based on the life of Michael de Freitas, a West Indian Black Muslim celebrity also known as Michael X and Michael Abdul Malik, who spent a number of years in London and was charged for using provocative language and was then sentenced to death in Trinidad for the murder of two people including a White English woman. Michael Abdul Malik, like Jimmy Ahmed, has been supported as a revolutionary leader by London liberals. But some London West-Indians scorn him also for being a *comic rogue*. His mother, like Malik's, is black, but his father is Chinese, a heritage resulting into clash and void in cultural identity. Jane is mistaken to anticipate an agrarian leader as someone: "... more physically awkward and more Negroid, someone at least as black as the boys. She saw someone who, close up, looked distinctly Chinese" (*Guerrillas,* p. 8). He has fled from law in London to pose as a liberator of agrarian interests in the island.

The title of the novel *Guerrillas* itself suggests the gap between the desire and capability to act—Roche and Jimmy are the appropriate figures to mark this in-betweenness. The so-called guerrillas are vulnerable and unresponsive. Roche seems to be a parasite that has lost whatever convictions he had but who uses his reputation as someone jailed and tortured for his commitment for the cause and the people. The novel, in fact, exposes the worthlessness of pioneering pretensions in the Third World societies. Revolution becomes only a new form of mimicry in such underdeveloped societies. Anthony Boxill observes: "The tone and atmosphere at the end of the novel is so similar to that at the beginning, that the reader has the impression after having finished the book that he has been in a static world awaiting decay."[3]

In fact, Naipaul's vision of colonialism in *Guerrillas* is gloomy as he finds the former colonizer in his declining Empire and the former colonized in his so-called turbulent independent state. The postcolonial critics like Frantz Fanon who, according to Edward Said, "... wants somehow to bind the European as well as the native together in a new non-adversarial community of awareness and anti-imperialism"[4] also advocate the utopian inter-mingling of the colonizer and the colonized. But here, both find themselves on the margins, each identifying the centre with the other or elsewhere. Naipaul presents the gravity and enormity of the cultural encounter resulting into the ultimate ambivalent status of the both. The guerrillas—Jimmy, Bryant, Peter Roche, and Jane, the displaced human beings—are found suffering from his or her own account of the annoyance of nonconformity, uncertainty, and homelessness. They have reached to the obvious conclusion that "to destroy the world is the only course of action that is now open to sane men" (*Guerrillas,* p. 42). This is because all attempts to realize selfhood and identity end up in disappointment as the degenerate society is opposed to any constructive change. The revolution as depicted in the novel is merely a part of the role created to deal with the greater disorder. Patrick Parrinder points out that though the novel is one "on the race problem and of cultural confusion, it is one which views every race and culture from the outside."[5]

The two major characters caught up with the protagonist, Jimmy are Peter Roche, a White South African, and Jane, his English lover. Roche, who was tormented in his homeland for his involvement in protests against apartheid, now works in public relations for Sablich's, a firm enthusiast to wipe down its history as slave traders by sponsoring Jimmy's so-called agricultural commune. Jane has come from England to join Roche, hoping to identify herself with a man with a cause. Chief among the other characters who enact the narrator's multifaceted conception of truth are Meredith Herbert, a Black journalist, solicitor, and politician and Harry de Tunja, a Jew in unending exile.

It is manifest here that the ambivalence among the Whites is equally terminal because in the postcolonial era, the imperial centre has lost its magnetism. The Europeans have started seeking delight among the recently decolonized people. Jane is attracted towards Peter Roche in London after reading his recently published book on his detention and persecution in South Africa. Purposeless, sterile, regarding herself as a victim, she considers him as one who: "… seemed to make accessible that remote world, of real events and real action … and through him she felt she was being given a new idea of human possibility" (*Guerrillas*, p. 43). He poses to be her liberator from the decay she observes in the middle-class environment into which she is born and which she blames for the stain on her early marriage, on her love affairs, on her very hopes for personal fulfillment. She imagines Roche as the *doer* who has chosen to leave London for "some new and as yet unsuspected centre of world disturbance … and not well paid job on the island with a firm that sounded like a firm of colonial shopkeepers" (*Guerrillas*, p. 44). She joins him on the island, only to discover that once again her homemade hero is no longer of any use to her and, like all her earlier choices—temporary. The narrator depicts her disappointment: "She saw that Roche was a refugee on the island … he was half colonial. He was less on the island than he had been in London … . She doubted whether half a dozen people on the island had read his book" (*Guerrillas,* pp. 45–46). Naipaul here, discloses how closely individual behaviour is linked to the political and social implications of colonialism. He sees the deep-rooted effects of colonialism on the individuals like Roche, Jimmy, Bryant, and Jane. They are engaged in a never ending conflict of *difference*. But in their case, "… differences do not only exist between outsider and insider—two entities—they are also at work within the outsider or the insider—a single entity."[6]

Strangely enough, Jane, a publicity manager at London who comes to the island assuming it to be the centre of movement, looks for excitement in the Third World. Her own imperial society no longer offers those like her any ideal to cherish. After leaving London, Jane has become just another displaced person, a stranger without acquaintances, movement or society. Dependent on pompous men for her purpose, ideology and a place in the world, she observes among the *doers* the typical anxiety for survival. Her passport makes clear her privileged position as she has the choice to return to London, unlike Jimmy or other West Indians. But she obtains this position from the former imperial order, which has been eroded in the postcolonial worlds. Jane is "adrift, enervated, her dissatisfactions vague, now centring on the world, now on men" (*Guerrillas*, p. 42). She is a woman filled with hazy ambitions which she wants to realize through her man; so she chooses Roche because she considers him a *doer*.

Ironically, on the very first day of her arrival on the island she starts feeling: "that she had come to a place at the end of the world, to a place that had exhausted its possibilities" (*Guerrillas*, p. 44). She does not take long to become conscious that her choice was wrong. "The city and the flat remained as unknown as it was on that first day; and nothing had happened to alter the conviction she had had, at the moment of arrival, that she had made a wrong decision" (*Guerrillas*, p. 41). She suffers from a sense of loneliness and reacts: "I have always been alone since I've been here" (*Guerrillas*, p. 176). The hymns on Adela's radio remind her of "the melancholy, the incompleteness, of all her time here ... ". (*Guerrillas*, p. 175)

As a result, she wants to leave the place at her earliest because she is lucky enough to have the option of returning to London open. She thinks that London will at least provide her a safer environment. The sense of insecurity is stronger in the island as the guerrillas occupy the brown hills. The Ridge where she is staying with Roche appears secure but she senses some strange personal unsteadiness there. Though she comes to the island to be with Roche and though she represents the colonial power to Jimmy, she is also one who derives her identity from an *'other'*—the man. Her irresolute and inconsistent mindset is extremely colonial as she fails to develop any enduring relationship with anybody in the island.

Moreover, the prevailing tone of dissipation, decay and exploitation intensifies the disillusionment in the relationship between Roche and Jane. Jimmy, Roche and Jane all three are preoccupied with finding satisfaction in their fake roles sincerely enacted before one another. Roche has undergone perpetual anguish for the Black people of South Africa before his arrival in the island. But, at times it seems that to boost his own repute as a leader Roche simply misuses the natives including Jimmy. Jimmy, who, on the other hand, was like a celebrity in London, is like a saviour loving and liking the common natives and inspiring fear in the rich White firms. In the process of writing, he fuses the memory of his brief triumph in London with his present fantasy. Jane whom he wants to get hold of and torture represents the world he envies and wishes to possess. The sexual encounters between Jimmy and Jane enact the most extreme effects of alienation on society's most vulnerable individuals—whatever is their race, origin or class. In his fictitious narrative of a white girl, he identifies himself to be involved with both victim and aggressor; he has fantasized himself to be involved in a conquest in which he asserts power through sexual cruelty and humiliation, thus incorporating what he hates and envies. The Black–White dichotomy holds a pivotal place as Jimmy is torn between the love-hate relationships. His conflict echoes the confusion of Fanon when he records his feelings:

> As I begin to recognize that the Negro is the symbol of sin, I catch myself hating the Negro. But then I recognize that I am a Negro. There are two ways out of this conflict ... I have only one solution: to rise above this absurd drama ... to reject the two terms that are equally unacceptable ... to reach out for the universal.[7]

Besides, the affluent capitalists on the island, in the form of the Sablich's, a firm with an unsavory history, realize that they must do something "to harness the energy of the idle and the rumbling masses, and to give the poor people a sense of purpose, surrounded as they are by disintegration and decay."[8] So they establish commune in the countryside to encourage the criminals and near criminal types from the slums to go back to the land and rebuild the country from scratch which is nothing but cynical gesture—a gimmick to show a concern which does not exist. The boys here are allowed to talk romantic revolutionary slogans which give an outlet to some of their anger and frustration. Thus the real problems are clouded in the rhetoric. It is to lead the boys on the commune that the Sablich's choose Jimmy Ahmed who is ironically caught up in his own private and bitter fantasies.

The Sablich's on the other hand hire Peter Roche to act as its social worker and officer between them and the commune. Peter Roche is not at all steadfast and therefore suits the Sablich's. It is not a question of dishonesty but he accepts the job without investigating the economic, political, or historical circumstances of the firm. His so-called revolutionary actions were carried out to give himself the image of a "man of action". The pertinent questioning of the motives of his actions leaves him miserable. The irony lies in the fact that Roche considers himself a *doer*. He pretends to have a very solid reason behind his enduring existence. He is even mistaken by his mistress Jane who takes him as a dynamic *man of action*. She wants to realize her unfulfilled dreams through her association with Roche. But she is utterly disillusioned when she observes:

> So Jane saw that on the island, which in her imagination had once been the setting of action that would undo the world, Roche was a refugee. He was a man who didn't have a place to go back to; he was someone for whom room had been made … . But she no longer believed him capable of passion. All that he seemed capable of was a cheap sarcasm, directed mainly at her … . (*Guerrillas*, p. 48)

Obviously, Roche is well aware of the mask he is using to fascinate others. He meets a well-deserved and much anticipated failure, as he himself was never sure of his success. His clarity of vision and openness, however remain remarkable. Even while falling apart, he manages to view the temporariness of his relationship with Jane very clearly. Roche, who was once in a South African prison as "the great white revolutionary and torture hero of South Africa," (*Guerrillas*, p. 36) works for Sablich's, a firm of West Indian "slave traders in the old days, they now pretend that black is beautiful" (*Guerrillas*, p. 36). He is concerned with helping dispossessed Blacks on this island, though, in fact, he is exercising a kind of control over them. Jimmy is one of his charges, and Sablich's supports his commune, Thrushcross Grange. He egoistically presents himself as a key figure on the island before Jane and Roche when he says: "They've got to support me, massa. Sablich's and everybody else. They've got to make me bigger. Because if I fail—hmm. I'm the only man they're afraid of". (*Guerrillas*, p. 20)

Likewise, Jane's arrival on the island further worsens the situation as she carries the typical colonial anxiety to the place and, without any deliberate attempt, intensifies the panic of Jimmy and Roche. Jimmy who has always been certain about his role in the island because, according the narrator, the government has to "build him up and pretend they are supporting him. The doer. And Jimmy has this English reputation. He can't just be got out of the way" (*Guerrillas*, p. 23). He feels emaciated and impotent as soon as he comes in close contact with Jane. She intends to use people for her own fulfillment, but ironically she herself is used and victimized by

Roche, Jimmy and Bryant. Having realized that Roche, the seeming enemy of imperialism, is actually its offspring and has become its propagator, a "refugee" and "half-colonial" (*Guerrillas,* p. 45) himself, Jane plans to return to London. She has got to understand not only Roche but also her life on the Ridge. The narrator describes:

> The Ridge was self-contained, shut off from the city; and at first the hysteria in which her neighbours lived had interested her. Here, where she had come as to the center of the world, the talk was of departure, of papers being fixed for Canada and the United States: secretive talk, because departure was at once like betrayal and surrender. (*Guerrillas,* pp. 44–45)

Besides, transient bureaucrats inhabit ridge and the expatriates here are demoralized by newspaper reports of guerrillas questioning the permanence the island has somehow offered them. Being homeless, she feels more insecure and vulnerable here on the Ridge surrounded by the brown hills occupied by guerrillas. The narrator brings out the intensity of the situation when he adds to the location of Ridge: "About the Ridge, so high, so seemingly secure, there was an unknown human turbulence" (*Guerrillas*, p. 51). It is a desolate place that had produced no great men, and its possibilities were now exhausted. Even the most settled and localized figure, Harry de Tunja, feels like escaping the fluid life of the island as, "during his many business trips to Canada, Harry had also been securing his status as a Canadian landed immigrant". (*Guerrillas,* p. 45)

Being disillusioned with her soulmate and the so-called island life of activity, Jane finds the sense of alienation and fragmentation prevalent among all the natives and outsiders in the novel. The relationship between Jane and Peter Roche is indicative of bleakness. Jane finds him incompetent, contemptuous and physically unpleasant. There is no love, little care and seldom sex between them. They are disdainful of each other, and gain little from their relationship, yet they are reluctant to break up. Jane immediately knows that coming to the island was a wrong decision, but she allows herself to be disillusioned in her relationship with Jimmy whom she considers a guerrilla leader.

However, now she is in a middle state, i.e., oscillating between the transient life of island and equally desolate life of London. She has become the metaphor of emptiness in the young women: "She saw the girls who were her friends as empty vessels, waiting to be filled by men, who in time appeared, their name echoing and re-echoing in conversation, Roger and Mark and John, as empty as the girls" (*Guerrillas*, p. 51). But she is contented to find herself privileged. Her in-betweenness is mixed with comfort. The narrator mentions her position:

> Not many people had that freedom: to decide, and then to do. It was part of her luck; in moments like this she always consoled ... she was privileged: it was the big idea, the one that overrode all the scattered, unrelated ideas deposited in her soul as she had adventured in life ... she would return to London; that society which she had given up, and whose destruction she thought she had awaited, continued. She would be safe in London, but she would be safe in the midst of decay. (*Guerrillas*, pp. 49–50)

But she delays her exit from the self-imposed expatriate life of island. It further leads her to catastrophe when Jimmy perpetually victimizes her. Being disinterested in the affairs of Jane, Roche feels injured and can not guide her about the misleading and deceptive image of Jimmy. He himself has a torn identity as, according to the narrator, "he worked with Jimmy Ahmed, whom he took seriously, more seriously than the people who gave Jimmy money; he bribed slum boys to go to Thrushcross Grange" (*Guerrillas*, p. 47). Her cynicism makes her inform Jimmy about her decision to leave the island without delay. But Jimmy hands her over to Bryant who consequently murders her in a mood of frenzy at the time of gang uprising.

Jimmy Ahmed, the half-Chinese Negro protagonist, is a victim both of colonialism and of moderate whites like Jane. Jimmy Ahmed is predominantly exposed to racial abuse and injury. He carries the wound of England on his back. He assumes to assert his identity through the advocacy of his negritude—but he is not even a Negro. In his native land he is the half-caste—a *hakwai Chinee* in the white world, in which he longs to be accepted, he is inescapably a "nigger". He explains his confused identity before Jane: "I was born in the back room of a Chinese grocery. I'm a *hakwai Chinee*. You know what a *hakwai* is? It's the Chinese for nigger" (*Guerrillas*, p. 20). Consequent upon his being persecuted for rape charges and after having been discarded by his White followers, Jimmy Ahmed flees London. In the island, Jimmy, the byproduct of inter-racial marriage is the leader of what is professed as an agricultural commune inhabited by wretched slum youths. He is left alone with his obsessions and eccentricities, "with the disintegrating remnants of an artificial personality created by his own aberrant egotism and consolidated by the overexcited British Press."[9] Yet Meredith, the sophisticated politician of the island, acknowledges him as a threat. He warns Roche to beware of Jimmy as, according to him, "He is dangerous because he's famous, because he has a lot of that English glamour still, and because he's nothing at all ... anybody can use that man and create chaos in this place. He can be programmed". (*Guerrillas*, p. 140)

To the surprise of the reader, in London Jimmy is feted and hailed as a leader of the Blacks. He imitates English life-style while projecting himself as the leader of the agriculture commune. Jane compliments him for his English style. He acknowledges his indebtedness to England when he says: "All the stuff here comes from England. You know what they say. You may not be able to make a living in England, but England teaches you how to live" (*Guerrillas*, p. 17). His mixed parentage and diverse influences make him behave some time as an orthodox Muslim and at other times as an advanced European. Being a true Muslim, he does not take wine offered by Jane. His loyalty keeps on shifting—he is the victim of perpetual doubt whether he should be faithful towards the Blacks or the Whites. He is, however, sharp enough to understand the casual attitude of Englishmen towards the revolution and revolutionaries. He is considered no more than a plaything in England. He himself admits:

> England isn't real ... . The problems aren't going to be solved there. You know what happens in England. Everybody goes to the demo and the meeting and then they leave you and go home to tea ... . I got away in time. I was lucky. Over there the black man can become ... like a play boy. They make you like a play boy in England. (*Guerrillas*, p. 19)

Afterward, in a letter to Marjorie, a lady with whom Jimmy had an affair in London and whom he considers a creative as well as destructive force, he admits that her prediction about his future is coming true. He writes: "You are the only person I can write to ... what you prophesied is all coming true, I am dying alone and unloved and I will die in anger, no other way is possible now. That is a bad way to die ..." (*Guerrillas*, p. 230). He feels grateful to her because he could realize his self with her. She has the credit to develop a sense of manhood in that child in the back room of his Chinese father's shop.

Nevertheless, he expresses disapproval of his mother's indulgence in interracial marriage which causes uninterrupted agony in his life. He asserts that the women like his mother don't have any sense of shame and they hardly ever care for their children who are destined to pay for the sins of their mothers. Jimmy is critical of his abnormal heritage, especially the mother who has deprived him of his black identity, his source of a genuine self. His ambiguous identity does not allow him to forget his personal alienation in social engagements and radical beliefs. His inherited disgrace never grants him reassurance. According to Meredith, discarded by his previous supporters in

London, Jimmy has been sent back to the island to realize his non-entity. Ultimately he finds himself a lost man—lost since childhood. Helpless against the government, Meredith, and Roche, he tortures Jane, the last object of his distorted fantasy and romance.

Ironically, unable to settle himself in his native land, he declares himself a native leader. He fights for the fundamental right of a man for the "portion of land on the earth". His ideology gets reflected in the words: "All revolutions begin with the land. Men are born on the earth, everyman has his one spot, it is his birth right, and men must claim their portion of the earth in brotherhood and harmony. In this spirit we came an intrepid band to virgin forest ..." (*Guerrillas*, p. 9). Similarly, Roche defines his aim explicitly when he says that he is looking for someone to lead. His purposelessness and meaninglessness is aptly depicted in this comment of Jane: "Of course, he's having everybody on .... And everybody is having him on. Everybody is pretending that something exists that doesn't exist" (*Guerrillas*, p. 23). The image of Jimmy as a *doer* is merely an eyewash, as he has no philosophy of his own. The boys who gather round Jimmy are derelicts and they have nowhere else to go.

Jimmy, who was earlier exploited by Whites in England, is transformed into a Black power leader. In the Caribbean island he is used by Roche to justify his place in liberal causes and he is consequently seduced by a liberal white, Jane. Jimmy has always been violent as earlier he faced a rape charge in England. His interaction with Jane, her sexual harassment and ultimate murder show his propensity for violence. In *Guerrillas* the sexual narrative is of a dismal and dreary nature. Commenting on the narrative of the novel Chandra B. Joshi adds:

> In *Guerrillas* the narrator's sympathies are with all the characters ... their psyches so that though they are critical of one another we see them as essentially victims of their situations: their greatnesses are measured against their failures. So that even the worst of them, the murderous gang leader, Jimmy, is a pathetic figure.[10]

On the other hand, sexual violence pervades the novel. The sex is totally devoid of any tenderness or sentiment in the novel—something that can be discerned in Jane and Jimmy's coming together. But it is meant for mutual comfort in Jimmy and Bryant's homosexual relationship. In Jimmy and Jane's sexual encounters there is no indication of any physical attraction. Jane's view of Jimmy, his home and his rebellious smartness—all these imply repugnance and revulsion. His desire for her is really a desire for racial revenge through sexual dominance. It is depressing the first time and viciously sadistic—a deliberate act of retribution the second time. This is the culmination of the novel—a ghastly picture of sexual assault followed by murder. Disgraced by his own sexual disappointment and infuriated at Jane's perceptible apathy on the first instance, Jimmy brutally sodomizes her. And then, he offers her up to Bryant, his homosexual partner saying: "Bryant, the rat! Kill the rat!" (*Guerrillas*, p. 245). The Black–White controversy and dichotomy is the guiding factor behind the abnormal conduct of Jimmy and Bryant towards Jane. She knows so little about herself emotionally and sexually. She could never apprehend the catastrophic end of her life in the hands of those she relied upon. She does not even resist when she is cut by Bryant and throttled by Jimmy. Having defined herself as a victim for most of her life, she goes to her final victimization submissively, as if she could experience herself in no other way.

After murdering Jane, Jimmy feels nothing except despair. He is lost in emptiness. Jimmy's malice and callousness in getting Jane murdered does not provide any solution to his basic dilemma. He might have realized a temporary sense of triumph over one of his tough opponents, i.e., white English culture. He might have considered himself the part of the enemy, and "by seeking the enemy within and executing him, he stood a better chance of being cleaned and renewed."[11] It is because of his penchant to find easy way out that Jimmy takes revenge on Jane, the representative oppressor of colonialism. Roche, one time lover of Jane, is least affected by the murder of Jane and wipes away her presence by setting her possessions on fire. Her unregistered entry in the island indicates her destined nonconformity and nothingness in the postcolonial world. His ultimate confession to Marjorie that he knows he is fooling himself and later to himself, after Jane's murder, that he doesn't know who or what he is, verify his lifelong conflict. He maintains hatred for the white English culture is in spite of the fact that he is captivated by the English tradition and culture. He even mimics the English way of life. In this context, Meredith rightly adds: "We're a dependent people, Peter. We need other people's approval ... some of us get taken up by certain people and are made famous. Then we are sent back here as leaders". (*Guerrillas*, p. 206)

Moreover, the circumstances of his birth and background make Jimmy the representative Naipaulian nomadic drifter, puzzled about his very individuality. But even the seemingly triumphant *doer* Peter Roche, a man with a standing as a radical who has fought and suffered for the Blacks in South Africa, is no less troubled with a sense of disappointment and pointlessness. He thinks:

> I've built my whole life on sand. He had thought of himself as a doer; it surprised him now to be so far from that self, to be a man who waited on events ... I've trapped myself. And he could neither act nor withdraw; he could only wait ... he had no political dogma and no longer had a vision of a world made good .... (*Guerrillas*, p. 87)

The man whom Jane had found as a *doer*, a man of achievement, sees himself at forty-five as quite adrift. And Jane finds her view of Roche altering. She sees him as a refugee on the islands: "a man who didn't have a place to go back to ..." (*Guerrillas*, p. 48). Her meeting with Peter Roche whom she considers a "doer", brings a ray of hope in her life. But it takes her no time to see that he too is as hollow as she herself is. He is indulged in the same job of public relations for Sablich's that she has deserted in London after having experienced a sense of meaninglessness of that job. His submissiveness and consequent unconcern make her decide to leave the island life.

Correspondingly, the association between Jane, Peter Roche, and Jimmy Ahmed also demonstrate the long-lasting effect of colonialism. Jimmy Ahmed, Peter Roche and Jane are the three major characters of the novel and all of them exemplify the sense of disappointment and defeat. Nevertheless, other characters also reflect the similar traits in their personalities. The boys like Bryant and Mannie in Thrushcross Grange, are the worst by-products of a postcolonial Creole society. They hang about with Jimmy because "they had no where to go. They were like Bryant, boys spawned by the city, casually conceived and after the backyard drama and ritual of their birth gradually abandoned ..." (*Guerrillas*, p. 27). The episode where a black man in island reminds Harry de Tunja of his Jewish origin marks change in his attitude. Earlier he is viewed as complacent and well-settled Ridge man, but he surprises everyone when it is revealed that he too has been planning to escape from the island. When his wife deserts him, Jane remarks: "Harry's cosy little world is breaking up." Roche replies: "It looked cosy to us. I wonder whether it was ever cosy" (*Guerrillas*, p. 154). Meredith Herbert, a Black solicitor, radio interviewer and politician, had at first appeared to Roche as a man with a dynamic personality. But very soon, Roche starts observing "an element of exaggeration and defiance ... strains behind the personality ... Roche began to have intimations of Meredith's own hysteria, of the rages, deprivations and unappeased ambition that perhaps lay behind that domesticity he flaunted" (*Guerrillas*, p. 134). His personality, once viewed in this way, could never emerge as perfect again.

It is in this way that the varied situations in the novel echo the most insidious circumstances in the lives of the colonials. Jimmy, after being admired for a time by progressives as a Black militant, flees England where he is an alien, because he is charged with rape. Roche is admired as a hero of South African resistance but flees England when threatened by a South African agent. In fact neither was a serious revolutionary with a philosophy. Both Jimmy and Roche attract women through their reputations as activists. Neither is at home on the island, Roche because he is a foreign white, Jimmy because he is part Chinese and taken as a product of England. Both make use of London ideas about how to liberate blacks. Harry's wife leaves him, Jane is planning to leave Roche, Harry will leave for Canada and Roche presumably will return to London. None of their decisions seem reasonable in the end. Roche flees England after the South Africans threaten him, and in the end he leaves the island in the face of threat by Jimmy. Due to her inconsistent nature, Jane always plays with fire. She is devoid of consistency, stability and meaning in life. When, in the end, Jimmy holds her for Bryant to put her to death, she never cries or struggles. Her surrender seems to be voluntary and anticipated. Naipaul is anxious to present the enduring presence of colonialism in the postcolonial age. He defends what Frantz Fanon has termed as "false decolonisation, legal independence without breaking down the colonial social and political structures."[12]

Guerrillas hence presents a narrative defining postcolonial disorder. Jane visualizes "the vision of decay, of a world going up in flames ... the world was not what it ought to be" (*Guerrillas*, pp. 96–97). The ambivalence of Jimmy may also be witnessed in his self-revelatory letter to Roy where he comments: "In my father's house there are many mansions ... . But the house is full up now Roy, there are no more mansions ... I fooled myself that there was a mansion waiting somewhere for me ... I always knew I was fooling myself. I knew there was no mansion, it was all going to end in smoke". (*Guerrillas*, p. 83)

In the novel, Jimmy is always uncertain as what he is fighting against. Ironically, the world he seeks to eliminate is the world that made him which in turn signifies his wish for self-abolition. The urge behind his desire to sacrifice himself and other nomads like him is the assertion: "... to destroy the world is the only course of action that is now open to the sane men ... I want to see fire everywhere ... there is no hope of creative endeavour being appreciated, it is all for nothing" (*Guerrillas*, p. 35). The intensity of this hopelessness can be observed further in the opinion of Meredith who observes: "If those people down on the beach were a little saner, don't you think they would burn this place down twice a year? Madness keeps the place going"

(*Guerrillas*, p. 138). These observations suggest the incapacity, insignificance, and nonconformity of a forsaken community of island.

Consequently, Jane has no charm left in her life as she has already experienced the utter disillusionment in her relationship with Roche and Jimmy. After breaking her ties with Roche, she indulges in another dispassionate relationship, this time with Jimmy who associates her with "those prostitutes who after defeat and degradation celebrate a triumph" (*Guerrillas*, p. 77). His disenchantment with Jane makes him find comfort in "Bryant's warm, firm flesh and his relieving mouth and tongue" (*Guerrillas*, p. 78). Jane shows frigidity when Jimmy is eager to get her, but unsatisfied, she turns to Roche for comfort, asking him to share her bed.

Though Jane always considers Meredith as a boring and a good for nothing fellow, Roche fails to understand his character. He resembles Ralph Kripalsingh as he poses himself as if he were a forgotten political hero. Though he is oblivious of his political disappointment, he is doomed to failure because of typical islanders' politics. He is in no way different from the inexperienced politicians in *The Mystic Masseur*, *The Suffrage of Elvira* and *The Mimic Men*. But, in Meredith's case, the political failure does not bring any ruination in his life, as he is an ingenious fellow with some standing as a solicitor and anchor of radio broadcast "Encounter". On the restoration of Meredith in the cabinet, Roche compares himself to Meredith who has been reinstated. Harry presents the predicament of Meredith's existence when he adds:

> A child could have told Meredith that they were calling him back just to throw him to the crowd … . They did terrible things to Meredith … . They strip him naked … somebody even put a knife to the man's balls … . He will have to hide now, you know. He can't live here after this. The place is too small. (*Guerrillas*, p. 189)

Further, Roche emphatically accepts that there are no guerrillas but only aimless gangs who, according to Harry de Tunja, "… don't know who they fighting or, who they fighting for. Everybody down there is a leader now. I hear there isn't even a government" (*Guerrillas*, p. 186). Violence and aggression dwell deep in the minds of these so-called guerrillas. After the death of Stephens, Bryant appears to lose his sanity and wants to kill Jimmy. Jimmy, on the other hand, leads Jane to see Bryant, claiming "he has something for you"; "Bryant and I are not friends now, Jane. You'll help to make us friends" (*Guerrillas*, p. 245), and when he notices Bryant with a cutlass in his hand, he cries "Bryant, the rat! Kill the rat!" (*Guerrillas*, p. 245). Jimmy sacrifices Jane to bring reconciliation in his relationship with Bryant, but the most important reason behind this heinous crime is his deep-seated hatred for the White women representing "superior" race.

Ultimately, after experiencing personal failure as a social activist in the island, Roche has no option left but to flee. Escape is the only solution with the displaced colonials and émigrés as they are always haunted by the sense of alienation, isolation, homelessness and meaninglessness in their lives. Roche has fled England to escape threats of the protesters on his views on race. In the end, he escapes the island to disown any responsibility for racial violence. All the politicians face utter failure because their ideology is borrowed and practically of no use. No organization or institution—political, legal, commercial or social, is competent to manage postcolonial turbulent situation of island. The radicals like Roche, Jimmy and Meredith can not contribute constructively in the colonial set up of island because they lack stability, purpose and creativity. Roche comes under the grip of personal panic of withdrawal and unfulfilled dreams while observing Meredith incapable of dominating others. The sense of deprivation and unrealized ambition that Roche perceives in his life, are opposed to his quest for totality in a disjointed society. Meredith's pipe dream to express himself fully is an continuing struggle against the subjugation of his race and class. In the same way, with the breaking out of riots in response to the killing of Stephens by the police, Harry is skeptical about the role of police and their capacity to control the riots. Police are abandoning their posts, the rebellion seems to have no centre and the rioters have no programme or a leader. Harry's remarks suggest the inefficiency and unruliness of colonial police: "I don't see how you can blame the police. They don't know who they fighting or who they fighting for. Everybody down there is a leader now. I hear there isn't even a government. You hear about Meredith? … they chase him" (*Guerrillas,* p. 186). The past of colonialism and subjugation has not loosened its hold on the present.

Later on, in the radio programme "Encounter" Meredith makes Roche acknowledge his helplessness to manage the affairs of Thrushcross Grange commune which Meredith names as "a cover for the guerrillas" (*Guerrillas,* p. 216). This interview lays bare the superficiality of his loyalty towards the mission of racial equality and of a life without meaningful aspirations. His purposeless indulgence in the affairs of Sablich's and Thrushcross Grange may be better understood when he affirms: "We were all misled. Perhaps we were all hoping against hope" (*Guerrillas,* p. 207). Responding to a query made by Meredith regarding his future plans, he admits that he has no plans for the future in the island and he will be back to London to get another job. His emptiness is revealed further when he confesses that he has left England not out of commitment but out of fear of a neo-Nazi who was bound to murder him. Thereafter, Jane feels all the more beguiled and betrayed by the so-called *doers*. The widespread bewilderment and ambivalence among the denizens is rightly observed by Lillian Feder:

> Down in the city, Jimmy, leading the rioters bearing Stephen's body through the streets, and Meredith, representing a government he mistrusts, are alike in denying what they know. Both pay for their compromises. Jimmy is soon dropped by the rioters, replaced by others who declare themselves leaders. Meredith is stripped and assailed by the mob.[13]

In *Guerrillas* there are merely leaderless individuals each of whom has his or her own hysteria, or as Jimmy writes: "When the leader himself begins to yield to despair, things are bad. The whole place is going to blow up. When everybody wants to fight there's nothing to fight for. Everybody wants to fight his own little war, everybody is a guerrilla" (*Guerrillas*, p. 87). The novel is a testimony of the individual in relation to society which is preoccupied with the idea of security and stability.

Hence, Jimmy's dilemma is the typical outcome of colonialism. Independence has left him to experience the contradictions, i.e., the assertion of native culture is confronted with the mimicking colonials who make an attempt to restore the native ideology. His posters indicate that he is neither a slave nor a stallion but the saviour of the others. The political chaos on the island symbolizes the cultural disintegration in the island. There is no fellow feeling among the residents of the island. The young folk of this Creole society seem to be troubled with self-contempt that shapes the personality of Jimmy. He is convinced that "all revolutions begin with the land" (*Guerrillas*, p. 9). He presents the colonial ambivalence through his observation that reminds him of the title of Fanon's first book: "… the people here have been betrayed too often, it's always a case of black faces white masks, you don't know who your enemy is, the enemy infiltrates your ranks all the time" (*Guerrillas*, p. 82). Jimmy's correspondence with his English associates named Roy and Marjorie best reflects the colonialism and its repercussions. Like Jane, Roy sees survival in England as subsidiary, away from the hub of valid action experienced by doers like Jimmy. Imperial-colonial dichotomy is observed at its best when Roy pens down in one of his letters to Jimmy:

> That place sounds ripe for something … I am beginning to feel that we are an incurably frivolous people and as a nation we seem

> resigned to giggling our way to oblivion … . We will continue to scan the newspapers for news of you and your doings which from the distance seem vastly exciting. (*Guerrillas*, p. 165)

And Jimmy's letter to Marjorie is written at the time of race riots, when Bryant is waiting outside to kill him for his betrayal. He writes: "you were my maker, you broke my heart, you made me and then you made me feel like dirt again, good only for dirt … you people sent me back here, to be nothing" (*Guerrillas*, p. 233). Jimmy lives for approval from what he identifies as the centre of the world viewing himself always at the margins. Roy and Jimmy both feel uneasy regardless of their locations. One feels lost in the island, and his counterpart is envious of Jimmy for enjoying the life full of activity.

However, Jimmy's inclination towards the Englishness is evident when he chooses a White English woman, Clarissa as the narrator of his fiction. Through his fictitious encounter with the White lady on the typical West Indian Island, his apathy towards the Black and affection for the Whites is perceptible. His is a confused personality as he establishes himself as the revolutionary leader among the Black natives of the island while fostering a strong antagonism towards the Whites. But his ambivalence asserts itself when he fantasizes about sadistically raping a White woman and then bravely helping the victimized. Jimmy's ambivalence asserts itself when he is seen identifying himself sometimes with English tradition and at other times with blacks like Bryant. He is overwhelmed by the story:

> … of the rape of a white girl at the beach by a gang. The girl had bled and shrieked and fainted. One of the men … using his cupped hands alone, to bring water to the girl … the most moving part of the story, and it had stayed with him … the bleeding girl on the front fender of the old Ford, the cupped hands offering water, the grateful eyes, remembering terror … wakened from his dream to the emptiness about him. (*Guerrillas*, pp. 60–61)

Jimmy's ultimate frustration with his twofold identity and Englishness makes him a sorry figure in the eyes of the natives like Bryant who intends to murder Jimmy for his adopting double standards. Being humiliated by Jane, he finds relief in the arms of a Black male. Jimmy's love for Bryant represents his affirmation of his Black self which he otherwise hides. Similarly, after his failure to establish meaningful sexual relationship with Jane: "He longed for the feel of Bryant, for Bryant's warm firm flesh and his relieving mouth and tongue" (*Guerrillas*, p. 78). Jimmy's homosexual relationship with Bryant presents his failure in finding carnal satisfaction in the white world.

Consequently, the discontentment of Jimmy in the absorbing world of English tradition and his involvement with Bryant presents his psychic enigma. Jimmy's involvement with Jane is indigestible to Bryant as he is hostile to her for her being the representative of white English culture. The children of "hell" who occupy the dreary landscape of Jimmy's commune are underdeveloped and deformed. Bryant, the most overriding comrade of Jimmy is of the *Medusa* head. The narrator is very much cautious while introducing Bryant whose "face was oddly narrow, and twisted on one side, as though he had been damaged at birth". (*Guerrillas*, p. 11)

So the novelist presents the ugly physical details to correlate the setting to the barrenness of the natives and expatriates alike. Roche meets a boy in the town with "the dull, close-set eyes, a pimple on the right eyelid: the mind half eaten away, human debris already, his cause already lost" (*Guerrillas*, p. 101). Peter Roche who is the pride of Jane, disappoints Jane with his laugh revealing: "the corners of his mouth rode up over the receding gums on his molars … it was like a glimpse of teeth in a skull, like a glimpse of a satyr … a glimpse of the inner man". (*Guerrillas*, p. 44)

For V.S. Naipaul, in the postcolonial scenario, the past and the present are at loggerheads as the native population is troubled and tortured by the postcolonial developments like industrialization, infiltration by the American capitalist market explorers, borrowed political standards and pseudo socialist movements. The slogans pasted and painted beside the roads are reminders of the basic mimicking tendency among the islanders. After observing the striking labels, even a stranger can smell the presence of the outside intruders in the island. The slogans like "*Basic Black, Don't Vote,* and *Birth Control is a Plot Against the Negro Race*", (*Guerrillas*, p. 1) are reminiscent of the clash between the old and new, native and alien, and the colonized and colonizer. The clash is all the more apparent when one notices that Sablich's the local bottlers of Coca Cola and the American Bauxite Company is the sponsor of these bills.

On the other hand, Jimmy's organization Thrushcross Grange reminds one of Emily Bronte's *Wuthering Heights* where Heathcliff, an orphan, when adopted by the natives of the Wuthering Heights, turns to be malicious in nature. Jimmy's borrowing of the term *Thrushcross Grange* pinpoints his predilection for the English culture. Jimmy resembles Heathcliff in his dislocation, sense of insecurity and in his vindictive nature. Anthony Boxill precisely observes the common trauma of Heathcliff and Jimmy when he remarks: "There can be no doubt that both Heathcliff and Jimmy have been slighted and made to suffer for reasons of race and class, but if Heathcliff can be taken seriously as a symbol of power and energy of the emerging lower classes, Jimmy never rises above the level of the conman and sham."[14] Like Heathcliff, the intense wounds of neglected and deprived childhoods mark both Jimmy and Meredith in *Guerrillas*.

Ultimately, the depressing mood of the novel dominates the psyches of the important characters. Meredith shows his utter annoyance in *Guerrillas* and for him, nobody will make a new life. Similarly, Jimmy Ahmed presents his hopelessness in his personal literary expression when he observes that there are no more *mansions* waiting for him anywhere in the world. The pain and disillusionment underlying this bitter cry has behind it a great deal of the felt experience of Naipaul himself after nearly twenty-five years of living in exile and functioning as a writer without a country, without roots, without a society. Chandra B. Joshi observes: "It is particularly after the visit to India which resulted in *India: A Wounded Civilisation* that the novelist seems to have become convinced of the folly of dreaming of 'mansions' awaiting one anywhere in the world and abandons finally his own hope to claim his Indian ancestry."[15] The main plot of the story, the background and the delineation of two of the three main characters are based on the story of the murder of an English woman, Gale Ann Benson, as narrated in "Michael X and the Black Power Killings in Trinidad".

Similarly, in *A Bend in the River* the African background is entirely provided by Naipaul's report on Zaire and the doings of its president Mobuto Sese Seko whose indirect presence as the Big Man looms large in the lives of the men of the town at the bend in the river. In *A Bend in the River* also, there is an apparent dichotomy between past and present. In this novel, Indar tells Salim that they will have to learn to trample on the past as it can only cause pain. This terribly grim and depressing world picture projects Naipaul's vision of the bleak future of half-made societies doomed to remain half-made.

Obviously, the terms in which these novels are structured—the violence in the form of murders, torment and sadism—become an absurd tragedy as the narrator presents his protagonist's memories of a structured past to hint at the essential conflict between the past and the present. The displaced denizens of island do not accept the enforced transformation in their lives and their apathy is presented in *A Bend in the River*: "They're going to kill everybody who can read and write, everybody who ever put on a jacket and tie ... They're going to kill all the masters and all the servants ... . They're going to kill and kill. They say it is the only way, to go back to the beginning before it's too late" (*A Bend in the River*, p. 293). The lonely people are seen searching for emotional richness ending up more alienated, insulated and ridden by fear if not hatred. Jimmy's ultimate disillusionment is reflected in these lines: "Then he was lost, lost since the beginning of time. But time had no beginning and he was disembodied. He was nothing more than this sense of loss that grew deeper and deeper as he awakened to it; he would have liked to scream, for the relief". (*Guerrillas*, p. 248)

Through his protagonists in *Guerrillas* and *A Bend in the River*, Naipaul shows that in a democratic world that emphasizes respect for the individual, survival is possible only in power groups. The individual not supported by power is always victimized and cowed down. The elements of choice and freedom, which gave dignity to existentialist thought, in today's political set-up, are no more the inherent rights of the individuals but of the man in the seat of power. The Big Man in *A Bend in the River* plays fast and loose with men and machines, ideas and history. And Jimmy in *Guerrillas*, the *hakwai* Chinese born in the back room of Chinese grocery, knows:

> They've got to support me, massa. Sablich's and everybody else. They've got to make me bigger. Because. Because, if I fail—hmm. I'm the only man that stands between them and revolution, and they know it now, massa. That's why I'm the only man they're afraid of .... I'm the friend of every capitalist in the country. Everybody is my friend. (*Guerrillas*, p. 9)

The disaffected existentialist protagonist, the victim of society, is also the destroyer of his community without which he can not survive—for the victim seeks affirmation and asserts himself as the destroyer. This ambiguity of human motivation underlies Jimmy's role in *Guerrillas*. The human dilemma evolves out of the conflict of cultures which themselves are not genuine as they have been prostituted by historical distortion or their inflexibility in the face of a growing and changing world. In these novels this confrontation of cultures takes place in recognizable third world countries which yet remain unreal to the people who congregate there. The *Whites* who have come to improve the colonial setup, bring their burden of a secure superiority with them while the *Coloureds* reject their misrepresented cultures as inferior and backward.

All the themes of *Guerrillas*, which build up a picture of despair and social breakdown, are dramatized by the dual consciousness of the narrator. His character is most rounded through his writings which enlarge on his fantasies regarding himself. Here, he exposes his present despair most truthfully as he realizes the distance between the imagined and the actual self.

In the novel, the narrator describes the two overtly conflicting social groups of disaffected people: the *Whites* versus the *Coloureds*, the expatriates versus the locals, and the Ridge versus the Grange. The various subjective realities of the expatriate society of the Ridge, through whose eyes the life of town and Grange life is seen, provide the outsider's view of Third World chaos, disorder and subhuman existence. Theirs is the despair of having come as messengers of goodwill to uplift and present a new hope on behalf of the western world only to find that they are at the mercy of their own analogous emptiness. Jimmy's, and indirectly Bryant's, consciousness pervades the novel from the beginning to end. Jimmy has become imbued with the spirit of self-examination and realizes that all, including himself, is a *rotten meat*, and consequently his will to fight gets subdued. Peter Roche and Jane occupy an ambiguous social position on the Ridge, the break-up of their relationship is one of the themes of the novel. They seem to be the true expatriates whereas the emotional orientation of Peter and Jane, unanchored souls, makes their sensibilities akin to those of Jimmy and Bryant who pose themselves as the true natives.

Sarcastically, in *A Bend in the River*, the adventurers like Raymond and the Big Man, literally and literarily, search for ivory at great risk to their lives. Ironically, Raymond tries to modernize the state with imported ideas without the knowledge of its needs and its potential. He conducts research and writes books on the tribes, and shows no sympathy with the land. Later Salim discovers that much of the research has been based on newspaper cuttings. Similarly Salim, Mahesh, Shobha, Noiman and Nazruddin, all outsiders though not expatriate, feel no bond with the town and make no efforts to establish them. For these people the town is an adversary that must be mastered and enslaved.

The sons of the soil, Ferdinand and the boys at the lycee, reveal the germs of growing disaffection when they question the White man's religion, culture and education which have transformed their former free life in the *bush*. They think seriously about the future of Africa but as Salim and Indar realize they are without the intellectual equipment that will translate their ideas into action. Their world of faith is powerless against the faithless White world, for they still revert to magic which, though it can exorcise spirits, cannot eject colonizers out of their state. Theirs is not a social vision in the contemporary sense of a society of responsible individual members. They serve in small, insufficient ways the members of their immediate community.

Quite often, V.S. Naipaul has been termed as an anti-conventional novelist with a keen postcolonial sensibility. Every writer, Naipaul opines, develops his individual predilections while being the part of the tradition. He finds the English language as his own but the English tradition is unfamiliar to him. In *Guerrillas* and *A Bend in the River*, Naipaul struggles with the ordeals and absurdities of living in new Third World countries. He is not obsessed with the idea of Western arrogance or nostalgia for colonialism. He is a tough-spirited writer, well aware of the unpleasant nature of contemporary history which holds out little hope for consequences. In addition to exposing the artificial and insecure role that a generation of expatriates played in several newly independent African countries, Naipaul also reiterates his thesis in *Guerrillas*, where he credits the importation of carelessly liberal ideas which help in the creation of political chaos. The purpose Raymond serves in the *A Bend in the River*, however, is more than just the mouthpiece of customary liberal attitudes. Rather, his failure also illustrates the efficacy of "the lie" that Salim identifies towards the beginning of the novel:

> ... Black men assuming the lies of white men. If it was Europe that gave us on the coast some idea of our history, it was Europe, I feel, that also introduced us to the lie ... the Europeans could do one thing and say something quite different; and they could act this way because they had an idea of what they owed to their civilization. (*A Bend in the River*, pp. 16–17)

In these two novels set in the Caribbean and Africa, Naipaul is in the grip of a complex vision which enables him to portray the ambivalence among the denizens of those unfortunate countries that have just toppled out of a tribal past, or freed themselves from colonial rule but cannot reach the uncertain blessings of modernity. He is obsessed with the shallowness of these proclaimed liberations. While reading these novels, one finds oneself driven to discomfiting reflections on how precarious is the very ideal of postcolonial civilization. In *A Bend in the River* Africa provides Naipaul with a setting within which he can further ascertain and develop his propositions about the collapse of the Third World. The canvas that Africa offers is at once fortuitous in as much as its demography reflects similar global migratory irruptions seen elsewhere in the former colonial world—such as the diasporic spread of sub-continental Indians. Its setting provides Naipaul with what happens to be another testing ground for his theories. Salim, the protagonist describes his dilemma of belongingness:

> Africa was my home, had been the home of my family for centuries. But we came from the east coast, and that made the

> difference. The coast was not truly African. It was an Arab-Indian-Persian-Portuguese place, and we who lived there were really people of the Indian Ocean. True Africa was at our back ... we looked east to the lands with which we traded—Arabia, India, Persia. These were also the lands of our ancestors. But we could no longer say that we were Arabians, or Indians or Persians; when we compared ourselves with these people, we felt like people of Africa. (*A Bend in the River*, pp. 10–11)

Naipaul's novels have shown an evolving complexity as his vision has deepened and his imagination has become more powerful. Allusions and parallels are increasingly used to bring together associations he has in mind and as he has come to see his own experience as universal and not solely the result of colonial Trinidad. Such universalizing is common to writers as they mature and is especially characteristic of writers in self-exile. But Naipaul also belongs to a generation of writers who received their university education during a time when the use of myth and literary allusions by Joyce, Eliot and Yeats was in fashion. In *The Enigma of Arrival* Naipaul says that because he dreaded change he "cultivated old, possibly ancestral ways of feeling ... and held on to the idea of a world in flux: the drum of creation in the god's right hand, the flame of destruction in his left".[16] Though *Guerrillas* is an agonized parody of societal existence and *A Bend in the River* is a similar parody of individual existence because a man fails to measure accurately the distance between ideas and actuality; the two novels depict the close links between the individual and his social environment which itself is moulded by geography, history and man's greed. The island and the town, the locales of two novels respectively, have been important only as economic assets of the first world. The natives imitate the actions and ideology of the colonial powers. These 'no man's lands' attract the disaffected of all cultures. And self-realization for such individuals can only mean knowledge of their own hollowness which induces extreme despair.

The in-between spaces of these novels, according to Homi K. Bhabha, "provide the terrain for elaborating strategies of selfhood—singular or communal—that initiate new signs of identity, and innovative sites of collaboration, and contestation, in the act of defining the idea of society itself." [17] In *Guerrillas*, Jimmy is destined to be a failure despite his well-known reputation since he is of mixed Chinese origin. It is one of the many ironies in the novel that the man regarded by the Britishers as a black leader is neither a Black nor a leader. Jimmy is one of the Naipaulian outsiders who, like Metty and

Ferdinand in *A Bend in the River*, is a half-breed, a product of the mixing of races as a result of colonialism. Moreover, Naipaul never defends the multiculturalism and creolization because, they, according to him, make the byproduct feel ambivalent and insecure.

A Bend in the River was written while Naipaul was living in a rented cottage in Wiltshire after his return to England following his disillusioning experiences with *The Loss of El Dorado*. It is set in an unnamed East African country, a bit perhaps like Uganda or Zaire, though finally Naipaul's own landscape. Naipaul, who had spent a large part of 1965–66 in East Africa and Zaire, returned to East Africa in 1971 and Zaire in 1975. Mobutu's international conference centre, Nsele, with its model farm and polytechnic college, is the basis of The New Domain in Naipaul's novel. In this African island, independence has been won and civil war has been concluded. The Big Man rules by rhetoric, craftiness, sorcery and fright. The first section of *A Bend in the River* titled "The Second Rebellion", is a portrait of the first generation of political and cultural refugees after decolonization. In the second section, "The New Domain", Salim is introduced into the prefabricated world of expatriates in Africa—Europe in Africa. The two chapters present the diverse pictures of traditional and modern Africa.

At the centre of the novel is Salim, a Muslim of an Indian family which has lived for several generations in a coastal town, trading quietly, and pitted in traditionalism. He identifies his family as Muslim, but as "a special group ... distinct from the Arabs and other Muslims of the coast; in our customs and attitudes we were closer to the Hindus of North-Western India, from which we had originally come" (*A Bend in the River,* p. 17). He elaborates the position of his family when he says: "When we had come no one could tell me. We were not that kind of people ... we seemed to have no means of gauging the passing of time. Neither my father nor my grandfather could put dates to their stories ... the past was simply the past". (*A Bend in the River,* p. 11)

Both from the narrative voice and dominant consciousness, Salim is a decent fellow, impressionable, thoughtful, but not at all intellectual. He is an outsider, watching with the outsider's nervousness. Salim's escape from small, restricted society for a new life in Central Africa is hardly rewarding as it is more suffocating and endangered than the life he has fled. In the new environment, his only contacts are with a few other aliens and expatriates. He develops an intimate relationship with an Indian couple—Mahesh and Shoba who live enclosed self-centred lives of their own, cut off from the

African world which surrounds them. This couple has escaped the foes of inter-caste love match, fearing family retaliation. Now they live only for themselves, obsessed as they are with the romance of their extraordinary union in a world preoccupied with the idea of racial discrimination and casteism. For them, the idea of *nation* and national identity has lost the meaning. A nation, according to Ernest Renan:

> ... is a soul, a spiritual principle ... one lies in the past, one in the present. One is the possession in common of a rich legacy of memories; the other is present-day consent, the desire to live together, the will to perpetuate the value of the heritage that one has received in an undivided form ... . The wish of nations is, all in all, the sole legitimate criterion, the one to which one must always return.[18]

The outsiders who constitute the bulk of the story in the novel are separated from the natives and thus remain outside the action of the plot, perhaps to locate themselves somewhere in the *nation*. The country, presumably Salim's too, has now entered modern history, or at least a coarse parody of it. Impressive buildings go up, for no clear purpose; young people are sent off to schools and universities; the population listens to three-hour radio orations by the Big Man. For the Blacks in the *bush*, for the Indians on the coast, even for the quavering elite supposed to run the country, everything is unsettled, dependent on the whim of the Big Man. Conceivably, it's a country without a coherent society. The fading of the tribes, the feebleness of all social classes in the towns, the absence of a self-assured intelligentsia: all lead to making the army the single source of power, and over the army, the Big Man. Rather then shipwrecked, then, Salim's Africa, even in its postcolonial phase is "still involved in the conditions of mere nature ... as on the threshold of the World's History."[19]

When Salim travels the interior, to a town on the bend of the river to set up a little shop selling cloth and linoleum, he encounters the first wave of African rage as if in answer to decades of imperial humiliation. The big lawns and gardens have been reduced to bush and the streets have disappeared. It's a ghost town, where rebuilding starts up, and Salim finds a modest niche. The *water hyacinth*, which is gradually but relentlessly claiming the river for itself, serves as the appropriate symbol in the novel. Salim explains the mystery when he observes: "The tall lilac-coloured flower had appeared only a few years before, and in the local language there was no word for it. The people still called it 'the new thing' or 'the new thing in the river' and to them it was another enemy" (*A Bend in the River*, p. 46). Here, in addition to providing a symbol for the history of invasion and incursion of the region, the water hyacinth also stands as a kind of fluid margin between the *old* Africa and the *new*. Its particular beauty is an ironic counter to its self-seeding and self-perpetuating capability which carries with it an inevitability of complete take over. The river dwellers' losing battle against the water hyacinth's spread also suggests the eventual futility of their historical struggle.

However, Salim's consciousness occupies the vital space, struggling conscientiously to understand the new Africa. On the surface, *A Bend in the River* emerges mostly as a web of caustic observation, less exciting than its predecessor, *Guerillas*; but it is a much better and deeper novel, as Naipaul has by now mastered the gift of creating an aura of psychic and moral tension. Each of the surrounding characters contributes to the manufacturing of this essentially Creole society which "is neither native nor derives directly from the culture of origin. It is used to describe both someone born in the colonies and some new cultural or linguistic forms created from the juxtaposition of diverse populations."[20] An Indian, Mahesh, tries will-fully to make family life into a safeguard against the assaults of history. A Belgian priest, Huismans keeps collecting tribal masks, though the masks are visibly decaying, like the world from which they came. A powerful woman from the bush, Zabeth comes to trade and begs Salim to look after her son, Ferdinand, now a student in the town and starts parroting the slogans of national pride.

Most spectacular of all is Raymond, a White intellectual who dresses up the Big Man's speeches with Parisian rhetoric. Lecturing his provincial admirers on the Big Man's greatness, Raymond asks them to listen to those continual speeches:

> I don't think many people know that earlier this year [the Big Man] and his entire government made a pilgrimage to the village of that woman of Africa. Has that been done before? Has any ruler attempted to give sanctity to the bush of Africa? This act of piety is something that brings tears to the eyes ... But piety is all we have to offer. (*A Bend in the River*, p. 147)

It is followed by Raymond's grief. The Big Man soon dumps Raymond, and he becomes another used-up intellectual whose phrases are no longer handy. It is imperative to act on the realities of changing situations, not on fantasy of imagination. When Salim first observes Raymond and Yvette at a party, he finds them as iconic symbols of social order and glamour, but when he happens to see their house by daylight at a luncheon, he is disillusioned to mark its dreariness. Raymond, a former school teacher and a famous historian in the vicinity and the Big Man's advisor, has been ignored by the

President just to make him struggle for recognition and survival. He has already been replaced by a new band of experts, while Africa has become historically insignificant on the world map. Raymond's research papers are decreasing in number and acceptability. Even his young wife Yvette, loses interest in him as he becomes socially insignificant. In the novel, love, like politics, is always in a state of change. His worthlessness suggests his sterility and futility in a challenging environment, and Yvette can not carry on with her dull relationship that will lead her to nothingness.

Absurdly, the Big Man has a genius for destructive manipulation, cutting down his army through a brilliantly evoked gang of White mercenaries in order to counter potential rivals. The country's new elite—raw, fearful, greedy, but touched with idealism—is kept constantly on edge. This newly emergent class is a tool in the hands of the Big Man, but it is a tool he has reason to fear. To the disenchanted Indian in Africa, Mahesh, "... it isn't an easy thing to understand. It isn't that there's no right and wrong here. There's no right" (*A Bend in the River*, p. 102). To the more patient Salim, the moral obligation of outsiders is to wait, be patient, and try to avoid passing judgement. Inevitably he is pushed into a kind of despair, saddened by a growing persuasion that, at least in the Big Man's country, human effort must burn itself out into waste, while ideas and ideals shrink to mere covers for power. Civilized norms are all we have to defend ourselves against ourselves, and they form, at best, a thin shield.

However, Big Man's policy of radicalization of businesses belonging to foreigners destroys property rights and introduces a further disorder and injustice beyond the simple corruption and violence depicted earlier in the novel. This is conscious corruption and perversion of truth and order. Africans are given businesses they do not own and the owners become managers and everyone becomes hysterical to amass wealth before the imminent chaos as the country slides quickly towards another rebellion. After his business is given to Theotime, for whom he now works, Salim increasingly becomes aware that he is defenseless and an easy prey for others. As he needs to save money to escape, Salim stops being able to help Metty:

> I could no longer offer him the simple protection he had asked for—Theotime made that plain during the course of the day. So the old contract between Metty and myself, which was the contract between his family and mine came to an end ... our special contract was over. He seemed to understand this, and it made him unbalanced. (*A Bend in the River*, pp. 273–74)

By the end, the Big Man has radicalized the country and assigned Salim's little shop to Citizen Theotime, who, according to

Salim, wants himself to be acknowledged as the boss. Arrested and thrown into jail, Salim is finally saved by the town's new commissioner, Ferdinand, only yesterday a stumbling boy from the village. Something has happened to this Ferdinand, some partial but significant access to truth. Rescuing Salim, he makes a speech that comes as a climax to this splendid novel: "We're all going to hell … . We're being killed. Nothing has any meaning … . Everyone wants to make his money and run away. But where? That is what is driving people mad. They feel they're losing the place … I wanted to be a child again, to forget books … . The bush runs … there is no place to go" (*A Bend in the River*, p. 291). Beyond this, Naipaul offers no intimations of hope or signals of perspective. It may be that the reality he grapples allows him nothing but harshness of voice. The severity of tone adopted by Naipaul is caused by the intricacy of the circumstances he observes worldwide.

Like *Guerrillas*, the principal characters in *A Bend in the River* are aliens. They are Asians, European settlers or expatriates, members of different tribes/ethnic groups, or people of a mixed ancestry that denies them authentic status. This displacement has always been one of Naipaul's themes and, for him, it serves as a device that allows him to narrativise the events from an outsider's point of view. In these novels he elaborates the tension and conflict among the expatriates owing to their differential identities. He is obsessed with the idea of presenting the chaos of inter-mixing of cultures:

> … the regulation and negotiation of those spaces that are continually, contingently, 'opening out', remaking the boundaries, exposing the limits of any claim to a singular or autonomous sign of difference—be it class, gender or race. Such assignations of social differences—where difference is neither One nor the Other but something else besides … that emerges in-between the claims of the past and the needs of the present.[21]

Analogous to *Guerrillas*, *A Bend in the River* is a fictional version of events Naipaul dealt with as a journalist. The titles of both novels refer to a leading figure, Michael X in the first instance, and Mobutu as "A New King for the Congo" in the second. Whereas Michael X is transformed into a leading character in *Guerrillas*, the new King, though his influence, like his photograph, is everywhere in the town where the novel is mainly set, but he does not appear as a character in *A Bend in the River*. The plot of the novel echoes Joseph Conrad's *Heart of Darkness* as Salim's narration is similar to that of a Conradian tale. Kurtz becomes Father Huismans, the collector of African masks who is killed by the Africans and whose head is *spiked*. It reminds one of the spiked heads by the hut of Kurtz around the *bush*. Salim is forced by his need for money to begin trading in ivory and gold. Secondly, Salim, like Kurtz, has a fiancée waiting for him in London.

In fact, the food for thought for the novel seems to come from Argentina where Naipaul spends considerable time between 1972 and 1977 examining how a formerly rich nation has degenerated into the destructive populist national-socialism of Peronism, political instability and the military government's dirty war against the guerrillas. He interviews guerrilla sympathizers and among others, one of the movement's founders. *Mimicry* of the then fashionable foreign notions of revolution has been grafted on to the problems left by European colonialism. His experience of the violent, irrational, guerrilla movement and the equally violent, irrational lawlessness of the government's war against the Guerrillas finds mention in *A Bend in the River*. He adds: "I transferred … the emotion of Argentina, and even the isolated police building in the bush of Jujuy, to my Central African setting."[22]

The protagonist-narrator of the novel, Salim embodies a period of history which he and Mobutu are a part. Through Salim's voice, Naipaul converts first person narration into the mental and psychological activity that creates individuality in contemporary history. His story begins with his flight from his family home to an unspecified town, no doubt Kisanganj, formerly Stanley Ville, in an unnamed country, obviously, Zaire, in the interior. The first sentence of the novel, "The world is what it is; men who are nothing, who allow themselves to become nothing, have no place in it" (*A Bend in the River*, p. 9), immediately conveys the narrator's adaptation to the historical, political, social, and cultural forces that shape his individual existence. The opening lines suggest the destructiveness, the lies, the self-serving ambitions and the continual struggle to survive. The notion of Africa as a new land, the wave of the future, the start of a postcolonial order, is thus treated with skepticism and irony. Little is found to be new. Whereas slavery has become the symbol of European injustice to Africa, *A Bend in the River* recalls the long history of slavery within Africa. It narrates the history of Arabs using African slaves, the privileged position of house slaves and the way slaves might feel more secure with a foreign master than freed among Africans of other tribes. This vision, an essentially amoral concept of life as achievement and of the strong and weak, runs throughout Naipaul's work. The meaninglessness of life in the African city gets highlighted when the narrator asserts:

> It seemed to me that men were born only to grow old, to live out their span, to acquire experience. Men lived to acquire

> experience; the quality of the experience was immaterial; pleasure and pain—and above all, pain—had no meaning; to possess pain was as meaningless as to chase pleasure. And even when the illumination vanished … I remembered that I had had it, that knowledge about the illusion of pain. (*A Bend in the River*, p. 229)

To remind the reader of Jimmy in *Guerillas*, Salim also is no hero; rather, he is a man whose background and temperament have provided him with little stability and few choices. Born in a family of merchants, he identifies himself neither with the religion or customs of his relatives nor with those of the Africans of the interior. Though his education is limited, he is bright, but with some intellectual and emotional constraints. Having understood that the way of life his family had established and maintained for centuries is doomed, he avails one opportunity to survive as an individual:

> I couldn't protect anyone; no one could protect me. We couldn't protect ourselves; we could only in various ways hide from the truth … To stay with my community, to pretend that I had simply to travel along with them, was to be taken with them to destruction. I could be master of my fate only if I stood alone. (*A Bend in the River*, p. 26)

More than the loss of his home, he foresees the end of the political system they had known. He also fears the mimicking tendency of the island people. The narrator presents his apprehension saying: "I feared the lies—black men assuming the lies of white men" (*A Bend in the River*, p. 23). In fact, Salim's most appealing quality is his uncompromising quest for the truth of whatever situation, problem or danger he encounters. Now admitting the dangers of inaction, he has planned to move on. But it is not only the historical truth that forces Salim to "carry on" (*A Bend in the River*, p. 75); rather, his undaunted desire to accommodate himself is superb.

Life, as seen in *A Bend in the River*, might be regarded as survival of the fittest; or it might be a hell of recurring patterns of useless activity in which nothing really changes. The three rebellions in the novel are not only the examples of an African rage to return to an imagined former racial and tribal purity, but they also represent an endless process of meaningless and misleading history. Fanon aptly describes the rebellious attitude of the natives:

> … divided into compartments, a motionless, Manicheanistic world … . The native is a being hemmed in … the first thing which the native learns is to stay in his place, and not to go beyond certain limits. This is why the dreams of the native are always of muscular prowess; his dreams are of action and of aggression.[23]

In contrast to this, there is also the human instinct among the rebels to achieve some important mark in the history by establishing themselves as individuals. Yet, as Indar learns by comparing himself to the wealthy American, and is shown by the contrast between London and the capital of the African state, or as is shown by the limitations reality imposes on Mr Biswas' attempted rebellion, a person's ability to accomplish and leave a mark on history is limited by environment, by the past and achievements of the culture. Salim knows, unlike Indar, that in the modern world there is no going back, and there is no home. He observes that there is no battle between good and evil; rather the only battle that continues is between the Big Man's *mimicry* of European order and those wanting to return to the purity of the African past.

In Naipaul's novels, choice depends on individual reactions to historical forces. Salim had been expected to remain in the family business and to marry the daughter of Nazruddin, a family friend. Instead he buys a shop owned by Nazruddin in the town at the bend of the river, which has been ravaged by internal conflict after independence with the hope of renewal. While the setting and the portrayal of a radically unstable society in *A Bend in the River* is based on his observation of Zaire and East Africa, many episodes in the novel are reminiscent of previous writings about Africa. In the novel the central characters are not protected by imperial power and their lives are endangered by the rapid changes and instabilities of postcolonial Africa. Like the new nations, they struggle for their independence and individuality, and they are often defeated by their own limitations, bad choices and illusions. Their lives are partly determined by the circumstances and the society in which they exist. One of the themes of the novel is the contradiction between the traditional culture rooted in the village life of the past and the modern European life. Moreover, the idea of separation marks the novel, and it is a separation "between races, cultures, histories, within histories—a separation between before and after that repeats the mythical moment or disjunction."[24] Yvette rightly comments upon the vulnerability of the European expatriates in Africa: "The man who jumps out and gets lost in the crowd is White" (*A Bend in the River,* p. 242). This conflict, which is inherent in most of the nationalist movements, is one of the important themes of Naipaul's writings.

As narrator, Salim is a partaker, spectator, and the creation of the turbulent scenario in the African town. Ironically, sometimes he is unaware of his drives and motivations operating unconsciously in diverse combinations with external circumstances despite his being an observant, conscious interpreter of his own thoughts and actions. Naipaul depicts both types of mental acts with extraordinary precision. In the beginning of the novel, as Salim drives from the coast to the interior in his Peugeot, the man at the wheel is himself driven through bush, feeling the madness of his aim, telling himself that he is going in the wrong direction as he persists in his need to create a new life in the ruins left by violence and anarchy. His ambivalence and in-betweenness come to the fore when he observes: "I was in Africa one day; I was in Europe the next morning. It was like being in two places at once ... both places were real; both places were unreal. You could play off one against the other; and you had no feeling of having made a final decision ...". (*A Bend in the River*, p. 246)

Naipaul has always been conscious of the difficulty of writing about societies he does not know from inside. *A Bend in the River* is a novel about Africa in which the lives, hopes and fears of foreigners are central. It is as much about expatriates and *diasporas* after decolonization as about national independence. *A Bend in the River*, like *Guerrillas*, is partly an attempt to understand the problems that have followed from decolonization. The leaflets distributed by the Liberation Army is a jumble of Marxist clichés, Fanonite calls to violence, black nationalism and black consciousness—the representative confusion of several decades of anti-colonial and postcolonial rhetoric of half-digested ideas often from outside Africa:

> ... and since war is an extension of politics we have decided to face the ENEMY with armed confrontation. Otherwise we all die forever. The ancestors are shrieking. If we are not deaf we can hear them. By enemy we mean the powers of imperialism, the multinationals and the puppet powers that be, the false gods, the capitalists, the priests and teachers who give false interpretations .... The schools teach ignorance and people practice ignorance in preference to their true culture. (*A Bend in the River*, p. 219)

A compassionate as well as a life-loving man, Salim thinks of the psychic compromises of slaves who in an earlier time had been forced to make a similar journey. However, Salim has grasped at the measure of freedom open to him. He reminds himself that he, after all, is going in the opposite direction; driving to the heart of the *bush*. Realizing that he is breaking faith with Nazruddin in breaking away from his commitment to marry his daughter, Salim also recognizes the ambiguity of the situation. Though Nazruddin is a stranger among his people for his exotic European manners, he stands for success and fortune. For Nazruddin, things seemingly work out beautifully but he always lives with a vision of things turning out badly. Loyalty to Nazruddin is, of course, a means of defining and defending his own needs. Salim fails to foresee the consequences of Nazruddin's actions. As soon as he approaches the town he recalls Nazruddin's stories of what the place was like. Knowing that the town is in ruins, he nonetheless allows himself to imagine its old life recreated for him by Nazruddin. The town he actually finds has turned to the bush. Being a successful businessman, Nazruddin knows when to flee Central Africa for Uganda and when to flee Uganda for Canada. But ultimately, he finds himself in an equally hostile and inhospitable world where he is cheated by other immigrants. His London apartments are filled with Arabs, East Europeans and small town English girls who do not pay him rent. London seems to consist of Arabs and other aliens on the streets seeking the jobs, opportunities, goods and safety not found in the places from whence they come. For them, every place appears the same place.

However, critics have questioned Salim's credibility because he seems to change his mind continually about issues without sufficient reason and, at other instances, his convictions seem to bear the authority of the trained, sophisticated intelligence of his creator. To be sure, Naipaul has endowed Salim with something of his own curiosity and skepticism, his commitment to seek out the truth within himself and to apprehend the corruption that political machinations and cultural pretensions would obscure. Naipaul's autobiographical allusions throughout his writings reveal that, for all his complaints about the narrowness of his background, he had the opportunity to transform his limitations into virtues.

So, Naipaul's portrayal of Salim embodies a fragile hope for a measure of individual assertion accommodating a history of obstruction. As the town begins to rise again and Salim rebuilds his store, he gets involved with other people, and it is in relation to them that he struggles to define himself. These people include Ali, a half-African family servant; Zabeth, a trader, one of Salim's first customers; Zabeth's son Ferdinand, a boy from the bush, now enrolled in the town's lycee; Father Huismans, the head of the lycee; Indar, a wealthy friend from the coast; Shoba and Mahesh, an Indian couple; Yvette, a Belgian with whom Salim falls in love; and Yvette's husband Raymond. The instability of daily life exert its influence on the very psychic processes and intimate acts of the characters. Mahesh and Shoba represent the dangers of romantic love, as they are from two different Indian castes; and so represent another version of the forbidden mingling of races. The expatriates are caught in a vicious circle resulting from a sense of estrangement which, according to Arnold Itwaru: "... touches upon the very notion of home, the lands and places of our birth. For that land, there, that region, lives in us as memory and dream, as nostalgia, romance of reflection, that which defines us as different, that to which we think we belong but no longer do".[25]

Characteristically, the suggestion that the Arabs of East Africa have lost their idea of themselves and have become weak by interbreeding with the Africans hints at the aftermaths of incoherent mingling of races. It can also be seen as reflecting the situation of the Indians and Arabs in East Africa, where after independence African leaders said that such foreigners can stay on only if they agree to assimilate into the African community. In Zanzibar Arab women were forced into marriage with Africans. The racial fears are connected to Naipaul's own fear of extinction, a fear which is expressed in terms of the Indian being wiped out by creolization in the West Indies.

Determined to establish a new way of life, Salim is aware that he has gone from one stifling environment to another. Observing Metty developing a new idea of his worth and Ferdinand trying out various images of himself, Salim feels compelled to demonstrate his separation from Ferdinand and the life of the *bush* about him. His utter loneliness is marked in the novel when he wishes to ascertain self-esteem through pretensions:

> It was partly the effect of my isolation ... . I knew there was something that separated me from Ferdinand and the life of bush about me. And it was because I had no means in my day-to-day life of asserting this difference, of exhibiting my true self, that I fell into the stupidity of exhibiting my things. (*A Bend in the River*, p. 49)

To get himself recognized, he shows Ferdinand his binoculars, his camera, and the popular science magazines that he reads. Through such exhibition, he reflects that he should have devoted himself to studying "the particular science or field I was reading about ... adding knowledge to knowledge, making discoveries, making something of myself, using all my faculties" (*A Bend in the River*, p. 50). Yet he knows that these aspirations will never be fulfilled and his potentialities will never remain unrealized.

By some means, Salim desires to explore and understand the limited realm available to him—the town and its people. During the new uprising, he is torn between compassion for the hotel workers who are abject in the presence of these strangers, and relief at the security these personnels offer. The predicament of the African colonials gets reflected when Salim observes:

> ... we all—Asians, Greeks, and other Europeans—remained prey, to be stalked in different ways ... it was in the history of the land: here men had always been prey. You don't feel malice towards your prey. You set a prey for him. It fails ten times; but it is always the same trap you set. (*A Bend in the River,* p. 62)

The person who introduces Salim to the range of Africa's hold on the outsider is Father Huismans, a Catholic priest who is enthralled by all things African—the food, the religious beliefs, the art and he reveres the remnants of European colonization. Salim is initially drawn to Huismans because of their differences. Father Huismans's interests, which Salim tries to comprehend, seem to him an avenue to the knowledge of the country and of himself. Using the motto of the lycee, "*Semper aliquid novi*" (*A Bend in the River,* p. 42), implying "always something new", Father Huismans explains that in the masks and carvings he collects, there is always something new, a unique religious purpose absent in copies. Salim is surprised to see Father Huismans's involvement in an art he himself does not admire. Unlike him, Father Huismans is indifferent to the dismal state of the country. For Salim, he is the man whose "Africa, of bush and river, was different from mine. His Africa was a wonderful place full of new things". (*A Bend in the River,* p. 68)

Naipaul soon uses a second Latin quotation to cast doubt on this idyllic picture of Africa and on Father Huismans's knowledge of the history of the land in which he feels so much at home. He tells Salim that the second motto of the town is a line from the Aeneid carved on the ruined monument near the dock gate: "*Miscerique probat populos et foedera jungi,*" which he translates as: "He approves of the mingling of the peoples and their bonds of union" (*A Bend in the River,* p. 69). Actually, in *Aeneid IV* (110–12), Venus tells Juno that she is uncertain as to whether Jupiter would approve of the blending of the peoples (Tyrians and Trojans). Naipaul sees it historically as part of the general political and social disorder, which results from the mixing of culture and the imposition of a European notion of the state on African tribes. The inherent postcolonial dilemma of expatriates in a fluid multicultural society is highlighted by Victor J. Ramraj when he observes:

> In this state of transition, some respond ambivalently to their dual, often antithetical, cultures or societies. Some attempt to assimilate and integrate. For others the luminal or transitional state is too prolonged or too excruciating to cope with and they may withdraw to their ancestral identity or homeland.[26]

Through the Virgilian reference Naipaul seems to highlight the adverse effects of inter-racial marriages, multiculturalism and mixed parentage. Though the European colonial settlers in the town reverse the meaning of the motto and defend the approval for the mingling of races which serves no purpose in an unstable colonial society fighting for its survival. This allusion serves numerous functions in the novel as it makes the sensitive natives question the European and Arab involvement with Africa. Further, it casts serious doubt on the sexual relationships involving various races, castes or tribes. The relationship between Salim and Yvette, Mahesh and Shoba, and the Arab men and African women is suggestive of unscrupulousness. Moreover the children of mixed parentage like Metty and Ferdinand are treated with repulsion. The children born out of such heterogeneous marriages are vulnerable as they belong to no established group, and they are bound to be treated as outcaste. All such marriages result into ultimate frustration and an ever-lasting sense of insecurity. Metty is caught in a trap after his marriage with an African woman. Salim becomes so responsive towards Yvette that he fails to observe the fast emerging political upheavals. He fails to guard his interests against the nationalization of his business. It further reminds the reader that Naipaul's account of love and sex is hardly ever gratifying. In the novel, sex diverts the attention of the people from their own best interests and brings disorder in their lives.

Like Naipaul, Chinua Achebe also blames the widespread corruption found in Nigeria [the heart of darkness] on the coming together of various cultures and the effect of foreign rule on previously self-contained tribal societies. If in Naipaul's novels there is, at times, a view that corruption, moral and political chaos, come from the mixing of peoples, it reminds that Trinidad has been notorious for corruption. Such corruption is not African specific; it is prevalent worldwide. For example, when Nazruddin moves to Canada he is swindled; and when he says that society can not exist if people do not keep to their words he is asked to go back to Africa. But there are suggestions that Africa has a long history of moral degradation due to irresistible temptation. This typically colonial degradation resulting from temptation is a common pattern evident in the cultures which have always been subjected to colonial exploitation. When Father Huismans explains that in the line on the ruined monument three words were altered to reverse the meaning, Salim is shaken by the audacity of the act. It reminds him of the town of Rome. Despite his wish not to offend Father Huismans, he comments:

> Twisting two-thousand year old words to celebrate sixty years of the steamer service from the capital! Rome was Rome. What was this place? To carve the words on a monument beside this

> African river was surely to invite the destruction of the town … . And almost as soon as it had been put up the monument had been destroyed … gibberish to the people … . (*A Bend in the River,* p. 69)

The imported ideas and norms can hardly flourish in the shaky environment of the island. He wonders at the lack of the anxiety that is perceptible in the original line of the Latin poem.

Nevertheless, Father Huismans reacts differently. The paired Latin quotations epitomize his role in Africa. He takes delight in each new revelation of the spiritual life of the country and uses the altered quotation from the *Aeneid* to place himself within an immense flow of history. In this flow the town at the bend in the river has always existed and will continue to exist, its history as a colony, to which he returns periodically is attractive for him. His equanimity is not enough to protect him from the reality of contemporary Africa, which hardly has any appeal. Soon after peace is restored after the second rebellion he is killed during his visit to the *bush*. His body is sent down the main river in a dug out and his head cut off and spiked. In the flow of history, the ruling powers and their subjects are placed in an ambivalent situation which is hardly advantageous to either side.

In Salim's eyes and, no doubt, in Naipaul's, Father Huismans is not simply a representative of colonial condescension. Salim mourns the loss of Father's "knowledge … and what to me was more than knowledge—his attitudes, his relish for Africa, his feelings for the beliefs of the forest. A little bit of the world was lost with him" (*A Bend in the River,* p. 89). These qualities, Salim believes, "had made him find human richness where the rest of us saw *bush* or had stopped seeing anything at all" (*A Bend in the River,* p. 90). Eventually, Salim, who has spent his life in Africa, realizes that Father Huismans's idea which made him rely too much on the mingling of peoples, has made Father Huismans pay heavily by his brutal murder. Father Huismans's innocence may have been instrumental in bringing about his death, but it hardly had the power to subvert the whole society, to which he actually paid too little attention.

Obviouly, in the boom that follows after the end of the rebellion, order and money are the framework provided by the ruling powers. This framework stimulates a sense of confidence in Salim, and his deeper concerns are further sensitized. Now on, the sense that he must somehow define his own role in the flow of history, becomes prominent. His observations of the president's new development, i.e., the establishment of Domain of the State at Nsele, and his relations with the people he meets there help him to visualize the possibilities open to him and also the hazards he must somehow meet. The introduction of the Domain may be considered as "synonymous with the promotion of the cultural values of the colonizer, and the development of so-called civilization ... a process of bringing the 'native' out of darkness."[27] His early reactions to the creation of the Domain, like Naipaul's in "A New King for the Congo," are full of ambivalence. It seems to be a town in itself that conveys instability even as it projects an image of power. It transmits the President's message that "Africans had become modern men who built in concrete and glass and sat in cushioned chairs covered in imitation velvet" (*A Bend in the River*, p. 110). For a while no one knows how the Domain, with its huge buildings, its farm, swimming pool, and conference hall, is to be utilized. Eventually, it becomes a university city and a research centre to train the future administrators of the nation.

In "A new King for the Congo" Naipaul, attempting to explain the extravagance of the Domain, and the "nationalizations" as an effort to heal the wound Africa has endured, finally admits that the domain is *shoddy* and the nationalizations *bogus*. Similarly, for Salim, it represents "shoddy grandeur ... a hoax" (*A Bend in the River*, p. 113), built out of foreign greed and African opportunism. In his own case, ironically, the deceptions seem to stimulate his interest in the African society into which he was born and the Africa he now inhabits. Salim is introduced to the New Domain by Indar, an old friend from the coast, who introduces himself as a guest of the government. In Salim's eyes, he is one of the new-style foreigners who stand for the new initiatives of the President. Salim and Indar resemble each other as both of them have escaped from their family to flourish in an alien environment. Ultimately, they return only to discover that their formerly affluent families have lost opulence. Their dislocation to some alien land proves to be fruitless. Indar's education in an English University and Salim's business enterprise bring them no sense of gratification. Nonetheless, Indar's imposing appearance, sophisticated manner and his appointment at the newly introduced polytechnic highlight the old distance between him and Salim. Eager for the knowledge of the world outside that Indar has to offer, Salim is all praise for Indar, though in words and not in spirit. For Salim, Indar becomes the guide to the strange world of the Domain, to which Salim becomes strongly attracted: "To travel those few miles between the town and the Domain was always to make some adjustment, to assume a new attitude, and each time almost to see another country". (*A Bend in the River*, p. 128)

Earlier, Indar flees from a threatened Indian community to a famous university in England and attempts to become a self-made man, a cosmopolitan, international expert, advisor on Third World problems and an independent intellectual. This is in contrast to Salim's quest for his independent identity as a businessman, the traditional role of the Asiatics in the diaspora. Paradoxically, Indar is bound to be dependent on American foundations and wealth, and at the same time nostalgic for the home he has fled from. At this point, Indar seems defeated by his awareness of his dependency. Salim's quest for independence and security takes him to London in another attempt to create a new life. There he finds many people like himself, aliens from former colonies, including Indians selling cigarettes on street corners. It reminds one of the typical Indian town where such *panwallas* are common. Bruce King interprets *A Bend in the River* in Indian context when he adds:

> As often in Naipaul's writings there is an Indian subtext. The title, *A Bend in the River*, suggests an analogy to the Indian classical epic, the Ramayana. Manohar Malgonkar's novel *A Bend in the Ganges* (1964), a love story set in the context of the Indian independence movement, independence and the horror of partition, probably gave Naipaul the idea of applying the Rama story to the problems resulting from decolonization.[28]

Bruce further correlates the African dilemma with that of Indians by finding identical instances of the fusion of Aryans and Dravidians in India. Naipaul could also have in mind the grandeur of the Aryan conquest with its supposedly ideal rule or the argument that the Aryans were discredited by India. Both visions—a view of imperial order and that the conquering people degenerate through inter breeding—are at times suggested by *A Bend in the River*.

Salim and the denizens of the town view the contemporary Africa as a place devoid of intellectual or aesthetic motivation, thus making their survival a tough task. Through the newly established institution of Domain, by contrast, another Africa has been created, and with it new African men like Indar and Raymond as the prototypes. Through the "educated talk" of Indar with his frequent references to "famous cities", Salim finds the Domain as a substitute for the lack of modern education he has missed. It offers him an opportunity to fulfill his desire to explore and learn. Bhabha justifies such transition in the decolonized territories when he adds: "The civil state is the ultimate expression of the innate ethical and rational bent of the human mind; the social instinct is the progressive destiny of human nature, the necessary transition from Nature to Culture."[29]

Salim who is used to witness everything fake and bogus in the stifling environment of African city, seeks the essential truth beneath the appearance. Though he is overwhelmed by the discussion at one of Indar's seminars, he questions the efficacy of the innovations like the Domain. He doubts whether Indar and he aren't fooling themselves and whether they aren't allowing the Africa they talk about to become too different from the Africa they know. As they are used to an environment full of the squalor, poverty, and the presence of the river and the forest all around, Salim feels as if the natives are trying to evade the truth by escaping their common past—the damaged life of their community, the past history that foretells their future. Whether the borrowed and mimicked ideology of the Domain is real or a fraud is the obvious question of debate among the natives and expatriates residing in the African city. Salim expresses his confusion: "I became confused myself. The Domain was a hoax. But at the same time it was real ... so I moved between the Domain and the town" (*A Bend in the River*, p. 135). The organization and its goals get popular among the masses because of the serious men who are associated to it. Salim may consider it as plot designed by a few men for their vested interests but for him these are not merely interesting philosophical enquiries; they are issues of psychic and physical survival, which become increasingly pressing as conditions in the country grow more precarious.

Naipaul's attempts to humanize the Big Man by referring to his lowly origins, his mother, and the patronage of Raymond, the imported Belgian historian, is constantly jeopardized by the fabulist atmosphere of sinister political adoration. The parallel development of Ferdinand as the evolving "new African man", furthermore, only serves to reinforce Naipaul's thesis of postcolonial mimicry. Raymond, who has been "someone close to power, the Big man's white man ..." (*A Bend in the River*, p. 152) praises the President as the most gifted of leaders, all the while knowing that he himself is no longer needed by the Big Man. His sensibility is typically colonial as he does not think beyond his master. His master has lost interest in him and he feels disillusioned and reacts, "that everything one does is just going to waste" (*A Bend in the River*, p. 141). He says, "We have no idea of the value posterity will place on the events we attempt to chronicle. We have no idea where the continent is going. We can only carry on" (*A Bend in the River*, p. 148). In spite of his generosity and loyalty, he is a sorry figure who has no real understanding of Africa and his knowledge of the country is chiefly of letters and missionary reports.

Moreover, the sentiments of love and sex are hardly valued among the displaced colonials like Salim. He experiences a unique sense of ecstatic joy and satisfaction in his involvement with Yvette. His past experience of "brothel sex" has produced only contempt for himself and his partners. But his relationship with Yvette is invigorating in which he feels the emergence of a new self. As he is preoccupied with the idea of winning Yvette, he is frightened by a vision of the decay of the man he has known himself to be. Feeling bound to Raymond through Yvette, Salim experiences the president's power "as a personal thing, to which we were all attached as with strings, which he might pull or let dangle" (*A Bend in the River,* p. 201). After his serious involvement and disillusionment with Yvette, Salim realizes that had he "understood more about Raymond" earlier, he might have seen Yvette more clearly—"her ambition, her bad judgement, her failure" (*A Bend in the River,* p. 199), and would not have become "involved with people as trapped as myself". (*A Bend in the River,* p. 199)

As Salim notices the hazards contained in the president's unvoiced dismissal of Raymond, and the unpredictability of life in the town, these become determinants of the self he enacts and observes: "We stood for ourselves. We all had to survive" (*A Bend in the River,* p. 207). Personal desires have hardly any significance in an atmosphere of political tensions, riots, and rebellion. But Yvette and Salim take a long time to understand the futility of their romance and ultimately they leave the country and leave each other as psychic and physical endurance demands the break.

Seemingly, Salim deliberately evades the knowledge of the world around him. Yet it asserts itself in his deeper ambivalence of the self manifested in his love for Yvette, which produces both self-esteem and "shame, to have reduced my manhood just to that" (*A Bend in the River,* p. 213). But this ambivalence leads to a more fundamental self-awareness: "She gave me the idea of my manliness I had grown to need. Wasn't my attachment to her an attachment to that idea?" (*A Bend in the River,* p. 218). His psychic growth demands recognition that the self he has tried to identify in relation to Yvette is itself a historical development, the persistent adaptation of cognitive and psychic processes to social and political necessity:

> And oddly involved with this idea of myself, and myself and Yvette, was the town itself—the flat, the house in the Domain, the way both our lives were arranged, the absence of a community, the isolation in which we both lived. In no other place would it be just like this; and perhaps in no other place would our relationship be possible. (*A Bend in the River,* p. 218)

The dramatic end of his life in the town and the tragedy of his affair with Yvette, make him feel ambivalent once more. As Salim and Yvette face this end, their talk is suggestive of waywardness:

> I had talked of Raymond's pain when I was thinking of my own, and Yvette had talked of Raymond's needs when she was thinking of her own. We had begun to talk, if not in opposites, at least indirectly, lying and not lying, making those signals at the truth which people in certain situations find it necessary to make. (*A Bend in the River*, p. 234)

Salim-Yvette relationship is as chaotic as that of Jimmy and Jane in *Guerrillas* where, eventually, Jimmy brutally rapes and murders her. During their last meeting Yvette's pomposity hints at her betrayal. Salim's ancestral Indian ideology seems to have asserted itself when he reaches to the conclusion that if Yvette is not faithful towards her gentlemanly husband then how he can expect her to be consistent towards him. Being enraged, he turns brutal like Jimmy and strikes her hard. His spitting at her is a violent reaction to what he sees as her untruthfulness, but also to his loss of love for a woman with whom he discovered sexual pleasure and grew in self-knowledge. This awareness makes Salim write to Nazruddin, now in London, to tell him that he wishes to see him. To recompense his isolated life in Africa, he accepts Nazruddin's daughter, Kareisha, a pharmacist, as a guide to the city and the new life for which this visit of Salim is a preparation. Before he can commit himself to a new beginning with his fiancee, however, he must return to Africa, supposedly to wrap up his business affairs, actually to relinquish what he clings to, a phase of his past, and the idea of the "Other" place. He also knows that "There could be no going back; there was nothing to go back to. We had become what the world outside had made us: we had to live in the world as it existed". (*A Bend in the River*, pp. 261–62)

But to his dismay, his shop has been nationalized under a policy of "radicalization". The town is in a state of insurrection, and he is placed in preventive detention. Knowing that he must leave immediately and stealthily after his release with Ferdinand's help, he escapes just in time. Though he admits that he is what the world outside has made him, he is not a subservient sufferer. Confined geographically, economically, socially, he develops what seems to him an amazing capacity to look outward from himself. Ironically he comes to realize that his superior friend Indar is in need of his support and guidance. He observes that the European experts are as vulnerable as he is, and he feels closer than ever to African fellow prisoners who have prepared themselves for death. Among the colonial derelicts and émigrés, he stands apart as his wish to survive is resolute and constant. In spite of the prevailing pessimism in decolonized Third World, there is a tragic optimism in Salim's individual struggle to create a self. Salim is indulged in continuous questioning and revision of his memories; his efforts to discover truths about himself and his place in the ever-changing world. He echoes Frantz Fanon who makes an appeal in his epoch making work *The Wretched of the Earth*:

> What we want to do is to go forward all the time, night and day, in the company of Man, in the company of all men ... it is a question of the Third World starting a new history of Man ... let us not pay tribute to Europe by creating states, institutions and societies which draw their inspiration from her. Humanity is waiting for something other from us than such an imitation.[30]

Unlike the African novelists, Naipaul does not have a similar commitment to Africa and is skeptical of its future. Although he does not attempt to create black African characters in depth, the Africa of corruption, a new insecure bourgeois, tribal conflict, food shortages and tyrannical governments predominantly govern his narrative. Naipaul's deepest sympathies are with the displaced Indians like Indar who are threatened by African nationalism and political disorder. He observes such disorder consequent upon the universal withdrawal of the older imperial order.

Salim learns from reading an encyclopedia that the universe may be nothing more than rubbish of some original Big-Bang that might have created it. This then is Naipaul's big bang novel although the instant focus is on the disorder of contemporary postcolonial Africa that has resulted from the disintegration of imperial order. Oppression of the underprivileged is the obvious outcome as the new inexperienced rulers attempt to enforce order on the natives. Ironically, the ruled are used to the primitive tribal and traditional village life in which the old animosities of tribes, and the cultural and economic insecurities of the new elite, are likely to lead to violent conflict. The modern state characterized by Nsele or the Domain, innovative technology and the Big Man's idea, is imported, and an act of *mimicry*. The institutions like the Domain are transplanted without testing the compatibility of the African soil, and the modern African state proves to be a threat to the traditional ways of life. For Fanon, it is a nerve wrecking experience:

> Colonialism is not simply content to impose its rule upon the present and the future of a dominated country. Colonialism is not

> satisfied with holding a people in its grip and emptying the native's brain of all form and content. By a kind of perverted logic, it turns to the past of the oppressed people, and distorts, disfigures and destroys it.[31]

The novel presents the political and social disorder of an African island where nothing is settled, and nothing is absolute or final. The episodic narrative of the novel allows the people to come and disappear immediately. Nothing stays there as the life of the colonials is characteristically fluid. Father Huismans who stands for a humanistic, larger, optimistic view of African history and traditional culture, annoys other expatriates, but he is brutally murdered. Salim observes that the father's idea of civilization was his vanity and "he paid for it" (*A Bend in the River*, p. 87). In this novel, Naipaul aims at projecting the complexity, ambiguity, and instability in the lives of the decolonized minds.

Indar makes an enlightening speech before Salim about the need for self-creation and trampling on the past, but he is frustrated by the circumstances so adversely that he is forced to leave the African town for the capital. Consequently, he lives an uncomfortable, humiliating and shipwrecked life with a crushed spirit. Being dispossessed, he dreams of a lost past, a lost home to which he can never return. Salim is an alienated outsider who, unwilling to accept fate, attempts to live fully. Ironically, Salim who follows the ideals of Indar to "trample on the past" (*A Bend in the River*, p. 123), attempts to become economically independent so that he can leave Africa soon. His revolt begins with awareness of the weakness and insecurity of the Asians of Africa in the face of the struggles for power following the withdrawal of the imperial order. His activism leads him to preventive detention only.

Although Salim narrates the story of his disordered and enervated life, the novel touches upon the lives of other heterogeneous figures also. Though the denizens of the town differ in their origin, race, background and aspirations, their present circumstances and disorder are common. The massacre of Arabs in East Africa, results into the escape of Metty for Metis, one of the slaves attached to his family, who joins Salim in the strife-torn city located in Central Africa. The conflicts and clashes are numerous in the novel—English versus African, African versus Arab, slave versus master, modern versus traditional, nature versus culture, and authentic versus borrowed.

Zabeth, an African tradeswoman, wants her son Ferdinand to be highly educated so that he may suit the requirements of the modern African state. Ferdinand, who is the byproduct of an interracial marriage like Jimmy in *Guerrillas*, represents the new generation of privileged Africans upon which the resources of the state are generously spent to provide a coveted Western higher education enabling them to get absorbed in the top positions in the bureaucracy. It is because of the vulnerable community life of the bush, and because of his tribally mixed parentage, that Ferdinand is at the mercy of the new political order.

Salim is curious to know the history of Africa through his wide reading of encyclopaedias. He being a representative of Indians, who came to work in Africa during this century, comes face to face with the similar duality among long established Arabs of East Africa. As he identifies himself with Indian culture and peoples, he finds a unique solace in the company of other expatriates from Indian origin—Mahesh and Shoba. Naipaul here highlights the intermingling of the most heterogeneous communities in a creolized and multi-racial African society. The amalgamation of the lost expatriates from different parts of the world is possible but rare. *A Bend in the River* is essentially an account of African colonial history and imperialism. Salim articulates his gratitude for the European chroniclers who have provided him with a seemingly truthful history of Africa and Africans:

> All that I know of our history and the history of the Indian Ocean I have got from books written by Europeans. If I say that our Arabs in their time were great adventurers and writers ... if I say these things it is because I have got them from European books. They formed no part of our knowledge or pride. Without Europeans, I feel all our past would have been washed away. (*A Bend in the River*, p. 18)

But this statement made by Naipaul through Salim seems to be ambivalent. It brings out the inclination of the natives towards the Eurocentric colonial education—suggesting the failure of the natives to write authentic history. Oriental knowledge is the only way for the decolonized denizens to become conscious of themselves. The nineteenth century Indian and African nationalists appropriated their Indianness or Africanness from European scholarship or Oriental studies.

Thus, *A Bend in the River*, which was written in England, is, in part, another deliberation on the problems and fate of the Indian diaspora in relation to the swift social and political changes that have followed decolonization. Those Indians who live by traditional norms are left at the mercy of the African desire to cleanse the land of others and avenge themselves for the degradation of the past. Figures like Ali, a representative mulatto, are no longer either Asiatic or a member of any African tribe, but a symbol of those who seek identity in an alien and inhospitable world. Naipaul is again preoccupied with the idea of projecting the diasporic ambivalence among the colonials with reference to the Indian diaspora. The Indian High Commission in London tells Indar that his group has enjoyed the benefits of working in Africa and now must accept his African fate. He is bound to live a life of a derelict as he can neither return to India nor can he get an assurance of security in an alien land.

In *A Bend in the River,* Naipaul has shifted his attention from Caribbean island to an African city representing a postcolonial wasteland after the collapse of a universal European order. Africa, like other colonies, has long been part of European consciousness but the consequences of the decolonization and African independence form the basis of the novel. The novel presents a vision of history of pointless repetitions, of empire being replaced by empire, of the strong conquering the weak and then themselves becoming weak and conquered by fresh blood, of a world of experience and suffering without purpose. The novel has a dramatic beginning—"The world is what it is" (*A Bend in the River,* p. 9), only to emphasize the futility of the efforts made by the rulers and the ruled in the pursuit of self-realization.

Therefore, it is evident from the study of *A Bend in the River* that there is an overall atmosphere of despair. The denizens of Central Africa can have no "leap in the dark" to a higher order of living as a permanent answer to existential anguish. Naipaul here suggests no angelic state of permanent joy for them. They cannot cherish any apocalyptic vision and nothing new enters to radically alter the structure of the world which seems unredeemable. Jimmy is trapped by his despair and wishes for death when he groans: "the corridor of time is now a room of mirrors, it just shows me forever picking myself up, and this time I want them to count me out". (*A Bend in the River,* p. 227)

The Caribbean-African novels, *Guerillas* and *A Bend in the River,* finally draw him compulsively into what Conrad has called *heart of darkness*, the jungles lurking inside the colonial White rulers also. Raymond and Yvette resemble Jane and Roche, second-rate Europeans who find exhilaration and the prospect of being near the centre of power in the third world. Yvette, Jane and Sandra are the prominent European women characters in Naipaul's fiction who follow their male partners to the third world expecting to find excitement and a better life but they are destined to be disillusioned. Yvette disappears dramatically after being condemned by Salim for her fickleness. Her whereabouts are unknown as the house occupied by them is now owned by an African.

As usual, sex and politics remind the reader of colonial destruction, brutality and humiliation. In her female masochism Yvette resembles Jane in *Guerrillas*, and she does not allow Salim to flourish in his business or career. From *Miguel Street* onwards Naipaul has remained constantly engaged in examining the causes of masochism and women-beating. In later novels one of the major themes of his novels is the way male impotence and colonial anxiety turn into sadistic rage against women.

A Bend in the River and *Guerrillas* thus present the repercussions of the loss of the imperial order rather than its achievements and celebration. Displacement and expatriation further intensify the chaos in the process of decolonization—Salim's flight to central Africa is emblematic of the essential disorder. The diverse mixing of peoples, the fall of imposing order and the aspirations of the people to assert their individuality are the major preoccupations of Naipaul in these two novels. Salim takes the wrong decision by undertaking the journey to Central Africa and getting involved with Yvette as it makes him experience an African hell. In these two novels the narrators portray the psychological reality of the association between the colonial west and the colonized Third World. The island of *Guerrillas*, almost exhausted of its economic potential, its human potential distorted through misuse, is a convenient junkyard for the discarded machines and unwanted men of the west.

It is obvious, therefore, that both *A Bend in the River* and *Guerillas* explore the beleaguered identities of the colonized and the colonizers alike in two different landscapes—Caribbean and African. While *Guerillas* highlights the consequences of contact between two antagonistic cultures in a Caribbean island, *A Bend in the River* chooses to delineate the trauma of an Eastern African's displacement towards the *bush* culture and resultant confrontation between the natives and aliens. Both these novels hence establish Naipaul as a novelist constantly evolving and exploring newer regions confronting certain colonial/postcolonial dichotomies.

Notes

1. V.S. Naipaul, *A Bend in the River* (London: Andre Deutsch, 1980) p. 206. (All the subsequent references for *A Bend in the River* have been taken from the same edition of the novel, cited hereafter, in the text with the corresponding page number(s) in parenthesis.)

2. V.S. Naipaul, *Guerrillas* (London: Andre Deutsch, 1980) p. 206. (All the subsequent references for *Guerillas* have been taken from the same edition of the novel, cited hereafter, in the text with the corresponding page number(s) in parenthesis.)
3. Anthony Boxill, *V.S. Naipaul's Fiction: In Quest of the Enemy* (New Brunswick: York Press, 1983) p. 65.
4. Edward Said, *Culture and Imperialism* (London: Vintage, 1993) p. 331.
5. Patrick Parrinder, "V.S. Naipaul and the Uses of Literacy," *Critical Quarterly*, 21.2 (1979) p. 12.
6. Trinh T. Minh-ha, "No Master Territories", *Post-colonial Studies Reader*, eds. Bill Ashcroft, Gareth Griffiths and Helen Tiffin (London: Routledge, 1995) p. 218.
7. Frantz Fanon, "The Fact of Blackness", *Post-colonial Studies Reader*, eds. Bill Ashcroft, Gareth Griffiths and Helen Tiffin, op. cit., p. 324.
8. Anthony Boxill, *V.S. Naipaul's Fiction: In Quest of the Enemy*, p. 65.
9. Francis Wyndham, "Services rendered: Review of Guerillas", *Critical Perspectives on V.S. Naipaul*, ed. Robert D. Hamner (London: Heinemann Educational Books, 1979) p. 255.
10. Chandra B. Joshi, *V.S. Naipaul: The Voice of Exile* (New Delhi: Sterling Publishers, 1994) p. 207.
11. Anthony Boxill, *V.S. Naipaul's Fiction: In Quest of the Enemy*, p. 71.
12. Frantz Fanon, *Black Skin, White Masks* (New York: Grove, 1967) p. 213.
13. Lillian Feder, *Naipaul's Truth* (New Delhi: Indialog, 2001) p. 220.
14. Anthony Boxhill, *V.S. Naipaul's fiction: In Quest of the Enemy* (New Brunswick: York Press, 1983) p. 65.
15. Chandra B. Joshi, *V.S. Naipaul: The Voice of Exile*, op. cit., p. 196
16. V.S. Naipaul, *The Enigma of Arrival* (London: Picador, 1987) p. 53.
17. Homi K. Bhabha, *The Location of Culture* (London: Routledge, 1994) pp. 1–2.
18. Ernest Renan, "What is a Nation?" *Nation and Narration*, ed. Homi K. Bhabha (London: Routledge, 1990) pp. 19–20.
19. Quoted by Fawzia Mustafa in *V.S. Naipaul* (Cambridge: Cambridge University Press, 1995) p. 148.
20. J. Michael Dash, "Psychology, Creolisation and Hybridisation", *New National and Post-Colonial Literatures*, ed. Bruce King (Oxford: Clarendon Press, 1996) p. 46.
21. Homi K. Bhabha, *The Location of Culture*, op. cit., p. 219.
22. V.S. Naipaul, "Argentina: Living with Cruelty," *The New York Review of Books*; 39, No. 3, 30 January 1992, p. 13.

23. Frantz Fanon, *The Wretched of the Earth* (London: Penguin, 1967) p. 40.
24. Homi K. Bhabha, *The Location of Culture*, op. cit., p. 82.
25. Arnold Itwaru, "Exile and Commemmoration," *Indenture and Exile: The Indo-Caribbean Experience*, ed. Frank Birbal Singh (Toronto: Toronto South Asia Review, 1989) p. 203.
26. Victor J. Ramraj, "Diasporas and Multiculturalism," *New National and Post-Colonial Literatures*, ed. Bruce King (Oxford: Clarendon Press, 1996) p. 216.
27. Gareth Griffins, "The Post-colonial Project: Critical Approaches and Problems," *New National and Post-colonial Literatures*, ed. Bruce King (Oxford: Clarendon Press, 1996) p. 166.
28. Bruce King, *V.S. Naipaul* (London: Macmillan, 1993) p. 133.
29. Homi K. Bhabha, *The Location of Culture*, op. cit., p. 43.
30. Frantz Fanon, *The Wretched of the Earth*, op. cit., p. 254.
31. Frantz Fanon, "National Culture," *Post-colonial Studies Reader*, eds., Bill Ashcroft, Gareth Griffiths and Helen Tiffin (London: Routledge, 1995) p. 154.

4

Reconciling Halfness

Unlike Naipaul's earlier fictional preoccupations such as the typical colonial clash between the natives and the expatriates, the colonized and the colonizers, and the Black and the White, the fictional works produced in the next phase of his creative expressions acquire subtler connotations. As observed earlier, in the works such as *Guerillas* and *A Bend in the River* where the novelist appears to have been obsessed with delineating a constant war between the European and the African cultures, in his later works, viz., *Half a Life* and *Magic Seeds*, he seems to have grown out of the single geographical territory and begins to articulate his experiences in the spirit of literary navigator. So far, the significant growth in the dimension of the novelist has been outlined through the study of his fictional works always advancing towards a broader perception. Jimmy Ahmed, Roche, Bryant and Jane contradict one another in *Guerillas* as they all represent different groups of people with different incongruities in life. Likewise, *A Bend in the River* shows the crucial disagreement between the European and African culture through the institution of New Domain and the character of Father Huismans. This novel with a quintessential African setting somehow echoes Conrad's *The Heart of Darkness* where Kurtz is shown occupied in a constant war with the native Africans. Moreover, *A Bend in the River* and *The Heart of Darkness* resemble each other because both of the novels discuss the issue of multiracialism or intermingling of the two heterogenous cultures. In the next phase of his literary career, Naipaul does not restrict himself to a single geographical territory; rather, he seems to sum up his experiences of a literary circumnavigator in India, Trinidad, England, and Africa.

The developed sensibility of the novelist gets reflected through his works such as *Half a Life* and *Magic Seeds* in which the territorial confinements are seen as diluting and eroding in the wake of a consciousness attained by the novelist. It is in this phase that the novelist asserts his vision in its totality with aplomb and ease. The theme of diasporic ambivalence in V.S. Naipaul's fictional works gets represented in an intense manner here in this phase. *Half a Life* and its sequel *Magic Seeds* are the novels which revisit the typical Naipaulian concerns—enigma of the nomads across the world, however with far more conviction. The novels present an account of Willie Chandran, the son of an Indian Brahmin mystic. The two novels are partially autobiographical as Willie, like so many of Naipaul's protagonists, aspires to escape from the dingy environment of his family. Like Anand in *A House for Mr Biswas,* Willie writes stories and fables in his school exercise book. These stories depict the shameful history of his family, his unflinching desire to flee, his father's reluctant marriage to a low-caste woman and its consequences. Willie Chandran's journey is also intended to be transformative like Anand Biswas, just as it was perceived in *A Way in the World* and *The Enigma of Arrival* where Naipaul zealously presents his own typical journey from the margins to the wider cosmopolitan world.

The publication of *Half a Life* coincides with conferring of the Nobel Prize for Literature to Naipaul in 2001. The novel emphatically records the author's first march into the horizons of heightened sensibility. This novel brings to the fore the most obvious and characteristic features of Naipaul's fiction—his recurring themes and concerns, his flair and his flaws. The young colonial Indian Willie Chandran, who fails to make sense of his life in India, escapes to London, and then to Mozambique. It is reminiscent of *A House for Mr Biswas, The Mystic Masseur* and most specifically of *The Mimic Men.* It is the novel in which Naipaul portrays and evaluates the lives of the people of mixed descent in three countries—India, England and Portuguese Africa and their struggle to discover their identities. The book is about the confused identities, a theme that Naipaul discusses in almost all the books he has written—people coming from small places, smaller historical contexts and struggling with the looseness of their selves and their lives. *Half a Life* delineates a powerful tale of one man's journey from childhood to middle age while at the same time creating a echoing tale about the convulsions of modern history, both the dying of old inequities and the rise of new illusions, and their spiritual legacy of homelessness and dislocation.

The autobiographical elements are once again predominant in Half *a Life.* Willie's circumstances resemble Naipaul's life as he was educated first in Canadian missionary school and later in a London university, and tried his hand at English short story writing in the early phase of his writing career. Chandran's childhood disgust seems at least a repetition of Naipaul's own life as he has also been to a missionary school at Trinidad only to develop apathy towards his family, native land and its culture. The book is not about a particular country, culture or issue rather it depicts the odyssey of Mr Chandran's life in such a way that the reader is caught between empathy and apathy toward Willie's enterprises. Perhaps this ambivalence is precisely the effect Naipaul seeks to produce in his novels. It's an attempt of an expatriate to establish the individual identity. Whereas *A House for Mr Biswas* is about an expatriate Indian's endeavour to assert his own identity in a Creole Caribbean world, and *Guerillas* is about a would-be West Indian revolutionary, *A Bend in the River* is all about the search for identity in a newly independent African nation, and *A Way in the World* represents the author's search for selfhood and for an understanding of the effect of inheritance. Similarly, *Half a Life* is all about the protagonist's persistent quest for roots and individual recognition. It is an odd tale moving from India to England to Africa and beyond. It is set firstly in post-independence India, at the politically protected court of the Maharaja, later in London, then in the pre-independence Africa in a nameless country modelled on Mozambique and briefly in Berlin. The novel follows Willie Chandran as he tries to find a place or role for himself across the world.

Half a Life is quite a departure from other novels of Naipaul. Instead of adopting linear narrative, he has adopted a circuitous narrative form. The story is told by several characters. There is, in the first place, an omniscient narrator, then there are Willie Chandran's father's and Willie's narratives. The story does not proceed in the conventional beginning-middle-end pattern. Naipaul's unconventional narrative technique in the novel alters the familiar sequence—with the end coming before the middle. Naipaul in fact, provides justification for breaking the conventional narrative pattern through Roger, the lawyer and a publisher's agent. Commenting on Willie's stories, he condemns Willie and his namesake Somerset Maugham saying:

> I know your great namesake and family friend says that a story should have a beginning, a middle and an end. But actually, if you think about it, life isn't like that. Life does not have a neat beginning and a tidy end. Life is always going on. You should begin in the middle and end in the middle, and it should all be there.[1]

The novel opens with Willie Chandran's curiosity to know about the genesis of his name. Willie impatiently asks his father, "Why is my middle name Somerset?" (*Half a Life*, p. 1). This inquiry forms the essence of Willie's perpetual ambivalence wherever he goes. The insubstantial and vague answer to this question highlights the irony of Willie's divided existence. *Mimicry* is obvious among the people like Willie's father who possess half-discovered self in the half-made societies. Multiple external forces play a vital role in breeding a sense of insecurity and alienation among the colonials like Willie who are destined to live just *half a life*. A lurking fear of annihilation torments the psyche of such half-grown figures.

Willie Somerset Chandran's curiosity and anxiety about his name, though a bit unusual, seems justified in the due course of his life. His name is connotative as it suggests his essential halfness in life. Half of his name is borrowed from the famous writer Somerset Maugham; his first name declares him as a Christian whereas his surname proclaims his mixed ancestry. The character of Willie is a testimony to the belief that a man's name predetermines his fate and circumstances. Willie is as much an amalgam of considerably diverse traits as is his name a combination of different and hostile sources. It further brings to the fore the tendency of the colonized to *mimic*. As a simple and general definition, mimicry implies "the action, practice, or art of mimicking."[2] Being dominant, the colonizer does not only want the colonized simply to imitate but also to absorb and adapt to its culture. Perhaps, for that reason, Homi Bhabha defines *mimicry* as "the process by which the colonized subject is reproduced as 'almost the same' but not quite."[3]

Willie's search for the roots takes him backward because his roots are entwined with those of his father's. The son of a half-rebel, half-acknowledged Brahmin father and a low-caste woman, Willie's denial of self begins in his childhood itself. His mother's low caste and the shaky status of his father inculcate a sense of shame in the boy, but his absurd determination to survive drives him into a make-believe world of falsehood. The choice of Willie to go against conventions is consistent with Naipaul's attitude towards his own colonial past. Naipaul broke all the shackles of conventions and did not let himself be victimized by the circumstances of his parents and native Caribbean island.

Willie Chandran's father explains Willie as how he has harmonized the different roles in life by negating the conventions and rejecting an excellent career, by marrying a woman of lower caste, and by becoming the "mendicant on the alms of the poorest of the poor" (*Half a Life*, p. 5). Afterwards, Willie starts abhorring his father and his halfness. He does not appreciate his father's ambivalence when he is caught between the negation-acceptance dichotomies. On the one hand, his father aspires to live a life of sacrifice but on the other hand he regrets his marriage with a low-caste woman. Similarly he talks about his determined oath of celibacy but ironically he begets two children. He is caught in a trap, i.e., whether he should stick to his vows or accept the tradition. Deploring what he has done, he likes to "go back" because he comes "from a line of priests" (*Half a Life*, p. 7). Willie's father complains that he has made himself unsuitable for life by turning his back on family and tradition. This negation makes him give up his education, and consequently compels him to be a mendicant. In another instance, he woos a backward caste female student at university, not because she is attractive or appealing, but because she fits into his image of the sacrifice he wants to make. This obsession to lead a life of sacrifice leads him to marry her. It, however, shocks and disappoints his son Willie Chandran who opens his outburst against his father.

Willie's father aims at living "a life of sacrifice" (*Half a Life*, p. 10). But, he laments his perpetual confinement imposed upon him for the certain roles he has created as husband, father, and mendicant. Consequently, Willie's father realizes that he "has fallen into ancestral ways" (*Half a Life*, p. 31). In an attempt to resist his tradition he marries a low caste woman only to find himself at the mercy of his own vehemence. He recollects the ambivalent pleasure of embracing an untouchable woman:

> Her very dark top lip slipped slowly—with the wetness of a snail, I thought over her big white teeth. For the first time I saw that she used powder. There was a thin white bloom on her cheeks and forehead; it made the black skin matt, and you could see where the powder ended and the shiny skin showed again. I was repelled, ashamed, moved. (*Half a Life*, p. 13)

The absolutely convincing character of Willie Chandran emerges from this discontented union. Peculiar like his father, he is eager to find something that will accommodate him both with his compatriots within the native history and expatriates far-off from their native world.

Memory, then, lurks underneath and continues to make Willie uncomfortable and ambivalent all the time. It has signified a burden for Willie and his father both because, as Willie says, "his shame was always with me, the little unhappiness at the back of my mind, like an incurable illness, corrupting all my moments" (*Half a Life*, p. 32). The father undergoes terrible mental anguish because, according to Simon Gikandi, "the voice from the past contains both joy and pain; it ensnares and liberates at the same time"[4] Willie feels embarrassed when he comes to know about his father being a mendicant. Gikandi rightly explains the causes behind Willie's embarrassment when he comments that "the past ... instead of functioning as a source of certainty and true understanding ... often generates fear and shame."[5] Disheartened and disillusioned, "he walked without seeing, thinking of the hopelessness of home and his own nebulous present. All at once, in the most magical way, he was lifted out of himself". (*Half a Life*, p. 50)

Willie comes from a mixed (inter-caste) marriage and is sent to a Christian school. Soon, Willie aspires to be a missionary and a Canadian like his teachers. In his English compositions he fantasizes himself as a regular Canadian boy with a *Mom* and a *Pop* and a *Car*. Negating the history, he reconstructs his life with such artistic skill that it becomes more than a riddle. In his compositions he pretends to be a Canadian and writes imaginary stories based on his understanding of American comic books and rebels against the knowledge imparted by his father. His day-dreaming makes his teachers reward him with high marks, but his father is wounded to find himself being humiliated in his composition. Willie dislikes his parents—more particularly his father and this sense of hostility in him, makes him *a sojourner*. As the compositions of Anand in *A House for Mr Biswas* determine his desire for wish-fulfillment, Willie's stories mock his parents and their contemptible circumstances.

While studying Naipaul from *A House for Mr Biswas* to *Half a Life*, one finds the two novels identical. What Gordon Rohlehr has commented on Mr Biswas in 1977 is strangely applicable to Willie's father in 2001. Rohlehr comments: "It is worth asking what is the social and universal significance of the rebellion of a mediocre ridiculous man. Biswas certainly is this ... he is forever trying to arrange his world, ending up more deeply immersed in the Absurd situation."[6] It is also an act of *mimicry* of his father who has been a radical in his own way. Like his father, Willie Chandran also finds the truth about his background repulsive; hence he takes to falsehood and pretensions. But, after the display of his anticipated image before the world, Willie starts living the image. He goes on creating and recreating lies because of his disgust on his realization of halfness in life. His compositions become a convenient medium to let his halfness expressed with assertion. His father soon discovers his dilemma and realizes that in order to avoid the worst, Willie must be allowed to flee. He reflects: "I used to think that you were me and I was worried at what I had done to you. But now I know that you are not me. What is in my head is not in yours. You are somebody else, somebody I don't know, and I worry for you because you are launched on a journey I know nothing of" (*Half a Life*, p. 49). Willie Chandran's father has stood at odds with the world aspiring for greatness. His father recollects his past when he has been obsessed with the idea of following Mahatma Gandhi's call for sacrifice. Most significant about the father's narration, however, is how convinced he is of the honesty of his attempts, and the validity of his personal sacrifices. The gap between his convictions and the reality of his life makes him at once a contemptible and a tragic figure. Both Willie Chandran's father and Willie represent drifting nomads in the absence of a purpose. Willie's father has tried to overcome it by joining the freedom movement, but the narrow life he has been forced to lead in that native state of the pre-independent India does not provide him any prospect to establish his individuality.

The lives of the characters like Willie are destined to be ridiculous. Willie's father finds the ground beneath his feet shaking as he marries a girl below his social status. Fighting the petty caste war, he reacts: "I was irredeemably tarnished, a fallen man of caste, and my path of mockery of sacred ways" (*Half a Life*, p. 32). Naming his son and daughter after the great English writer William Somerset Maugham and Sarojini Naidu respectively, proves to be a mockery as both of his children are unable to attain their individuality in life. The disappointment of Willie's father reminds the reader of the story of Naipaul's father—his ambitions and failures. Jha finds the novel as typically Naipaulian when he comments that it: "... delineates the traumas of a tainted and troubled past, of attempting to find some meaning and purpose of life. It beautifully analyses the pangs of exile, their living a half-life, their sense of alienation, and their cultural traditions."[7] Willie realizes that his personal failures mirror those of his father and these failures ultimately mirror the failures of colonialism.

The novel is all about the consequences of mimicking by Willie and his father. Mimicking Gandhi, he is obliged to marry a low-caste woman whose very sight breeds repulsion in him. Because of his insubstantial ideals he has to marry in haste. Willie Chandran finds himself caught between dilemmas owing to his father's contempt for Willie's mother, his mother's coarse attempts at warm affection, and the Canadian sensibilities of the mission school he attends. The novel keeps on exploring different cultures in a pursuit to catch the typical halfness prevalent among the colonial expatriates and the natives alike. Willie, who is born and raised in India, attains self-awareness of his past, and by drawing essence from that past he reconstructs a background on which he can set his new life. Through the father's life story, Willie learns about his ancestry and the circumstances responsible for his father's absurdity. His sense of history makes him believe that "he could, within reason, remake himself and his past and ancestry". (*Half a* Life, p. 57)

In the novel, Willie is made to accommodate himself in different foreign cultures endeavoring to appreciate it all the way through further subcultures. Like other protagonists of Naipaul, he is also caught between conflicts—love-hate, rejection-acceptance, and native-alien. Jessica Lee Thomas remarks: "Naipaul tells a half-finished story, one that begins in the middle, ends in the middle, and contains within its folds the understanding of an uncompleted beauty, which, like a half-finished portrait, holds the promise and potential of greatness."[8] Here one can observe the slight distinction between Naipaul's early works and *Half a Life*. The novel primarily focuses the typical colonial/postcolonial issues—displacement, insecurity and disorientation. These concerns are incorporated in the novel through the drifting existence of the protagonist.

Negating history is a sin which brings its own punishment. Willie's father sets the example of the half-lived life and his son Willie follows his footsteps. He, being the representative of the next-generation, does not learn from his father's mistakes and allows history to repeat and even re-repeat itself. Willie's father bears the punishment of the negation of history. Willie's father asserts:

> My decision was simple. It was to turn my back on our ancestry, the foolish, foreign-ruled starveling priests my grandfather had told me about, to turn my back on all my father's foolish hopes for me as someone high in the Maharaja's service, all the foolish hopes of the college principal to have me marry his daughter. My decision was to turn my back on all those ways of death, to trample on them, and to do the only noble thing that lay in my power, which was to marry the lowest person I could find. (*Half a Life*, pp. 10–11)

Despite not having finished his own convent school education, he gets scholarship to a college of education for mature students. Willie flees to London to launch himself as a man with enterprise, but ironically in his search for wholeness, he loses even the half-life that has been within his reach. This is the escapist tendency of Willie to get away from what he is familiar with. The world he enters is completely an unfamiliar one. He gropes for friendship, sex and recognition which he hardly ever achieves.

London offers him no opportunity to realize eternal sense of gratification, rather he finds himself all the more lost. The education that he is getting in London is hardly consequential. He is attracted towards the immigrant community of postwar London, its dull West-End Clubs and sexual encounters. After coming into contact with the world of sex in London he compares his father's life-style in India to the life-style he himself has been acquainted with in London, and feels pity for his father. To his Indian sensibility the world of sex appears rather brutal. Naipaul's delineation of the London scenes and the penetrating descriptions of Africa are hard to beat. He finds nothing significant in western education and shows only half-hearted interest to attain it. His indeterminate state makes him observe:

> The learning he was being given was like the food he was eating, without savour. The two were inseparable in his mind. And just as he ate without pleasure, so, with a kind of blindness, he did what the lectures and tutors asked of him, read the books and articles and did the essays. He was unanchored, with no idea of what lay ahead. (*Half a Life*, p. 58)

In London, he discovers that British manners too are as ridiculous as the Indian customs. What makes him confident and assertive in London is that now he has understood both India and England. His opinion that the English people have no acquaintance with Indian etiquettes makes him feel free to say what he likes about his native land. He reconstructs an entirely different and less disgraceful past for himself. He introduces his mother as "a full Christian" (*Half a Life*, p. 58) and his father as the son of a courtier. In search of his identity in a strange world Willie again projects a borrowed, make-believe identity and endeavours to carve a new image. In college, Willie gets himself adjusted by rebuilding himself and his past. And he tells lies to re-make his past, avoiding those elements of his life for which he has been ashamed. He has no firm objectives and ambitions. There are moments of promise. In England "Willie began to understand that he was free to present himself as he wished. He could, as it were, write his own revolution. The possibilities were dizzying. He could, within reason, remake himself and his past and his ancestry (*Half a Life*, p. 60). Willie Chandran can't take advantage of the opportunity. Most promisingly perhaps, he finds that he can become a writer, a story-teller, but he allows this ambition to be thwarted. He chooses simply to flee again into a world that is entirely fragmentary. His wife Ana leads him to her home, a province of Portuguese Africa, a country whose inhabitants are all apprehensively living out the last days of colonialism.

Because of his mother's education at the mission school, he sees her as an orthodox Christian. In addition, to disengage himself from the mission school, and interpreting from memory what he has read, he adjusts his behaviour to certain things suited to the manners of a Christian. He adds that his mother belongs "to an ancient Christian community of the subcontinent … almost as old as Christianity itself" (*Half a Life*, p. 58). He also claims that his father is a Brahmin and that "his father's father was a 'courtier'" (*Half a Life*, p. 58). By recreating himself intentionally, Willie invents a myth of origin centred on his family's history in an attempt to gain acceptability and to manage his developing new world.

> … he adapted certain things he had read, and he spoke of his mother as belonging to an ancient Christian community of the subcontinent, a community almost as old as Christianity itself. He kept his father as a Brahmin. He made his father's father a 'courtier'. So playing with words, he began to re-make himself. It excited him and began to give him a feeling of power. (*Half a Life*, p. 61)

During his stay in London, Willie encounters a few people each of whom is panicked by the typical halfness in life. In the novel, Naipaul presents a series of characters who are waiting for something to happen which actually never happens. The account of these characters; their terror and fear; and their marginality are the key concerns of the novelist to assert that emigration and resultant creolization can ensure no satisfaction. Percy Cato, Jamaican of mixed parentage and more brown than black, resembles Willie in more than one way. He is a Jamaican born and brought up in Panama. Like Willie, he is also ashamed of his background and instead of giving true account of his life, he too believes in presenting the fictitious image of himself. When he tells Willie about his father's migration to Panama as a clerk, Willie very well understands that he's lying: "That's a foolish story. His father went there as a labourer. He would have been in one of the gangs, holding his pickaxe before him on the ground, like the others, and looking obediently at the photographer" (*Half a Life*, p. 62). Similarly, Percy's predilection to dress flawlessly is to be seen as a precaution to evade the disclosure of the true identity of the expatriates like him. Such strategies adopted by Willie and Percy Cato illustrate the painful sense of shame, fear and humiliation that characterizes the unique expatriate sensibility which Naipaul's characters try in vain to camouflage. Their fictional recreation of their lives makes them more ridiculous and their ambivalence becomes more evident.

The novel is full of characters who are exiles in their characteristic modes, who have no proper place in the world. Percy Cato,

Marcus, Graca, Ana, Sarojini, Jacinto, Ricardo, Carla, the Noranhas, the Correias, Alvaro, etc., are all searching for the fullness of their lives. Roger escorts him to an intellectual London dinner party and there he introduces Willie as a literary star to be. There he meets Marcus, a Negro "dedicated to inter-racial sex" (*Half a Life,* p. 89); Richard "a bedroom Marxist" (*Half a Life,* p. 91); Peter, a Latin American women-expert; Serafina, the wife of a pederast man. In this quest for fullness and self-realization, they find themselves clamped to unforeseen situations. Having no other choices, they continue to thrive on whatever comes their way. Willie is the most fitting example of this halfness of life and the characteristic ambivalence among the expatriates.

Sexual promiscuity is a common feature prevalent among the third world expatriates who have moved from the conservative society to a liberal Western world which is not infected with such reservations. The exiles in the novel lead a *half-life*. Willie desires to discover some purpose in life, though temporarily, through his sexual encounters in London and the Portuguese African colony. But he realizes the futility of life through his varied experiences. All the exiles realize that an exile is bound to experience the halfness in life as they don't have more of a personal life. Willie may conceal himself by projecting a false image of his descent, but he can not destroy his reality and at all critical moments his halfness becomes apparent. His sexual frustrations are not his own; they are the frustrations of a society, of a race and of a culture. His cultural background and awareness of his incompleteness breeds in him a sense of susceptibility and reticence. The bohemian culture of Notting Hill is unfamiliar to Willie but not being able to safeguard his own culture, he seeks to adjust to the Notting Hill culture. Willie is torn within himself in his efforts to absorb himself in the alien culture which is the only alternative left to the immigrant in order to survive. An émigré is destined to experience a state of divided identity—divided by culture, history and circumstance.

Whatever freedom Willie attempts to enjoy, he remains dissatisfied because he needs constant support of someone to guide him in the alien setting. Even the girls Willie sleeps with are not his friends but the lovers of his friends. Willie keeps planning to declare his love before Percy and the world when June marries her childhood friend neglecting both Percy and Willie. Similarly, Richard's friend Perdita deserts Willie after the frustrated experience of one night. Willie's half-realized attempts at sex, the lack of money mixed with the poverty of his experience, are subjects that Naipaul has dealt in his previous novels also. Willie's rejection of a vicarious existence has been seen as "coming of age" of Naipaul's hero. The protagonists of Naipaul's fiction may be different persons but a thread of continuity may be observed in their fate and limbotic status. Willie in Naipaul's twelfth novel may be in many ways different from Mohun Biswas in *A House for Mr Biswas,* Ganesh in *The Mystic Masseur* and Ralph Singh in *The Mimic Men* but essentially they all stand for the crisis of the same race as their sense of ambivalence, inadequacy, unease and uncertainty presents the different aspects of the same cultural mindset. Naipaul has once said:

> I said earlier that everything of value about me is in my books. I will go further now. I will say I am the sum of my books. Each book, intuitively sensed and, in the case of fiction, intuitively worked out, stands on what has gone before, and grows out of it. I feel that at any stage of my literary career it could have been said that the last book contained all the others.[9]

All his major protagonists suffer the tragedy of displacement and separation from their land. Their separation from their native land leads them to a disorder and their consequent search for land is associated with the search for order. There are a number of writers whose central preoccupation is the anguish and pain of diaspora but what makes Naipaul truly inimitable is his unique sensibility. His fictional characters are moved not as much by anguish as by angst. Though quite akin to many a writer whose works primarily delineate the anguish and pain of diaspora, what makes Naipaul stand head and shoulders above his peers over others is his firsthand experience of the ambivalence and in-betweenness among the displaced. The second part of the novel is typically Naipaulian as it reproduces writer's rather unhappy student years in England. Naipaul himself has mentioned depression and suicidal tendencies during his student life in London. The protagonists of Naipaul take refuge in clumsy sexual encounters whenever they experience difficulty in putting aside their sense of unwholesomeness. Willie is in no way different from Ralph Singh, Jimmy Ahmed or Salim in *The Mimic Men, Guerillas* and *A Bend in the River* respectively. Thrown in such difficult situations, they all look alike. His sexual encounters with prostitutes are disgusting and nerve-wrecking: "She was a big girl in a tight skirt that showed off her hips. She filled the small room with her perfume ... that mingled smell of excrement and sweat and deep, piercing, many sided sweetness from no simple source" (*Half a Life,* p. 66). "Brothel fantasies"[10] offer the temporary comfort to the agonized souls. Even Alvaro, who lives happily with his African wife in a grimy house, enjoys the excitement of wild sex with a number of mistresses or concubines or pick-ups from the surrounding villages. He gets a fresh crop of innocent teenager girls every month. Though he poses himself as a hardcore imp and a *doer*, Willie Chandran finds him nervous and asks for his support. Naipaul here presents the naked picture of racism and sexual promiscuity in England. The character of Alvaro somehow unearths the dirty picture of Naipaul who has been reportedly enjoying sexual relationships with prostitutes for long. Express India reports:

> Nobel Laureate Sir V.S. Naipaul tormented his first wife for nearly four decades, regularly visited brothels in London and kept a mistress for almost 24 years before suddenly leaving her to marry a Pakistani scribe, according to his biography … has admitted in his biography that he frequently humiliated his first wife (Patricia) … . The book, penned by Patrick French who was given free access to all of Naipaul's papers, claims that the novelist started visiting prostitutes when the couple were living in London three years after they married. In the summer of 1958, turning imagination into reality, he [Naipaul] started to have sex with prostitutes.[11]

Another typical expatriate is the African Marcus with his peculiar desire to have white grandchildren. He sees nothing strange in his plan. He has also shown as how the inter-racial sexual relationship has changed the demography in some places. For him, it is simply the repetition of something that has happened on a large scale in England a hundred and fifty years ago.

> In the eighteenth century there were about half a million black people in England. They've all vanished. They disappeared in the local population. They were bred out. The Negro gene is a recessive one. If this were more widely known there would be a good deal less racial feeling than there is. (*Half a Life*, pp. 94–95)

The common postcolonial concern of multiculturalism and interracial relationships characterize *Half a Life* also. Referring to South America, Marcus says, "… there were large Negro populations in Buenos Aires and Uruguay in 1800. They disappeared in the local population. They were bred out. The Negro is recessive. Not many people know that" (*Half a Life*, p. 97). The displacement or expatriation is not the usual and painless phenomenon rather it results into essential alienation. Freedom from the native frustration leads an expatriate to experience the loss of identity and individuality. Assimilation of the émigrés is all the more hazardous as it may challenge the uniqueness of all the races and groups alike. About the varied characters drawn from different backgrounds in *Half a Life,* V.S. Naipaul comments:

> ... they are not really free men. The niche of the world is too confining ... within their own little territories, their life is as confined as it was before. At the end of colonial times, people were subjected to petty tyrannies. They have fewer rights and fewer possibilities. The smart people want green cards. They want to come 'to your country, run restaurants and talk about revolution.[12]

For these nomads, the world is full of slippery substances, and for them time is as slippery as the *self* itself. Naipaul's works derive their strength from his own life and the Swedish Academy has very correctly recognized this in its Nobel citation: "He became an explorer, not of the wilderness but of societies—everywhere at home and a stranger, a Ulysses ... ."[13] The Academy has rightly called V.S. Naipaul a *nomadic* literary man. He is a writer with world perspective, and he has never stopped travelling. These travels have inspired more than twenty four books of fiction and non-fiction. His travels to India, Trinidad, Africa, South America and the Muslim World provide him with the stuff for recreation. But, he has been primarily concerned about the narration of "the areas of darkness".[14]

Willie fails to see his prospects in London after completing his studies. Like a typical expatriate, he readies himself for the next journey—the journey to Ana's African country. Willie has come to Britain in search of a foothold but failing to find one he navigates to Africa which bears more affinity to his colonial experiences. Thus passing away from one destination to another, from one continent to another, he feels that he has lost his language. In his pursuit to establish identity, he is pushed towards quietness. According to Chris Colin:

> *Half a Life* meanders interestingly in this way buildungsroman to travel book, England to Africa and Naipaul is offering us a character with a similarly unstable centre. The novel and its protagonist alike drift along with the convulsions of postcolonial Africa and England, but Willie never reduces to a simple metaphor, and the drifting isn't in service of some glib point. He is, instead, a believable and likably sad man, with half a life left and probably more peripheries to visit along the way.[15]

An emigrant is threatened with the loss of native culture and language to which he tries to stick desperately. Wearing away of heritage language further aggravates the ambivalence among the colonized. For them, survival is worthless unless it is expressed appropriately in their native or first language. The expatriates are dispossessed of this power and it intensifies their sense of alienation. An emigrant is always preoccupied with the idea of his/her malleability to that which is for all intents and purposes alien. In this process of accommodation, the language proves to be the most effective device to come to his help. But again, he is caught in another predicament, that is, he starts developing love-hate relationship with the native language. Naipaul himself touches upon the issue of the extinction of native language when he observes:

> They have adopted the language of the sheltering country and their own language has become a secret gibberish. Immigrants are people on their own. They can not be judged by the standards of their older culture. Culture is like language, ever developing. There is no right and wrong, no purity from which there is decline. Usage sanctions everything.[16]

Naipaul being a representative diasporic writer can very well comprehend the anguish of losing one's language. Willie being the mouthpiece of his creator comes to realize that his native language has almost gone, that his London-English is going, that he is left with no proper gift of expression. In the African colony, he observes that even the ordinary people he meets on the streets know the language and the customs of the place. Being ashamed of his insufficiency, he does not disclose his linguistic insecurity to his wife, Ana. Naipaul honestly highlights the trauma of migration and consequent loss in his Nobel Lecture in these words:

> The world outside existed in a kind of darkness; and we inquired about nothing. I was just old enough to have some idea of the Indian epics, the Ramayana in particular. The children who came five years or so after me in our extended family didn't have this luck. No one taught us Hindi. Sometimes someone wrote out the alphabet for us to learn, and that was that; we were expected to do the rest ourselves. So, as English penetrated, we began to lose our language.[17]

Naipaul's personal consciousness of the loss of language gets articulated through the character of Ana. She is a Portuguese-African woman, with whom Willie falls in love and has a pleasurable, satisfying sexual relationship. She considers the language as the only medium to severe her ties with constricted colonial atmosphere of her native land. This understanding makes her flee to England so that she may be proficient in global English. She finds her grandfather helpless in becoming a cosmopolitan because he is not proficient in the language of the world. The justification Ana gives to her family shows the impact of the language in the culture of diaspora:

> I wanted to breakout of the Portuguese language. I feel it was that that had made my grandfather such a limited man. He had no true idea of the world ... in his mind because of the Portuguese language, all the rest of the world had been stained away. And I didn't want to learn South African English, which is what people learn here. I wanted to learn English. (*Half a Life*, pp. 154–55)

In Conradian terms, her grandfather represents purity of experiences as he doesn't think beyond Portugal and Portuguese Africa, Goa and Brazil because of the Portuguese language which he adores limitlessly.

During his trans-continental journey from Southampton to Ana's African country, Willie's mind is preoccupied with the alarming uncertainty and confusion to which he is leading himself through this migration. His ambiguity is well-illustrated by the narrator:

> He thought about the new language he would have to learn. He wondered whether he would be able to hold on to his own language. He wondered whether he would forget his English .... Willie was trying to deal with the knowledge that had come to him on the ship that his home language had almost gone, that his English was going, that he had no proper language left, no gift of expression. (*Half a Life*, p. 132)

Willie's loss of his language becomes even more paradoxical when the reader looks back to the moment when he is acclaimed as an emerging writer by Roger sometimes in the past. On the publication of his first book Willie is introduced as a new subversive voice from the subcontinent (*Half a Life*, p. 122). The loss of language does not only challenge his individual identity but his identity as a writer is also at stake. With his remigration to Africa Willie's language itself becomes a victim to repressive forces.

The relationship of Willie and Ana who is heir to an estate in Mozambique, is not based on any romantic attraction. Willie comes closer to Ana because in her he finds the source to provide him wholeness. Moreover, their circumstances are almost alike and Willie discovers a kind of reciprocity in her. Their colonial experiences, expatriate status and sense of constant alienation make them sense some resemblance. It is their *halfness* that establishes the tie between the two. When his stories are rejected by Roger with the comments: "... you don't want to write about real things ... I feel about these stories that the writer has secrets. He is hiding ... ." (*Half a Life*, p. 79), he gets a letter, from Ana with the remarks: "In your stories for the first time I find moments that are like moments in my own life" (*Half a Life*, p. 79). They become emotionally involved as they find parallel between their backgrounds. Ana's grandfather, a Portuguese, marries an African, and later when he grows rich, he chooses Portuguese sons-in-law. Ana's mother has left her Portuguese husband only to remarry a man of mixed race. Ana's father dupes his wife to get her money and leaves home. In her stepfather's home Ana is seduced. Because of all these experiences, Ana develops emptiness in her mind and longs for love that will eliminate her lonesomeness. She marries Willie with the devotion of a loyal wife to lead a purposeful life. Willie's torn identity corresponds to Ana's vacuity and after winning her love he acknowledges that he has found a complete recognition. With no plans for the future as his scholarship at the college comes to an end, Willie Chandran takes up with Ana and follows her to the Portuguese colony of Mozambique.

Willie, the protagonist, is simply presenting a world of make-belief through his stories, but Ana appreciates him as a writer because she values his halfness. Willie himself is aware of the strong reason behind Ana's praise of his stories. He suspects Ana's genuine love towards him as, according to him: "It was possible that she belonged to a mixed community or stood in some, other kind of half and half position" (*Half a Life*, p. 124). He feels contented about his undertakings as a London student where, according to the narrator, "he had made an active and mixed London life for himself and was an author with a book soon to be published" (*Half a Life*, p. 114). But soon after he contradicts himself when he says: "Let the book die. Let it fade away. Let me not be reminded of it. I will write no more. This book was not something I should have done, anyway. It was artificial and false" (*Half a Life*, p. 115). Ana's *halfness* makes him forget his own insecurity temporarily. However, they get together only to fall in love.

Their association takes a definite shape when Willie agrees to follow Ana to Africa and spends eighteen years in a Portuguese-African colony as Ana's man. He also confesses that he depends on Ana for being a man. When he decides to go to Africa with her, it is an agonizing attempt to escape London, but it does carry anticipation for hopefulness. He follows Ana to Africa in an effort to run away from his own aimlessness. The unknown motive drives him mad. The narrator adds, "... and what was most intoxicating for Willie was that for the first time in his life he felt himself in the presence of someone who accepted him completely. At home his life had been ruled by his mixed inheritance. It spoilt everything" (*Half a Life*, p. 125). Ana has African blood and a family estate in the country. It ensures him that her company will enable him to forget his failures which otherwise predominate his life. He loves her and lessens his fear by granting him full realization of manhood.

On his arrival at Mozambique, Willie discovers it to be "a little low built concrete town" (*Half a Life*, p. 134) and he doesn't feel like staying there permanently. Disillusioned with his fate, he reacts: "I don't know where I am. I don't think I can pick my way back. I don't even want this view to become familiar. I must not unpack. I must never behave as though I am staying" (*Half a Life*, p. 135). In Ana's city, he is "walking as if in wilderness" (*Half a Life*, p. 134). His much-hyped arrival as *Ana's man* leads him nowhere and his ambivalence is further intensified. His rudderless drift makes him irresolute and despite initial lack of enthusiasm he stays with Ana for eighteen years. He observes the great emptiness in this Portuguese-African colony, and he asks Ana to narrate the history of her country. Willie comes to sense Ana's special way of looking at people as she classifies the people as African or not African. Ironically Willie finds himself as someone who is not an African. Moreover he observes the typical eccentricity among the Africans who seem to be afraid of one another. With the break out of the Civil War, Portuguese African colony is about to face a bloody revolution. Ana warns Willie: "Africans may not be afraid of you and me, but they are afraid of one another ... even the humblest has power. In that way they are better off than the rest of us" (*Half a Life*, p. 159). It makes Willie leave Ana and Africa and he goes to Germany, to Sarojini who has married a radical German photographer.

Willie's experience and realization of halfness in life are reflected in his transcontinental migration and multi-dimensional socio-cultural environment. Wherever he goes, he realizes that a man searches for wholeness but becomes only half-successful. Similarly, Ana is an extension of Willie's ambivalence. His ultimate failure as an expatriate twice displaced from his native land, comes to the fore when he shares his loss with his sister. He informs her that he has made his life more vulnerable by escaping London. He regrets his loss of independence he enjoyed in London where he had made himself known as Willie Chandran but in Africa he has become simply "Ana's London man". (*Half a Life*, p. 145)

All the same, Willie's experiences in London and Africa carry some similarity, that is, on reaching London, he is traumatized to see that the city won't help him to meet his expectations. Similarly when he arrives in Africa its splendour worries him. He doesn't think that he is in a position to cope with it. He longs for prominence and magnificence, but when he experiences it, he shies away. He is destined to experience disillusionment whenever he dreams of grandeur. In London, Willie faces the sense of disappointment and in African colony he finds himself gullible. Willie Chandran's fear of the *bush* and *half-made* societies is, nonetheless real:

> I often thought back to the terror of my first day that picture of the road and the Africans walking was always with me—and wondered that the land had been tamed in this way, that such a reasonable life could be extracted from such an unpromising landscape, that blood, in some way, had been squeezed out of stone. (*Half a Life,* p. 149)

With his frequent transmigrations, he finds himself busy in playing with words to remake and readjust himself. As the narration of the novel primarily oscillates between the account of Willie Chandran and his father's, one always feels himself in the middle of things throughout the novel. But, even more than for his storytelling prowess, Naipaul is famous for his searing, unforgiving and controversial portraits of formerly colonized societies struggling towards self-realization in the postcolonial world. Horace Engdahl, permanent Secretary of the Swedish Academy and the member of its Nobel Committee asserted:

> Sir Vidia! Your life as a writer calls to mind what Alfred Nobel said of himself: 'My homeland is where I work, and I work everywhere.' In every place, you have remained yourself, faithful to your instinct. Your books trace the outline of an individual quest of unusual directions. Like a Nemo piloting a craft of your own design, without representing anyone or anything, you have manifested the independence of literature. I would like to convey to you the warm congratulations of the Swedish Academy as I now request you to receive the Nobel Prize in Literature from the hands of his majesty the King.[18]

The excellent narration enhances the sense and spirit of this rather bleak story. The author's serious message seems to be that those with biographies like Willie's—and, it must be deduced, Naipaul's own—are condemned to displacement and consequently to only "half a life". They are destined to live disoriented and disordered lives because of the inherent disorder that the novelist feels within. Naipaul has experienced the sense of disorder in his life since his escape from Trinidad. He admits: "Disorder within, disorder without. Only my school life was ordered; anything that had happened there I could date at once. But my family life—my life at home or my life in the house, in the street—was jumbled, without sequence."[19]

Willie's father, an Indian of the priestly Brahmin caste is stupefied as his life turns from a carefully imagined *life of sacrifice* into a vague existence after his marriage to a woman of the lowest caste. Willie frequently comes across individuals leading a half-life as exiles. His story is set in post-independence India, then in London and then he travels to a pre-independence African country which is closely modelled on Mozambique, and then for a brief period in Berlin. He feels at home with people who are caught in the web of identity crisis because of the affinity he shares with them.

The characters interacting most intimately with Willie are like half men, half beasts. His half-African, half-Portuguese lover; Ana moves in a circle of people trying to reconcile themselves to a world that presents no final solution to the drifting expatriates. In Africa, the estate owners pretend to the status of the full Portuguese, while most are only half, and many of the foremen on the estates have mixed blood in their veins. The prostitutes Willie encounters during his stay in Africa and the women he tries to see back in London always present numerous, apparently contradictory fronts. He observes thirteen-year-old African girls posing as lascivious, experienced women as they seduce the soldiers in bars. Willie himself desires to do something meaningful in life—to compose some story that is yet to be written. Naipaul expresses his purpose through Roger when he rejects the idea of a fair beginning, middle or end in life.

The incomplete nature of an individual life emerges as the ultimate end of every enterprise undertaken by the displaced emigrants and the natives alike. Naipaul shows a society where action is futile, cloaked in self-delusion, and where people have no ability to progress. Critics praise Naipaul for the extraordinary vision that marks his writing. Being a rootless wanderer, as a man without heritage, Naipaul consistently ridicules the romantic views of the places he journeys to, be they England, Trinidad, India or Africa, in favour of a bitter contradictory truth. Though he has endured harsh criticism from the Third World for his often scathing portrayals of India or the Caribbean, he has simply used his truthful and penetrating observation to portray the civilizations of the world. According to Paul Theroux, "The novel ends nowhere. It is about nothing, just an assortment of Naipaul situations and remarks. Anyone who does not know his work will find it clumsy, unbelievable, badly written, willful and weird."[20] Like Ganesh, Mr Biswas, Mr Stone and Ralph Singh—the protagonists in Naipaul's earlier novels—Willie Chandran is also projected as a writer from the beginning and the distinguishing quality of Willie is his courage to expose the pretences he finds around him. Through his compositions like "Life of Sacrifice", he exposes the pretences of his father and his disgust for the native.

Ambivalent and alienated life is the destiny of the colonial expatriates. Despite all adverse circumstances, Willie finds some relief among the Africans. He reacts: "In Africa I had after a while let those London lies drop, in our half-and-half group they seemed to have no point" (*Half a Life,* p. 179). Here he seems to have established oneness with his past and with himself. Willie comes to realize the futility of all his efforts in a half-made society. He is expecting to be acknowledged as a man with strong foothold but, according to the narrator, he finds that: "there was no special reaction to me. It was curiously deflating. I was expecting some recognition of my extraordinariness and there was nothing" (*Half a Life,* p. 144). Gradually he finds some solace in the realization that he is not the only one who is devoid of identity rather there are many like him who suffer due to the sense of double exile.

The description of the local, colonial expatriate community, many of them bearing Portuguese names, indeed, adds to the strength of the book. It is a life of colonial ease, with servants and sex available at little cost. African's natural affinity for dance and the availability of easy sex offer Willie a whole new world of personal experience and liberation. But the old inhibitions haunt him all the time when he indulges in sex and promiscuity. In another sense, his Indian background turns out to be helpful because it has permitted him to deal with his circumstances in Africa and, also, it has rescued him from London. As he tells to his sister how he comes to understand his role, he concludes that he: "... was helped in this understanding by [his] own background—that the world [he] had entered was only a half-and-half world" (*Half a Life,* p. 150). In Ana's country, people accept his new self based on his London construct of a life. Once more, his memory reminds him of his former times: "They seemed not to know that I was once something else" (*Half a Life,* p. 139). He has always been role-playing, hiding the truth and adjusting his historical past to construct his life. He reacts: "... all the old ghosts were already with me, the ghosts of home, the ghosts of London eleven or twelve years before ... all the shame and incompleteness" (*Half a Life,* p. 187). He discovers that he is in a "half-and-half world" (*Half a Life,* p. 160) with "half-and-half friends" (*Half a Life,* p. 162) who had come to reconcile with their position as "people of the second rank" (*Half a Life,* p. 160). He meets Correias, Ricardo, Luis and his wife Graca. These people are burdened with the divided selves owing to the alien and inhospitable circumstances in Mozambique. The African colony is characterized by the Creole society consisting of Portuguese like Noronhas and the Correias who are exploited by the Portuguese. In his letter to his sister Sarojini, Willie

Chandran elaborates the typical multicultural and Creole society of Portuguese-African colony. There is easy racial acceptance here for Willie Chandran:

> Most of the shops we used were Portuguese. One or two were Indian. I was nervous of going into them at first. I didn't want to get that look from the shop people that would remind me of home and bad things. But there was never anything like that, no flicker of racial recognition from the family inside. There, too, they accepted the new person I had become in Ana's country. They seemed not to know that I was once something else. (*Half a Life*, p. 148)

The Correias are used as the scapegoats and the second rank citizens in the Portuguese colony. The anonymous ruler resembles Big Man in *A Bend in the River*, who represents the imperial forces. In Berlin, describing the plight of Correias to Sarojini, Willie says:

> To destroy a Portuguese like himself would have been to break caste, according to the code of the colony, and to become disreputable. There was no trouble at all in throwing a man of the second rank into darkness, someone from the half-and-half world, educated and respectable and striving … . (*Half a Life*, p. 74)

All the denizens and expatriates residing in Mozambique lack order in their lives. Mozambique is at best, a *half-and-half* world. The colonized are bound to live "makeshift and ambivalent"[21] lives. Naipaul has created the world of make-believe and the disintegrating half-formed society. The ambitions of the people and the ideal they strive for is Portugal or Portuguese—the colonizers. They are not fully Portuguese, often children or grandchildren of some mixed sort of marriage, or simply emigrants, neither truly native in the country they left nor the country they live in. Willie finds the Portuguese community as constricted and disorganized as the Indian one which he has sought to flee.

The loss of identity, sense of alienation and exile is the fate of the mixed, unspecified class. The stigma of being a second rate citizen hangs around Willie and other pipe-dreamers like him. The love-hate relationship between the colonizer and the colonized is evident here. Graca, third generation migrant and the beautiful pure Portuguese wife of Luis stays back in Africa when the Portuguese leave the country. She has been born and brought up in Africa so she feels a sense of belongingness with the Portuguese colony but her children go back to Portugal where they have to give documentary proof of their Portuguese identity. Loss of identity is then, an inevitable outcome of colonization which afflicts both sides—the colonizer as well as the colonized.

Willie feels aggrieved to find his Indian passport and twenty pounds stolen by the local Africans. He was procuring his passport and the meager amount safely to ensure himself with a choice to escape once more. But when Willie loses his passport and Ana advises him to write to his Indian relatives for another passport, he recalls the Government offices in India and Naipaul gets an opportunity to criticize the way the Indian bureaucracy works. Willie recaptures the image of a typical Indian office:

> ... the pea-green walls shiny with grime ... . The floor black with dirt, the pan-chewing clerks in their trousers or lungis, each man correctly marked on the forehead with a fresh caste-mark (his principal duty of the day), on every desk the ragged stacks of old files in many faded colours, poor-quality paper crumbling away—and I knew that I would wait a long time in far-off Africa, and nothing would come. (*Half a Life*, p. 158)

He suffers long as an easy victim to unpredictable circumstances but after having spent eighteen years in Africa, he comes to realize that at forty-one, it's high time he stopped fooling himself. Feeling lost in Africa, Willie, at forty one, once again admits, "I have been hiding from myself. I have risked nothing. And now the best part of my life is over" (*Half a Life*, p. 140). Willie's state of exile reminds one of Said's pointed observations:

> Exile is strangely compelling to think about but terrible to experience. It is the unbearable rift forced between a human being and a native place, between the self and its true home: its essential sadness can never be surmounted. And while it is true that literature and history contain heroic, romantic, glorious, even triumphant episodes in an exile's life, these are no more than efforts meant to overcome the crippling sorrow of estrangement. The achievements of exile are permanently undermined by the loss of something left behind forever.[22]

As Willie grows away from Ana, he attempts to find freedom in squalid sexual encounters with African prostitutes. His sexual encounters with Graca remind the reader of Salim-Yvette relationship in *A Bend in the River* as Willie owes Graca his assertion of manhood when he admits: "I had died without knowing this depth of satisfaction, this other person that I had just discovered within myself. It was worth any price, any consequence" (*Half a Life*, p. 204). He doesn't hesitate to reveal his relationship with Graca before Ana, his wife. His instability can be correlated to his shifting loyalty from Ana to Graca. When he finally leaves Ana, it is with the full realization that his life with her has been merely another sort of protected half-life. He wants to emerge out of the shadow of the image of "Ana's London man" which has been thrust upon him without his knowledge. He is resolved that there are not going to be any more slips for him. Resolutely he tells Ana: "I mean I've given you eighteen years. I can't give you any more. I can't live your life any more. I want to live my own" (*Half a Life*, p. 136). Ana is sailing in the same boat and she too shares the agony felt by him. She has herself been leading a borrowed life. She tells Willie: "Perhaps, it wasn't really my life either" (*Half a Life*, p. 128). Here again Willie makes a radical cut when still only just over the age of forty, he gives up his life with Ana and goes to Germany, where his sister, Sarojini is living. When the book ends, there might be hope for Willie Chandran. But that is not Naipaul's concern: his focus is on the past, and on what Willie turns to be. Willie Chandran seems something of a lesser Naipaul here.

Half a Life being a depressing work, the predominant theme of the novel is rootlessness. It ruthlessly depicts how human beings continue to live with a feeling of displacement, insecurity, and disorientation due to a social environment, which is half-developed and half-eradicated. These are the leitmotifs that carry through the characters of *Miguel Street*, *A House for Mr Biswas*, *The Mystic Masseur*, and *Half a Life*. Willie's escape to England to get out of the situation never helps him. Despite his marriage to Ana and flight to Portuguese Africa, he fails to strike roots there and after eighteen years' stay, leaves that country telling Ann, "I am forty-one, I am tired of living your life" (*Half a Life*, p. 227). For Willie, as for Said: "Exile is never the state of being satisfied, placid, or secure ... exile is the life led outside habitual order. It is nomadic, decentred, contrapuntal; but no sooner does one get accustomed to it than its unsettling force erupts anew."[23]

Being contemplative, on the last page of the book, as he talks to Ana he evokes his memorial burden and recognizes his wastefulness when he says: " ... pain that had been with me for months, and perhaps for years ... now the best part of my life has gone, and I've done nothing" (*Half a Life*, p. 211). In this way, William Somerset Chandran ends his half a life by admitting his suffering caused by the burden of his memorial past and by his myth of origin. Amit Chaudhary rightly observes:

> This short novel, then, captures in miniature the exceptional trajectory of Naipaul's oeuvre; the figure of the father, the life of the writer, and, finally, an enquiry into the origins of the colonial landscape itself ... . *Half a Life* is not one of Naipaul's major undertakings, but I don't think it was meant to be. It is intended

> to give us yet another perspective on his corpus, in which one detail illuminates another.[24]

Naipaul sharply dissects the difficulties of cultural displacement within his novels. Most of his works deal with the portrayal of *ambivalence* among the third world denizens and its varied effects on the common man. His allegiance is to the real, to real history as borne by real people. Willie Chandran is used here as a medium for representative vignettes of colonial life. Nevertheless one is left at the end of *Half a Life* with the feeling that not only Willie Chandran but Naipaul himself does not know what will happen next. The Michigan Daily reported that with:

> In *Half a Life*, V.S. Naipaul has succeeded in furthering society"s consciousness of race, identity and failure. Willie Chandran is not a particularly interesting character, but he is endearing and arguably universal. In a way, his discoveries are our own. And perhaps, like he, we all waste half our lives searching for the intangible.[25]

In *Half a Life,* Willie is preoccupied with various dislocations, migrations, exile, the idea of being unanchored and displaced, the enigma of a decentred and disorientating experience in the explosive and disconcerting realities of half-London, half-Portuguese and half-and-half world with their different linguistic, cultural ecologies, sociological hues and nostalgia. Willie tries to run away from his background but he is reminded of his origins that always remain with him as he can not severe his links with his past. Sarojini proves instrumental for Willie to strike a chord with his cultural tradition, caste and class. Being confused in the postcolonial social matrix of Trinidad, India, Portuguese province of Africa and London Willie, according to Dom Moraes: "... is trying to say that to live in post-colonial countries addles people's mind. This is possible, but it is not a great discovery. And if, as the title suggests Naipaul is saying that most people, in the true sense, only lead a half-life, it is a statement of the obvious."[26]

Nevertheless one is left at the end of *Half a Life* with the feeling that Willie Chandran echoes Naipaul's personal enigma of arrival which he experiences wherever he goes. Willie's life is by no means over, nor does his own narrative provide a closure to his story of Africa. It simply ends without reference to the previous story of Berlin. The displacement of the novel's characters forms the tension in the story. There are the exiles like Percy Cato, Marcus and Ana who appear to have no proper place in the world Willie meets in London. They mirror Willie's own sense of being on the margins of life, homeless and directionless.

> *Half a Life* ... portrays and evaluates the lives of the peoples of mixed descent in three countries—India, England and Portuguese Africa (modeled on Mozambique) and their struggle to discover their identities. Partly autobiographical, the novel delineates the traumas of a tainted and troubled past, of attempting to find some meaning and purpose of life. A major theme running through the novel and supported by its structure is that of 'exiles living a half-life.'[27]

The very theme and the setting of the narrative are likely to raise issues such as Naipaul's attitude to the colonial power and the colonized people, multiculturalism, colonial politics, postcolonial ambivalence, identity crisis, etc., which are equally relevant to Naipaul's previous writings. There is a constant evaluation of India and the Indians in Naipaul's works. *Half a Life*, too, defines his relationship with India in a unique way. In this novel Naipaul deconstructs the myth of Indian spirituality.

Willie comes close to the figure of the postcolonial migrant intellectual signifying a universal condition of hybridity. Homi Bhabha's views on the migrant experience as a postcolonial metropolitan *assimilation* may be recalled in this context: "The space of the translation of cultural difference at the interstices is infused with that temporality of the present which makes graphic a moment of transition, not merely the continuum of history."[28] The existential suffering of the exile that Willie has to undergo in the multiracial society of the Portuguese Africa prepares him to assert his individuality. He describes his experience when his desire is fulfilled: "Graca's need matched my own .... I thought how terrible it would have been if, as could so easily have happened, I had died without knowing this depth of satisfaction, this other person that I had just discovered within myself. It was worth my price, any consequence" (*Half a Life*, p. 205). Naipaul finds a pretence and negation of life in such casual relationships. He has all along striven for self-awareness and this striving of half a life is recorded in the novel. The task of a historian and an anthropologist is once again incorporated into the task of a novelist. Just like his creator, "Willie runs away from his background, and even when he gets to Africa, this Portuguese province, he is reminded of the background from which he came."[29] Paul Theroux comments on V.S. Naipaul's movements: "He is a tireless but reluctant traveller, like an unsponsored explorer without a compass in his work as in his life—for his characters share his homelessness."[30]

Praised for his creative use of autobiography in his travel narratives and for converting autobiographical material into poignant fiction, Naipaul's protagonists emerge from different social classes.

They are linked to each other and to their progenitor by an impulse to pursue the truth about themselves and their world. In its Nobel citation to Naipaul Swedish Academy rightly remarks:

> He is to a very high degree a cosmopolitan writer, a fact that he himself considers to stem from his lack of roots; he is unhappy about the cultural and spiritual poverty, of Trinidad, he feels alienated from India, and in England he is incapable of relating to and identifying with the traditional values of what was once a colonial power.[31]

The novel is the essence of all that Naipaul is known for—the unaccepted people longing to belong. In the novelist's own words, he has "tried to make it easy, and light, and a small book, and yet full of things."[32] According to Farrukh Dhondy: "… it's a very powerful work of the imagination. It takes us through three different settings, and three different eras, and we meet people in different ways. We follow its central character Willie, from pre-independence India, to post-war London, to a Portuguese province in Africa".[33]

Naipaul's novels express the *ambivalence* of the exile, a feature of his own experience as an Indian in the West Indies, a West Indian in England, and a nomadic intellectual in a postcolonial world. The pivotal themes in Naipaul's works stem from the damaging effects of imperialism upon the people of the Third World, exemplified in cultural alienation and illusory freedom. "*Half a Life* takes its name from the overarching concern of the book: characters caught in a cusp of history, ambition and love; characters who live at half throttle and without complete self-knowledge."[34] As a writer he has been compared to Joseph Conrad because of similar pessimistic portrayal of human nature and the themes of exile and alienation. He is popular for his searing, unforgiving and controversial portraits of formerly colonized societies struggling towards self-realization in the world torn in certain dichotomies. The novel *Half a Life* aims at making people understand that the expatriates are bound to live only fractions of life. Edward W. Said accepts Naipaul as: "… too remarkable and gifted writer to be dismissed. So great has the pressure of western ideas become in Naipaul that any sympathetic feelings he might have had for the things he sees have been obliterated. There is no life in what he writes about—only hard lunacy, despair."[35]

As the story of Willie Somerset Chandran's first forty years is narrated in *Half a Life*, *Magic Seeds* continues the story of Willie Chandran. It picks up where *Half a Life* left off, Willie living with his sister in Berlin. *Magic Seeds* is the most recent novel by V.S. Naipaul and it does not present the wholeness of life; rather, it continues to focus the halfness of Willie's life. Saddened with the cold response of the readers, Naipaul announced at a speech in New Delhi in 2004: "I have no faith in the survival of the novel. It is almost over. The world has changed and people do not have the time to give that a book requires."[36] Moreover, Naipaul does not see the book particularly as a sequel because it is based upon quite a separate idea. Anne Sheridan comments on Naipaul's oeuvre:

> Naipaul's India is abstract and his London sketchy, but his Mozambique is convincingly realized. Mozambique of colonial times produced no writers of stature. The country's best writer, Mia Couto belongs to the post-independence generation, and is anyhow too much under the sway of magic realism to be a reliable chronicler. Thus Naipaul would seem to be free to invent a fantasy antebellum Mozambique of his own. His allegiance is to the real, to real history as borne by real people; the second part of *Half a Life* has a strongly journalistic flavor, with Willie Chandran used as medium for representative vignettes of colonial life.[37]

The genesis of the first half of *Magic Seeds* may be traced in his visit to India where he meets some middle-class vain and foolish people who have been involved in this guerrilla business. He finds no revolutionary grandeur in their movement. The reference is to the Bengali Communists that he interviews for *India: A Million Mutinies Now* (1990). These two men, a science professor and a company executive, go from Calcutta to the villages of Bengal as part of the Naxalite movement: a Maoist peasant rebellion that has started in 1967 and spread across India, feeding off the discontents and earlier rebellions of the poorer, lower castes. Their story follows the trajectory of much of Naipaul's political writing: the movement goes from a raw, humiliated concern with the poor and India, to cultural and economic suicide, new compulsions and violations, and a cause far removed from the peasant's hunger. Soon the party line sanctions individual killing of class enemies; generally, the easy targets were lone policemen, the smaller landlords who don't have much protection. In an interview Naipaul makes his perception regarding *Magic Seeds* clear:

> I don't feel I can speak with authority for many other people ... one gets so tired here, in London and elsewhere, of meeting people from the subcontinent who've completely remade themselves, who've manufactured stories for themselves to keep their end up. It's like a national illness actually ... India will not have full mental health ... unless people truly possess their history.[38]

Magic Seeds is the despairingly comic story of Willie Chandran who responds to the angst of his own dislocation by trying to find "his war". Now he returns to India and joins up with a Maoist revolutionary group, lives in the jungle, wondering all the while he loiters there. Nomadic Willie Chandran reverses his direction back to the land he escaped in his childhood to join a guerilla group in India after being motivated by his sister, Sarojini. She always nags and persuades Willie to do something and join the revolution in India as a Maoist guerrilla. On the advice of his sister, he joins the movement headed by Kandapalli. Reaching India, he locates Joseph, an educated revolutionary with a degree from an English university, who sends him to a kind of commune, where he's introduced to others who pack him off to a camp in the forest. Finding himself among the unorganized rebels, Willie feels disappointed. The narrator projects his agony: "... Willie cried, tears of rage, tears of fear, and ... filled him with grief for the whole world."[39] However, later he finds himself trapped by joining the wrong guerrillas. It is too late for him to react, so he decides to remain silent and goes with their struggle and action. Willie becomes the movement's courier, living in the forest with the movement's poor camp, doing the movement's pointless struggle—liberating villages, terrifying the landlord and bourgeois.

It is a novel that revisits the themes—*ambivalence* among émigrés, identity, and the precariousness of civilization—that the novelist has been tackling with over the past five decades. The title refers both to the futile revolution run by the revolutionaries with whom Willie associates himself in India and, perhaps, to the seed that will produce, through miscegenation, a raceless society. Like so many of Naipaul's protagonists including Ganesh, Mohun Biswas, Ralph Singh and Jimmy, Willie is a writer. As a student, he writes stories and fables in his exercise book that portray, in symbolic form, the appalling history of his family: his father's unenthusiastic marriage to a low-caste woman and the births of his father's two unwanted children, Willie and his sister, Sarojini. Disillusioned with the disgraceful life of India, Willie escapes to London. Naipaul himself analyses the Indian concept of illusion at the end of *An Area of Darkness* where he philosophizes:

> The world is illusion, the Hindus say. We talk of despair, but true despair lies too deep for formulations. It was only now, as my experience of India defined itself more properly against my own homelessness, that I saw how close in the past year I had been to the total Indian negation, how much it had become the basis of thought and feeling ... .[40]

Willie never knows exactly what he actually aspires to do. His hard-won sense of purpose collapses. He is unexpectedly released with the help of his English lawyer friend, Roger. The setting changes to London when he forms a series of affairs, realizes the pointlessness of his own life by listening to Roger's story of his relationship with council estate woman Marian. Through the relationship of Roger and Marian emerges the broad issues of racial discrimination and multi-cultural Britain.

Sarojini makes him reconsider himself and his past life and makes him undo his previous depravity. Being motivated by his sister, he experiences a true pride within him, pride to struggle and rejects everything he sees in Berlin. For him, Berlin is the place for people who live for pleasure and terrible simplicity. During his life in Berlin, Sarojini: "had given him the daily mental exercise of thinking himself back into more desperate places of the world he had seen or known" (*Magic Seeds*, p. 24). He joins the movement to prove himself a *doer* only to find out that things are not as ordered as he has expected. Though he sometimes rejoices the settled life in Berlin, Willie seems to have been influenced by Fanon's call:

> Come then, comrades, the European game has finally ended; we must do something different. We today can do everything, so long as we do not imitate Europe, so long as we are not obsessed by the desire to catch up with Europe ... throw us off our balance ... let us try to create the whole man, whom Europe has been incapable of bringing to triumphant birth.[41]

Fanonian call inspires Willie to prove himself a crusader for his native compatriots in India. The repelling cultures and circumstances attract him at the same time. When he sees the Indian passengers on airport, he feels a great distance from them:

> He studied the Indian passengers there-people mostly likely wasn't going to see again after a few hours- more fearfully than he had studied the Tamils and other Indians in Berlin. He saw Indian in everything they wore and did. He was full of his mission, full of the revolution in his soul, and he felt a great distance from them. (*Magic Seeds*, p. 29)

His enterprise simply leads him to prison from where he escapes to England once again. The Indian authorities release him because he is now a postcolonial Indian author and they cannot have him in prison. His sister gets his previous book republished after some time. His circuitous movements establish his identity as a man lost and confused. Perhaps he is very much sure about his destined *halfness*. The opening lines of the novel take the reader back to where Willie has been left in the previous novel:

> It had begun many years before, in Berlin. Another world. He was living there in a temporary, half-and-half way with his sister Sarojini. After Africa it had been a great refreshment, this new kind of protected life, being almost a tourist, without demands and without anxiety … . Willie said, 'I don't see what I can do. I don't know where I can go.' (*Magic Seeds*, p. 2)

His constant ambivalence tortures his psyche to the extent that now he finds himself questioning his decisions: "What could I have done in India? What could have I done in England in 1957 or 1958? Or in Africa? … I was always someone on the outside. I still am. What could I do in Berlin?" (*Magic Seeds*, p. 2). After reaching India, Willie realizes that he is now a different person. He tries to convince himself that India is the world he comes from. During his struggle with the movement, Willie experiences the strangeness of his native land and its people. When he comes closer with people of his nation and ethnicity, he feels he does not know them. He is among strangers and feels alienated:

> He had been away from India too long. He couldn't assess the background of the people around him. He could only try to read faces and physiques: the too full, sensual mouth in some speaking of some kind of sexual perversion, the hard mean eyes in others, the bruised seeming eyes of yet others that spoke of hard or abused childhoods and tormented adult lives. That was as far as he could read. Among these people seeking various ways to revenge themselves on the world, he was among strangers. (*Magic Seeds*, p. 53)

Willie's life seems purposeless after his brief stay in Berlin and his instability irritates his sister. She convinces him to start a magnificent life marked by activity and variety. Sarojini admires an Indian revolutionary named Kandapalli, mysterious ideological fanatic who has come up with a new ideology on the class struggle. For him, "revolution was to come from below, from the village, from the people. There was to be no place in this movement for middle-class masqueraders" (*Magic Seeds*, p. 15). Willie, now in his forties and at loose ends, is an easy mark, ready to be recruited for a cause—any cause which can stabilize his unstable and irregular life. Willie intends to join his guerrilla movement. Naturally, things go wrong from the start, and he actually winds up becoming a member of a different faction. Almost immediately he realizes: "There has been some mistake. I have fallen in among the wrong people. I have come to the wrong revolution …". (*Magic Seeds*, p. 49)

Willie echoes Jimmy in *Guerillas* who talks about the protection of the agrarian rights but Naipaul deftly penetrates deeper to explore the stimulus behind these pseudo-revolutions. Naipaul sees no beauty in the orthodox Marxist Cheddi B. Jagan's rebellion to become Prime Minister of Guyana and in the ideology of Michael X, the black power leader who ends up a murderer in Trinidad. Earlier, these revolutionaries have been ridiculed by the novelist in the novel *Guerrillas*. The novelist seems to believe that the revolutionaries like Jimmy and Willie propagate their vision of the land, the dignity of labour and egalitarian society but only at the cost of innocent human lives. Naipaul seems to discredit their make-belief, the falsified progressive ideology that conceals their will to power. For these pseudo-revolutionaries, joining the revolution is an adventure. Rather, it seems that their futility further humiliates and enrages the novelist.

Willie represents the nomads who live in a world of flux which never allows them to stay permanently at one point. While in Berlin, Sarojini reminds Willie of the essential instability of their lives when she says:

> You have been here for six months … you may not be able to stay here. That is the way the world is made. You can't object to it. You've got to start thinking of moving on. Do you have any idea of where you can go? Is there anything you feel you want to do?" (*Magic Seeds*, p. 1)

The metaphors of *packing* and *unpacking* are prominent and catchy in the novel. The aimless guerillas like Willie commit unremitting mistakes and inadvertently repeat them until they are reduced to nothing. Willie is well aware of the vulnerability of his London associations; he is never duped by the callousness of Mozambique; he reaches Berlin only for a passing relief, and he never regrets leaving any place—native or alien. Bhagabat Nayak rightly adds about the cosmopolitan outlook of Naipaul:

> His writing has often been seen in the Third World as caustic and personal, but it takes his readers into the farthest reaches of the third-world—Africa, the Caribbean, Asia and the Central Asia and all the way to South Africa, to test one or both his obsessions what it means to become and finally to be a writer; what happens to post-colonial societies when the imperial power recedes, leaving cruelty and chaos to fill the breach.[42]

Chandran has been migrated from India to England to southern Africa, mostly in search of a free sex life. The sex scenes in the novel are as dreary as these have been in *Guerrillas*, where Jimmy and Jane make love submerged with anger and constitute an ambivalence that renders the sexual intercourse traumatic. He is never mistaken about his insubstantial existence but his urge for wish-fulfillment propels him towards different destinations. Naipaul condemns the misguided figures like Willie when he says: "It's a calamity, it's a great period of boredom and nothing happening and life being eaten away and mind being eaten away. And probably people like Willy are always in that position because they have no idea of history—very few Indians have an idea of history, the history of India."[43] When asked by Ramchandra as to why he has deserted his wife, he himself gives an account of certain accidents which he meets in life: "I began to feel that because of my insecurity—the insecurity I had been born into, like you—I had yielded too often to accidents, and that these accidents had taken me further and further away from myself". (*Magic Seeds*, p. 115)

The guerilla revolutionaries pose as if they are fighting for a noble cause but they are devoid of any purpose in their lives. The ideology they fight for is the usually confused and blurred philosophy of many a revolutionary movement across the world. Their propaganda gets exposed through the comments of the narrator:

> There was to be a renewed emphasis on the old idea of liquidating the class enemy. Since the feudal people had long ago run away, and there was strictly speaking no class enemy left in these villages, the people to be liquidated were the better off .... Willie ... became disorientated. He remembered the time when it consoled him, gave him a hold on things, to count the beds he had slept in. Such a hold was no longer possible for him. He wished now passionately only to save himself, to get in touch with himself again .... (*Magic Seeds*, p. 143)

By the time Willie becomes a guerrilla—roughly at the end of the 1970s—the disintegration has set in long ago. He goes with the intention of joining Kandapalli (probably a reference to Kondapalli Seetaramaiah, founder of the People's War Group, in the forests of Andhra Pradesh). Eventually, after a meandering recruitment process, he arrives at the rebel training camp in a teak forest where he realizes that he has fallen among the wrong people pursuing the wrong revolution. These people are dropouts from the towns and cities, playing as guerrillas, and playing at killing. This is soon confirmed by a letter from Sarojini. She accepts that there has been a mistake: "The movement, as you know, has split, and what has happened is that you are among psychopaths ... The comfort is that you are all serving the same cause in the end, and the time may come one day when you may be able to cross over and join Kandapalli's people" (*Magic Seeds*, p. 63). Willie spends seven years among these psychopaths. He lives a boring, occasionally violent and, above all, pointless and purposeless life. The guerrillas haunt the forests, railway towns, and filthy tanneries, recruiting, carrying messages or arms, or waiting for orders that never come. They push deeper into the forest to extend the liberated areas, to occupy and re-educate. They fail as the peasants do not want to be liberated. These people are desperately poor, *half-tribals*, *matchstick people*, and *tanners*—their bodies flimsy and their minds hollow after centuries of slavery, abuse and bad food.

The revolutionaries are frustrated with the revolution and the opposition of people for whom they volunteer. Frantz Fanon is justified when he remarks:

> The peasant who goes on scratching out a living from the soil … do not manage … to convince themselves that anything has really changed in their lives … the masses have no illusions. They are hungry … they turn away from this nation in which they have been given no place and begin to lose interest in it.[44]

At their many meetings, the guerilla leaders debate their lack of progress, and complain about the poor human material they have to work with. The guerillas devote their maximum time to make people understand their objective which is so hazy that it hardly ever appeals to the proletariat class. When they are utterly disappointed, a guerrilla suggests that the peasants will begin to understand the revolution only when they start killing them. But, that leader, according to Fanon, is unaware of the suggestion that "no leader, however valuable he may be, can substitute himself for the popular will … and … a prospect that is human because conscious and sovereign men dwell therein."[45]

Willie is not oblivious of his position among the guerillas and he is well informed that he is with the wrong crowd, but being directionless, he sticks with them for some seven years, beguiling not only himself but his comrades also. His latest escape repeats the story of his multiple failures across many countries so far. His constant flights are marked by the ambivalence and uncertainty. His confession of his disappointments makes his guerilla companions feel good as they start establishing a sound rapport with him owing to the oneness of their past. He shares his predicament of losing his wife Ana with Ramchandra:

> … because of the insecurity I had been born into … I had yielded too often to accidents, and that these accidents had taken me further and further away from myself … I was leaving her [Ana] because I was tired of living her life … she said it wasn't really her life … her life was as much a series of accidents as I thought mine was. (*Magic Seeds*, p. 115)

The gang of leaders includes numerous frustrated fellows like Joseph, Bhoj Narain, Einstein and Ramachandra who have joined the movement just to attain their position as *doers*. Largely following Willie's experience, Naipaul also offers others' stories, suggesting circumstances that lead to such fates and the senseless wastage of life caused by this activity. The great detachment that he feels clearly emphasises his ambivalence. He is preoccupied with the success of his new mission yet he finds himself poles apart from them. His vision and perspective have already changed due to his exposure to the western life in London. While observing a woman mopping the floor, he finds himself a transformed person and confesses:

> Twenty years ago I wouldn't have seen what I am seeing now. I am seeing what I see because I have made myself another person. I cannot make myself that old person again. But I must go back to that old way of seeing. Otherwise my cause is lost before I have begun. I have come from the world of waste and appearances. (*Magic Seeds*, p. 30)

Willie, and many of his comrades, remain outsiders; hardly ever feeling safe in the protective and vulnerable network that makes up the movement. Their personal whims and inhibitions drive them to join the movement. The activists come from all sorts of backgrounds. Many of them are, like Willie, lost souls, unable to find a hold in the real world.

There are clashes and mixings of cultures, and value systems resulting into the phenomena of acceptance and rejection. According to Ashcroft, ambivalence is "a term first developed in psychoanalysis to describe a continual fluctuation between wanting one thing and wanting its opposite. It also refers to a simultaneous attraction toward and repulsion from an object, person or action."[46] To elaborate the state of in-betweenness and ambivalence, Homi K. Bhabha "describes the complex mix of attraction and repulsion that characterizes the relationship between colonizer and colonized."[47] Willie's westernized personality dissuades him from getting mixed with Africans also. He admits: "I always had sympathy for Africans, but I saw them from the outside. I never really found out about them. Most of the time I saw Africa from the eyes of the colonists" (*Magic Seeds*, p. 38). Mimicry being the obvious outcome of expatriation, Willie's stay in London makes him experience mimicry, consciously or unconsciously. It is in this context that Homi Bhabha suggests that the colonial *mimicry* "is the desire for a reformed, recognizable Other, as a subject of difference that is almost the same, but not quite … the discourse of mimicry is constructed around an ambivalence … mimicry is, thus the sign of a double articulation".[48] When asked by Willie as how Ramachandra has turned a guerilla, the story of the factors shaping Ramchandra as a guerilla is the tale of suffering owing to a person's mimicking tendency. As it has already been observed, concealing the personal identity and name are the common tactics adopted by a dejected colonial in the novels of Naipaul. Keeping in consonance with this firmly engaging pattern of Naipaul's work when Ramchandra's story unfolds, one discovers that in his college, he respects a professor and wants to offer him dinner. But to hide his poverty and wretchedness, he leaves his teacher at some rich stranger's house. When his teacher asks him: "Why did you kidnap me last night and take me to those people … I didn't know who they were, and they didn't know anything about me" (*Magic Seeds,* p. 122), Ramachandra justifies himself saying: "I am a poor man sir. I can't give someone like you dinner, and I wanted only the best for you … I was full of shame" (*Magic Seeds,* p. 122). What humiliates the student is not the shame he feels for his poverty but the reply of his teacher: "But, Ramachandara, my background is like yours. My family were just as poor as you" (*Magic Seeds,* p. 122). The admittance of his real past by the teacher humiliates him all the more. He reacts: "… I was full of shame. I hated myself. I wanted to wipe out everyone who witnessed my shame. I felt I couldn't live in the world unless those people were dead. Unless my professor was dead. I have almost forgotten what they looked like, but that shame and anger is still with me" (*Magic Seeds,* p. 122). Similarly, Willie, the *mimic*, is at his best when he stops in the great shopping avenues with a masterly understanding of western dressing sense. The narrator finds him altogether changed when he says: "Willie stopped in front of the Patrick Hellman shop to look at the Armani clothes in the window. Twenty years before he had known nothing about clothes, he had no eye for cloth or cut; now it was different" (*Magic Seeds,* p. 15). Similarly Willie reads Hemingway, Kipling and Blake only to find himself "very far away" (*Magic Seeds,* p. 22) from him. This state of *ambivalence* is evident not only in Willie but also in other characters like Roger, Marcus, Ramchandra, Einstein and even Sarojini. Naipaul presents them as anything but heroes, or people who clearly know what is right; instead, they are all damaged souls, ill at ease in the contemporary world and incapable of playing a meaningful role in it. Naipaul's analysis of the pointlessness sounds valid, even if the justifications and explanations he offers are, erroneous. He finds his revolutionaries deluded and self-absorbed. Willie helplessly responds to Ramachandra's mimicry through his explanation: "Little things drive people more than we sometimes imagine. I have so many causes of shame. In India, London, and Africa. They are fresh after twenty years. I don't think they will ever die. They will die only with me" (*Magic Seeds,* p. 123). Their willingness to offer themselves to the Movement is symbolic of their desperation. While narrating the futility of the revolution and the revolutionaries in the colonial setting, Naipaul becomes so sentimentally obsessed, ruthless and crude that the critics like Alok Rai are compelled to observe the unpleasant twist of Naipaul:

> ... there is something sad about the fact that someone who is, beyond doubt, a major literary figure of our times—someone whose honesty and courage has been enabling and formative for so many—should be exiting with such a weak book. It is also the case that even the failures of someone as engaged ... as Naipaul are worth attending do.[49]

The revolution in *Magic Seeds* isn't the world's most imposing revolution; rather, it's simply a typical organization with rotten, unsure, dented and detrimental agenda. In *Guerillas,* Jimmy's commune is located in a Caribbean rural locale with the slogan—"FOR THE LAND AND THE REVOLUTION."[50] In the same way, the revolutionary group in India has the ability to establish hold over villages, in the area they are active. There is nothing challenging there as their area of command is too far from cities or even real towns, that the government fails to establish any easy control. The guerrillas may have some success, but it is limited, with little hope for change. Willie's reaction on the death of his comrade Ramachandra is revelatory of the destined futility of such hollow rebellions. He thinks: "Now I am truly lost. In every way. I don't know what lies ahead or behind. My only cause now is to survive, to get out of this". (*Magic Seeds,* p. 125)

The deep-rooted duality of these so-called revolutionaries comes to the fore when Keso intends to murder the villagers merely to force them to serve the revolution around them. He suggests: "We would have achieved a lot more if we had killed a few of these people whenever we liberated a village. We would also have been safer now" (*Magic Seeds,* p. 127). Their success is measured not in actual accomplishment but in the destructive tit-for-tat with the authorities: "Murders of class enemies—which now meant only peasants with a little too much land—were required now, to balance the successes of the police" (*Magic Seeds,* p. 143). Much of the time Willie is simply a courier and his is an exceptionally monotonous and aimlessness life, but he deliberately endeavours to search for a purpose so that he may convince himself about the worth of his association with a lost and archaic movement and to develop his ability to look at home everywhere. Willie, being an Indian native with western education and life, feels that he needs to struggle for his nation. He knows that his opinion of the nation is different from the graceful people with simplified life in London, Berlin and Africa. They live for pleasure and he feels joy when he rejects them in everything he sees when he is walking in Berlin. Nevertheless, he is excited about the movement that he is about to join. His eagerness to join the movement is vividly portrayed by the narrator: "For the first time in his life he began to experience a kind of true pride. He felt himself, so to speak, taking up space when he walked in the streets; and he wondered whether this was how other people felt all the time, without effort, all the secure people he had met in London and Africa" (*Magic Seeds,* p. 24). He experiences a love-hate relationship towards India. Willie Chandran's ambivalence is caused by two opposite attractions in his life, i.e., his life in the colonizer country and his English education makes him experience mimicry in his life. His life is marked by mimicry in order to accommodate himself in the Western society. On the other hand, Willie asserts his nationalism by undertaking the tough task to transform the lives of the peasants. Willie wants one thing while seeking the opposite as well. At the airport of the unnamed Indian city, "... the black-bladed ceiling fans were busy; the metal rods or shanks that fixed them to the ceiling were furry with oil and sifted dust" (*Magic Seeds,* p. 27). In his hotel, Willie notes the impact of globalization in hotel marketing clichés: "A room service menu standing upright on the small table promised food around the clock, with dishes 'from our baker's basket' and 'from the fisherman's net' and 'from the butcher's block'"(*Magic Seeds,* p. 32). Thinking back wistfully to his childhood, Willie contemplates with pain that there is no true place in the world for him to retrieve his lost identity.

Though Naipaul has earlier deplored Gandhi's vision of a nonviolent revolution as a fairy tale, reducing people to their functions and simplified characteristics—in other words—totalitarian, *Magic Seeds* presents Gandhian autobiography as a great source of strength for Willie. After reading the autobiography of Mahatma Gandhi, he makes up his mind to struggle for his poor native fellows and feels regretful. In *Magic Seeds* Willie reads Gandhi's autobiography, *The Story of My Experiments with Truth*, and finds it a healing book. Gandhi's example imbues him with a kind of true pride. He says:

> I wish this healing book had come my way twenty-five years ago. I might have become another man. I would have aimed another

> life. I wouldn't have lived that shabby life in Africa among strangers. I would have felt that I wasn't alone in the world, that a great man had been there before me. Instead, I was reading Hemingway, who was very far away from me, who had nothing to offer me, and doing my bogus stories. What darkness, what self deception, what waste. (*Magic Seeds*, p. 22)

But, somehow, he wishes to reconcile his twin identities. Sometimes, he poses as the representative of Western outlook, but very soon he holds back. His *ambivalence* signifies a complex relationship between the colonizer and the colonized since "the colonized subject is never simply and completely opposed to the colonizer".[51] Willie's ambivalence comes to surface when he often misses his western life and its comforts while fighting for the cause of proletariat class in India: "I thought the two worlds, and I had a very good idea of the world which I belonged. But, now, really, I wish I could go back a few hours and stand outside the Patrick Hellman shop in Berlin, or go to the oyster and champagne at the bar in the KDW". (*Magic Seeds,* p. 29)

Naipaul can sense the hollowness behind the movement but it gives him an opportunity to depict the perverted revolutionary idealism and zeal convincingly. He highlights the insurgency and the consequent violence, and those affected by it—activists and villagers alike—extraordinarily well. Characterized by fear and boredom, it turns out to be a precarious struggle, rather than an exciting adventure for Willie. Like all revolutions, this one is fuelled by illusory hopes. They are in the state of indecision and find themselves helpless to correlate their past with present. Theirs is a myopic vision. Willie questions the guerilla ideology—"They all want the old ways to go. But the old ways are part of people's being. If the old ways go people will not know who they are, and these villages, which have their own beauty, will become a jungle" (*Magic Seeds,* p. 120). In a BBC interview with Harriet Gilbert, V.S. Naipaul condemns the so-called guerillas and guerilla movements:

> They (guerrilla groups in India) believe revolution is the answer. They have no idea what would follow revolution, and in fact where they liberate these areas they become centres of tyranny. They blow up the bridges, they cut the telephone wires to the world outside. So the peasants who should have been liberated are really imprisoned as in the old feudal days. It is an intellectual folly these guerrilla movements, they have nothing to offer.[52]

Ultimately Willie and Einstein surrender their arms themselves to the police. Willie takes it lightly as, according to the narrator, he, "confused the idea of surrender with amnesty. He has thought that after surrender before the police, he will be released" (*Magic Seeds*, p. 152). He is slightly disappointed to find himself sentenced to ten years in jail. Here again, Sarojini's resourcefulness helps him get relief out of this mess as well. As luck would have it, his freedom from Indian jail takes him back to permanent exile in England. However, his seven years with the movement proved his nationalism. When Bhoj Narayan asks him why he has joined the movement, Willie answers, "I suppose it's the story of my life. I suppose it's the way the world is made" (*Magic Seeds*, p. 61). He knows where he comes from but he still holds it. Willie realizes the co-existence of the two worlds, the East and the West, and his own ambivalent position between the two. The narrator adds:

> The two worlds coexisted. It was foolish to pretend otherwise. He was clear in his own mind now to which world he belonged. It had seemed natural to him twenty and more years ago, at home, to want to hide. Now all that had followed from that wish seemed to him shameful. His half-life in London; all his life in Africa, that life when he was permanently in semi-hiding, gauging his success by the fact … his second-class, semi-Portuguese group he didn't particularly stand out and was "passing"; all that life seemed shameful. (*Magic Seeds*, p. 14)

After his release, he moves along his old friend, Roger and adds to the depth of his disorder when he simply accepts what comes his way without any consequential effort to shape his life. He finds his existence in England more precarious as he sees no beauty in the land he has deserted thirty years back. Now he comes to the realization that he doesn't like going about the routine life of London any more:

> Time lay heavily on his hands, and there was little he found he wanted to do. He had seen enough of London. His new way of looking no longer offered surprises. It no longer excited him to see the London of his past. To see it too often was to strip it of memories, and in this way to lose precious pieces of himself. (*Magic Seeds*, p. 197)

He shares his ambivalent state of mind with Sarojini when he writes: "I am a man rescued and physically free and sound in mind and limb I am also a man serving an endless prison sentence. I don't have the philosophy to cope" (*Magic Seeds*, p. 49). Willie is yet again displaced and lives a marginal life—removed from reality in all senses. But Naipaul sees this ambivalence as the most common characteristic among all the colonials—rich or poor, natives or expatriates, and colonizers and the colonized alike. Roger rightly points out:

> The common people are as confused and uncertain as everybody else. They are actors, like everybody else. Their accents are changing. They try to be like people in the television soaps, and now they've lost touch with what they really might be … . Women had no real idea of the little unconsidered things that make them attractive, and I suppose the same is true about what women like in men. (*Magic Seeds*, p. 247)

Naipaul's focus here is to underline the burning postcolonial issue, that is, everyone is at sea irrespective of varying roles they perform. Naipaul has been observed as very harsh and straightforward in his treatment of the postcolonial issues especially those related to the emotional turmoil and instability experienced by the immigrants. Theo Tait observes:

> *Magic Seeds* confirms the forbidding drift of Naipaul's talent: since *A House for Mr Biswas*, doomed to be more admired than loved, and since *A Bend in the River*, probably more respected than read. As Thackeray said of Swift, Naipaul leaves the reader with conflicting desires: wanting both to damn him—'filthy in word, filthy in thought, furious, raging, obscene'—for having, as it were, given up on being human; but also to acknowledge a gloomy genius: 'So great a man he seems to me, that thinking of him is like thinking of an empire falling.'[53]

Roger plays as the mouthpiece of the novelist when he constantly tries to define and explain the changed world around him. At the end of the novel, Willie goes with a friend to a wedding, a mixed-race celebration that conveys to Willie not only celebration but also the true look of a world in which traditional lines of division, of social expectation, have been erased and redrawn so much as to be no longer useful. Roger offers his vivid explanation of the transformed Londoners and expatriates like Willie and Marcus on the occasion of Lyndhurst's marriage with a white girl. Naipaul's view of Marcus is cynical. Naipaul is suggestive of the fact that the racial and ethnic fate of a person is pre-determined; one cannot escape who one is, and must learn to live with his destined identities whether he likes them or not. It's not a consoling vision; neither is it despairing. He comments:

> They're confused. They're not too well educated. That was the smart thing at one time. But now they don't know who they are and what's expected of them. The world has changed much too quickly for them. Perhaps they don't feel a great deal about anything, and have been confused for the last hundred years. (*Magic Seeds*, p. 291)

The perplexed modern world and its more baffled inhabitants are deviously presented by Naipaul. It is not an amusing picture, but it sounds awfully true. Naipaul feels that lack of a guiding principle is the root of the problem. Roger refers to a laborious writer who lives penniless and dies unnoticed and unrecognized. But Roger is sorry to react that he "could see this writer's predicament very clearly. But I couldn't see my own" (*Magic Seeds*, p. 281). Naipaul suggests the panacea for all ills through Willie's ultimate understanding of the present disorder when the penchant for *mimicry* is ridiculed by him:

> My friend here says that the happiest and most successful people are those who have very precise goals, limited and attainable … . Our African friend at an early age … developed one ambition … and this was to have sex only with white women and then one day to have a white grandchild. He has succeeded in both things. His half-English son, Lyndhurst, now a man of about thirty, has had two children by a pure-white aristocratic lady … it is the fashion here, babies before wedding bells. (*Magic Seeds*, pp. 285–86)

A taxi-driver deftly highlights the futility of an attempt to transform the society in which one lives when he asserts: "You can change the houses. You can't change the people" (*Magic Seeds*, p. 276). The guerilla ideology and their ultimate extinction perhaps germinate from Roger's reaction to taxi-driver's comprehensive statement: "Yet, I feel, taking the taxi-driver's point now … our ideas of doing good to other people, regardless of their need, are out of period, a foolish vanity in a charged world … the nicer sides of our civilization, the compassion, the law, may have been used to overthrow that civilization" (*Magic Seeds*, p. 276). By the end of his literary career, Naipaul occupies the image of "a literary colossus".[54] Here he asserts his opinion about the drifted and directionless colonials admitting no reform. The idea of reform repels Willie and he counters positive thoughts when he adds: "I don't wish to cultivate anybody or to be cultivated by them. I had to … survive". (*Magic Seeds*, p. 210)

Though Willie is intermittently drawn to better-world initiatives, he is unable to carry them out with much conviction or enthusiasm. Through his constant struggles and consequent failures, he comes to conclude that: "It is wrong to have an ideal view of the world. That's where the mischief starts. That's where everything starts unraveling" (*Magic Seeds*, p. 294). Ironically his conviction not to cherish an ideal view of the world, fails him. In fact, at the end of the novel Willie seems to be on the verge of doing exactly the opposite of what his well-wishers like Sarojini and Roger maintain as necessary, i.e., turning away from artificial ideals and expectations. Paradoxically, to fulfill the dream of her father, Sarojini has made an *international marriage*, to

Wolf, a radical German documentary-maker. She talks convincingly about Lenin and Mao to encourage him to take up a sadistic revolutionary cause.

Magic Seeds seems to be a somewhat ill-humoured tirade against modernity and what has become of postcolonial civilization across the world. Willie witnesses the disastrous transformations in India where he fears that the churning of the castes is a more vital issue than any other agenda to establish democracy in true sense. The incongruity of Indian situation lies in the fact that people here do not know their place and the responsibilities are assigned at random irrespective of capability or aptitude. It will certainly lead the country to calamity. The intellectuals like Willie, Einstein and Joseph are fascinated towards a guerilla movement searching for its own foothold. Moreover, Willie's ambivalence is caused by his mimicry and his nationalism. Meanwhile, he also holds his sense of nationalism through his struggles for his own nation and its people, though purposelessly. Willie laments his constant failures before Sarojini:

> I am coming to the end of my mental resources ... But my mind is letting me down now ... I've thought of our parents and my childhood ... I've thought of London. I've thought of Africa. I've thought of Berlin ... I've thought of my years in the movement. If I were a religious man I would say that I was putting my spiritual life in order. Counting the beds I slept in. (*Magic Seeds*, p. 169)

Naipaul does not ignore the pertinent issues like casteism, factionalism, racialism and their consequences in a postcolonial milieu. Ramachandra narrates the story of a *harijan* boy who ends up as a senior teacher, leaving Ramchandra pursuing a quest for purpose in life. Being well-versed in Indian ways of life, Naipaul presents a lucid account of the lopsided treatment meted out to a *harijan* boy at the house of Ramchandra. He narrates the episode with lamentation and a sense of loss:

> My mother ... refused point blank to wash any cup or glass the boy used. So I washed any glass or cup the boy used. I wonder if the boy knew. You know what happened to him? He was ambitious—my father was right. He is a senior teacher now, that boy, as oily as a paratha and as fat as a barrel. And I am here. (*Magic Seeds*, p. 110)

Similarly, Roger comments harshly on the establishment of ancillary council estates. The class difference, according to him, is noticeable in England also. Roger doubts the extinction of servant class because he sees its existence in some other form. He says:

> The servant class has vanished. No one knows what they have metamorphosed into. One thing we can be sure of is that we have not lost them, that they are still in varying ways with us, in culture and attitudes of dependence. In every town and large village we now have ancillary council estates, clusters of subsidized dwellings meant originally for the poor … . They have a deliberate socialist ugliness, a conscious suppression … . (*Magic Seeds*, p. 250)

Magic Seeds presents the self-indulgent and self-pitying flawed characters who deserve no attraction or appeal. Naipaul's narration is equally unusual as the protagonist and his ever-changing companions are shown in a desolate world, each man cherishing his own ambivalence. Mike Phillips argues: "*Magic Seeds* seems to represent some sort of struggle to reassess and defend his life's work. In the end the enterprise is a failure, largely because the author has nothing new or interesting to offer. There may be many reasons to admire the body of Naipaul's writing. This book is not one of them."[55] Quite often it is a journey back and forth to ascertain the roots somewhere in the world. Naipaul, even more than most novelists, is driven back again and again to his origins. In *Magic Seeds,* the territory he covers is global: India, England, Africa, and the Caribbean. Naipaul has temporarily occupied a *portion of earth* in these territories, and they dig deep in his psyche. In an interview with Rahul Singh he says, "… I was born in Trinidad, I have lived most of my life in England, and India is the land of my ancestors. That says it all. I am not English, not Indian, not Trinidadian. I am my own person".[56] The idea of *Universal Civilisation* came into formulation by his keen understanding of the cultural traditions of India, Caribbean, Western world and of colonialism.

The novel repeats the theme of constant search of a foothold in a marginal world characterized by expatriation, multiculturalism, displacement and colonial ambivalence. Willie's concern about his displacement resembles the predicament of Mohun Biswas. Willie laments:

> I have never slept in a room of my own. Never at home in India, when I was a boy. Never here in London. Never in Africa. I lived in somebody else's house always, and slept in somebody else's bed. In the forest of course there were no rooms, and then the jail was the jail. Will I ever sleep in a room of my own? (*Magic Seeds,* p. 185)

A House for Mr Biswas presents the trauma of Biswas when the narrator exclaims as how terrible it would have been for a man to have lived without one's *portion of the earth*—unconnected and unaccommodated. The same idea of insecurity and dislocation marks the beginning of *A Bend in the River* (1979): "The world is what it is; men who are nothing, who allow themselves to become nothing, have no place in it."[57] In the beginning of *Magic Seeds*, Willie has left Africa and is living in Berlin with his sister Sarojini, "in a temporary, half-and-half way" (*Magic Seeds*, p. 1). His search for a *portion of the earth* in the world starts again as if from a scratch. Finding nothing unusual in *Magic Seeds*, Mike Phillips rightly adds:

> ... *Magic Seeds* seems to represent some sort of struggle to reassess and defend his life's work. In the end the enterprise is a failure, largely because the author has nothing new or interesting to offer. There may be many reasons to admire the body of Naipaul's writing. This book is not one of them.[58]

At the beginning, Naipaul might have appeared in unique occupation of a marginal and peripheral world, but his vision is fixed upon the brutal collision of the cultures, the elaborate paralysis of *areas of darkness* and *wounded civilizations*. Now he has passed beyond India, Trinidad, or Africa to a *universal darkness*. Chinua Achebe comes with the vivid description of this universality which marks the later novels of Naipaul:

> In the nature of things the works of Western writer is automatically informed by universality. It is any others who must strain to achieve it. So's-and-so's work is universal; he has truly arrived! As though universality were some distant bend in the road which you may take if you travel out far enough in the direction of Europe ... if you put adequate distance between yourself and your home.[59]

By the end of his career, Naipaul's work is a creative reflection of the anguished countries and their denizens without seeking after any homeliness. Naipaul constructs an entirely new metaphor for dislocation, fragmentation, ambivalence, rootlessness and the quest for a viable identity because, according to M.S. Nagarajan, he is: "... eternally an outsider—an Indian in the West Indies, a West Indian in England, and as described by many ... a nomadic intellectual in the non-descript Third World".[60] His Indian-Caribbean ancestry, the enigma of a decentred and disoriented experience in the explosive and disconcerting realities of the postcolonial world anywhere and everywhere, and the knotted relationship with his own cultural identity from Indian and his Caribbean and Western identities help him to remain as a kind of literary outsider in the postcolonial realities. He remarks:

> The universal civilization has been a long time in the making ... the extra-ordinary attempt of this civilization to accommodate the rest of the world, and all the currents of that world's thought ... because my movement within this civilization has been from the periphery to the centre, I may have seen or felt certain things more freshly than people to whom those things were everyday.[61]

Willie represents the "anguish of whole countries and people unable to cope."[62] Said feels the pulse of the writer by confirming his universality when he writes: "here was an author who had seen the new politics of half-made societies that seemed doomed to remain half-made."[63]

Through the last two novels, V.S. Naipaul aims at projecting a change in his worldview, gradually expanding the compass with time, travels and consequent experience. While he is very critical towards the native population of Trinidad in his early works, he shows a deeper understanding of cause and effect in his later novels. Naipaul himself observes the change in his later novels as the change "from the comedy of street life to a study of a kind of widespread schizophrenia."[64] For him, simple has become complicated. In *Half a Life* and *Magic Seeds*, he shifts his focus on the various social, financial and religious pressures which make a colonial undertake certain enterprises only to experience absolute failure in the scheme of colonial/postcolonial world. Though his preoccupation is to explore the "suppressed histories"[65] of the world, he goes beyond the colonies to witness the schizophrenia among the colonizers too. Naipaul's journey starts from Trinidad, "a dot on the map of the world",[66] to his navigations across the world. Exploring *the dots*, he manages to spot the bond among them all. His physical travels signify the extension of his inner being. By the time he writes *Magic Seeds*, he has lost the passion and intensity of a typical diaspora writer preoccupied with the portrayal of romantic *mimicry*, nostalgia and mystery hovering round the nomads. Consequently, the last novels are criticized for Naipaul's lack of warmth and empathy for the émigrés. Willie being the mouthpiece of the novelist, advocates the idea not to seek home anywhere, but to feel at home everywhere.

Notes

1. V.S. Naipaul, *Half a Life* (Delhi: Picador, 2001) p. 83. (All the subsequent references for *Half a Life* have been taken from the same edition of the novel, cited hereafter, in the text with the corresponding page number(s) in parenthesis.)

2. "Mimicry", *Merriam-Webster Online*, 3 June 2008.
3. Bill Ashcroft, *Key Concepts in Post-colonial Studies* (London: Routledge, 1998) p. 140.
4. Simon Gikandi, *Writing in Limbo: Modernism and Caribbean Literature* (New York: Cornell UP, 1992) p. 192.
5. Ibid., p. 172.
6. Gordon Rohlehr, "Character and Rebellion in A House for Mr Biswas," *Critical Perspectives on V.S. Naipaul*, ed. Robert D. Hamner (Washington D.C.: Three Continents Press, 1977) p. 84.
7. Parmanand Jha, "Exile, Alienation and Cultural Tradition: V.S. Naipaul's *Half a Life*," *The Indian Journal of English Studies*, Vol. 39, 2001–2002, p. 47.
8. Jessica Lee Thomas, "Naipaul revels in the space between extremes," *Half and Half*, 9 January 2008<http://www.yalereviewofbooks.com/archive/spring02/review16.shtml. html.
9. V.S. Naipaul, "Two Worlds," *Literary Occasions: Essays*, ed. Pankaj Mishra (Delhi: Picador India, 2003) p. 190.
10. V.S. Naipaul, *A Bend in the River* (Delhi: Clarion Books, 1980) p. 187.
11. *Express India*, "V.S. Naipaul Kept a Mistress for Almost 24 Years," 21 March 2008, London, 10 October 2008<http://www.expressindia.com/latest-news/V-S-Naipaul-kept-a-mistress-for-almost-24-years/287179/.
12. Mel Gussow, "V.S. Naipaul in Search of Himself: A Conversation," 24 April 1994. *The New York Times Archives*, 25 August 2006 <http:www.nytimes.com/books/98/06/07/specials/Naipaul/-38k.
13. The Swedish Academy, "The Presentation Speech," *V.S. Naipaul: Critical Essays*, Vol. III, ed. Mohit K. Ray (New Delhi: Atlantic Publishers, 2005) p. xiii.
14. V.S. Naipaul, "Two Worlds," Literary Occasions: Essays, ed. Pankaj Mishra, op. cit., p. 192.
15. Chris Colin, "Half a Life by V.S. Naipaul", 12 June 2001, *Salon.com Books*, 14 April 2008 <http:www.Salon. Com/books/review/2001/12/06/Naipaul/-23k.
16. V.S. Naipaul, "East Indian," *Literary Occasions: Essays* (Delhi: Picador India, 2003) p. 41.
17. V.S. Naipaul, "Two Worlds," *Literary Occasions: Essays*, op. cit., p. 188.
18. Horace Engdahl, "Prose in the Style of Naipaul," 14 December 2001, *The Nobel Prize in Literature*, 5 January 2007 <http:www.tehelka.com/channels/literary/2001dec./14/ir/b 2140/speech/html-22k.

19. V.S. Naipaul, "Prologue to an Autobiography," *Literary Occasions: Essays* (Delhi: Picador India, 2003) p. 73.
20. Paul Theroux, "From the Critics," 3 March 2002, *The Guardian*, 24 October2008<http:www.members.tripod.com/brendajer/gnalid22 – m.html.
21. Amit Chaudhuri, "The World of V.S. Naipaul," *V.S. Naipaul: An Anthology of Recent Criticism*, ed. Purabi Panwar (Delhi: Pencraft International, 2003) p. 190.
22. Edward W. Said, *Reflections on Exile* (London: Granta Books, 2001) p. 173.
23. Ibid., p. 186.
24. Amit Chaudhuri, "Times Literary Supplement," 21 September 2001, *The Times of India*, 12 October 2005.
25. Neal Pais, "Naipaul's *Half a Life* a Prize-winning Exploration of Isolation," 22 February 2002, *Daily Books Editor: The Michigan Daily*, 25 November 2007.
26. Dom Moraes, "*Half a Life*", *The Hindu* (4 November 2001) p. 3.
27. Dr Parmanand Jha, "Exile, Alienation and Cultural Tradition: V.S. Naipaul's *Half a Life*", "Souvenir", *All India English Teachers' Conference* 24–26 January 2002. Department of English, Government Girls P.G. College, Bilaspur, p. 3.
28. Homi K. Bhabha, *The Location of Culture* (London & New York: Routledge, 1994) p. 244.
29. Farrukh Dhondy, "Interview with V.S. Naipaul", 13 August 2001, *Indian Writers Don't Know Why Their Country Is In Such a Mess*, 15 July2008<http://ontology.buffalo.edu/smith//courses01/rrtw/vsnaipaul.htm.
30. Paul Theroux, "V.S. Naipaul", *Modern Fiction Studies*, 30: 3 (Autumn 1984): 450.
31. *The Hindustan Times*, Delhi, 12 October 2001.
32. V.S. Naipaul, "Interview with V.S. Naipaul", 13 August 2001, *Indian Writers Don't Know Why Their Country Is In Such a Mess*, 15 July 2008< edu/smith//courses01/rrtw/vsnaipaul.htm.
33. Ibid.
34. Shoma Chaudhary, "A Fantasy of Nobility", *Tehelka*, 15 March 2007<http://www. tehelka.com/ channels/literary/2001/Oct.12
35. Edward W. Said, "Bitter Dispatches from the Third World," *Reflections on Exile* (UK: Granta Books, 2001) p. 102.
36. Manish, "Naipaul's *Magic Seeds*", 2 June 2008, *NYT Book Reviews*, 6 September 2008, para 4.

37. Anne Sheridan, "Half a Life: V.S. Naipaul," 2001, 4 March 2002, *Culture Vulture*, 5 May 2007<http: culturevulture. net/books/*Half a Life*.html.
38. V.S. Naipaul's Interview with BBC, http://www.bbc.co.uk/ pressoffice/ pressreleases/stories/2004/09september/23/naipaul.shtml.
39. V.S. Naipaul, *Magic Seeds* (Delhi: Picador, 2004) p. 49. (All the subsequent references for *A Bend in the River* have been taken from the same edition of the novel, cited hereafter, in the text with the corresponding page number(s) in parenthesis.)
40. V.S. Naipaul, *An Area of Darkness* (Delhi: Picador, 1964) pp. 266–67.
41. Frantz Fanon, *The Wretched of the Earth* (London: Penguin, 1967) pp. 251–52.
42. Bhagabat Nayak, "Disorientation of Identity in V.S. Naipaul's *Half a Life*," ed. Mohit K. Ray, *V.S. Naipaul: Critical Essays* (Delhi: Atlantic Publishers, 2005) p. 250.
43. V.S. Naipaul, "VS Naipaul talks to BBC World Service about threat to Britain from 'council house culture,'" 23 September 2004, *BBC Press Office*, 25 October 2007<http://www.bbc.co.uk/pressoffice/ pressreleases/ stories/2004/09september/23/ naipaul.shtml.
44. Frantz Fanon, op. cit., p. 136.
45. Ibid., p. 165.
46. Bill Ashcroft, *Key concept in post-colonial studies* (London: Routledge, 1998) p. 12.
47. Ibid., p. 12.
48. Quoted in Julian Wolfreys, ed., *Introducing Literary Theories: A Guide and Glossary* (Delhi: Atlantic Publishers, 2005) p. 214.
49. Alok Rai, "Not much magic", *The Hindu*, Sunday, 24 October 2004.
50. V.S. Naipaul, *Guerillas* (New Delhi: Picador, 2002) p. 4.
51. Bill Ashcroft, op. cit., p. 12.
52. V.S. Naipaul, "VS Naipaul talks to BBC World Service about threat to Britain from 'council house culture,'" 23 September 2004, *BBC Press Office*, 25 October 2007< http://www.bbc.co.uk/ pressoffice/ pressreleases/ stories/2004/09september/23/naipaul.shtml.
53. Theo Tait, "Vicious Poke in the Eye," 4 November 2004, *London Review of Books*, 8 October 2006<http://www.lrb.co.uk/ v26/n21/tait01_.html.
54. Rajnish Wattas, "Spectrum," *The Tribune*, Sunday, 20 April 2003.
55. Chinua Achebe, "Colonial Criticism," *Post-Colonial Studies Reader*, eds. Bill Ashcroft, Gareth Griffiths and Helen Tiffin (London: Routledge, 1995) p. 59.
56. Mike Phillips, "Growing pains," 25 September, 2004, *Guardian*, 24 October 2008.

57. V.S. Naipaul, *A Bend in the River,* op. cit., p. 9.
58. V.S. Naipaul, *The Times of India,* Delhi, 19 February 2002.
59. Mike Phillips, "Growing pains", http://books.guardian.co.uk/print/0,3858,5023072–99930,00.html op. cit.
60. M.S. Nagarajan, "Home and Exile," *The Hindu*, 5 May 2002, p. 4.
61. Edward Said, *Reflections on Exile,* op. cit., p. 101.
62. V.S. Naipaul, "Our Universal Civilisation," *The Writer and the World*, ed. Pankaj Mishra (Delhi: Picador India, 2002) p. 517.
63. Edward Said, *Reflections on Exile,* op. cit., p. 108
64. V.S. Naipaul, "Two Worlds," *Literary Occasions: Essays*, op. cit., p. 194.
65. Ibid., p. xi.
66. V.S. Naipaul, *A Writer's People: Ways of Looking and Feeling* (Delhi: Picador India, 2007) p. 4.

Conclusion

V.S. Naipaul has been rightly acknowledged as a "nomadic literary sojourner" by the Nobel Prize Swedish Academy. His extensive travels form him as a writer with a world perspective. His fiction is a creative reflection of anguish and pain of the countries that people find unable to cope with. His journeys have taken him to India, the birthplace of his grandfather; to Trinidad, his birthplace; African continent, Joseph Conrad's area of darkness; South American lands; and back to England, and in each country he has found the cultures confronting disorder and anarchy. Besides, Naipaul's literary talent has been shaped by the acute perception of his own rootlessness and displacement. He enjoys all the advantages of portraying the cross cultural relations in the postcolonial era objectively. After his utter disillusionment with Trinidad and India during his travels back to the land of his birth and that of his ancesters respectively, he identifies himself with no alternative community. Though he has been preoccupied with marginal and peripheral world, his vision is fixed upon the brutal *collision of cultures*. His fiction deals with the typical postcolonial themes of the fragmentation of the social order, the sense of void, the meaninglessness of human endeavours in an amoral universe, and the absurdity of man's situation. In his Nobel Prize acceptance speech, he maintains that everything of worth mentioning about him lies in his books and he is simply the sum of his books.

Naipaul has remained persistently devoted to his own colonial experiences in Trinidad. He writes in English about what he has called 'half-made' societies in the Caribbean, India, Africa and Asia. He has rightly been termed as a literary navigator for his portrayal of some of the world's old colonies hitherto unexplored by many Westerners. His pursuit for discovery and investigation earned Naipaul the recognition throughout his career. Naipaul more than anyone else, chronicles the displacement, both at physical and emotional levels, that came immediately after the end of colonialism. He was the first to put his finger on something that is fairly common now. Naipaul is himself an explorer and wherever he has gone, his role has been "to look and to look again, to re-look and rethink". In his fictional works, he has discovered with great compassion the dilemma of the exile—the pain of homelessness and of loss of tradition.

His works are characterized by the portrayal of representative diasporic ambivalence. Exile has been the spur as well as the subject of his writing. His shifting absorption and anxieties however, mark a remarkable shift in the presentation of *ambivalence*. Homi K. Bhabha's interpretation of diasporic ambivalence is quite relevant while analyzing the depiction of half-made societies in the novels of Naipaul. Though Naipaul primarily presents a consistent image of social reality in the non-Western world, where dispossessed people search for order in their lives, he does not ignore the callousness and monotony in the lives of the Westerners. He is a twice-displaced diasporic writer whose quest for identity bespeaks the search of many colonial peoples occupying what Naipaul contemptuously calls "half-made societies". He presents an unfailing image of social reality in the non-Western world where dispossessed people search for order in their lives. His own search for home represents the collective search of the generation of colonial peoples. Naipaul's writings deal with the cultural confusion of the Third World and the problem of an outsider, a feature of his own experience as an Indian in the West Indies, a West Indian in England, and a nomadic intellectual in a postcolonial world. Writing as a dispossessed person who has been culturally uprooted and forced to create his own world, Naipaul finds personal resonance with the worldviews of the homeless nomads, the former colonial subjects in search of a unique identity. Well acquainted with the colonial/postcolonial anguish haunting the psyches of the natives and expatriates alike, Naipaul has also provoked much controversy because of his partial views of the "half-made societies". Caryl Phillips criticizes Naipaul for his undisguised contempt for the people of the Third World, and Edward W. Said denounces him as a "native informer", defending the metropolitan view of the Third World. The recent criticism of Naipaul took everyone by surprise when Nigel Reynolds, the *The Daily Telegraph* correspondent discloses that in the biography by Patrick French, V.S. Naipaul's reputation would be further maligned. The biographer presents a lucid account of Naipaul's heinous deeds of tormenting his first wife for four decades, visiting prostitutes and keeping a mistress for twenty four years. According to Nigel, his arrogance and rudeness have already lost him many friends in the literary world. His tendency to indulge in "brothel-sex" gets reflected in *A Bend in the River* and more openly in *Half a Life*. His range of characters includes displaced mimic men and derelicts who further represent the negative effects of living in a world devoid of spiritual, moral and emotional support. He applies the terms like "human debris", and "rotten meat" to signify the essential halfness of the colonial people around the world.

His fiction is marked by four perceptible phases, i.e., starting with his concern with self and "a dot on the map of the world", his fictional works acquire an utterly contemporary, universal significance with the last work of fiction. The early novels and short stories, based closely on his personal experiences in Trinidad, have been much-admired for their narrative skill, colourful use of West Indian dialect, and sardonic humour as they express themes of individual rootlessness and cultural deprivation that are the effects of colonial history. The characters in his early fiction are often depicted as alienated from the societies in which they are born, for they spend their lives trying to escape or to build a place of refuge they can identify themselves with. The first phase includes his Trinidadian-tetralogy—*The Mystic Masseur, Miguel Street, The Suffrage of Elvira* and *A House for Mr Biswas*. What preoccupies Naipaul in these novels is the portrayal of twice-torn and displaced immigrants oscillating between home culture and alien culture with their simultaneous fascination for sophisticated culture of the West. The early fictional works are to a large extent an attempt at defining his personal enigma during his formative years in Trinidad which is ironically the home of the exiles—Africans or Indians. These novels underline the essential *ambivalence* of East-Indian emigrants at Trinidad, at the same time seeking the belongingness and affiliation in West. Naipaul's escape from Trinidad and corresponding inability to find a foothold elsewhere has been the recurring theme in his fictional works but in his tetralogy, he is more obsessed with the issues pertaining to Caribbean island—the land inhabited by the expatriates.

V.S. Naipaul's novel *The Mystic Masseur* has been made into a film directed by Ismail Merchant with the script of the film by Caryl Phillips, a younger West-Indian novelist. Having failed as a masseur and author, Ganesh, the protagonist of *The Mystic Masseur,* aspires to be the mystic. Dressing himself in a turban and *dhoti* (loincloth) and burning incense, Pundit Ganesh attracts a following lured more by his affectations than by his wisdom. His is a tale of an expatriate making and re-making his identity. The mainstay of Naipaul's vision is his sensitivity to the power of the past. Traditional cultural forms relentlessly reassert themselves; social habit takes over where mimicry fails. The past, in Naipaul's scheme, asserts itself in a fascination with things medieval and an appreciation for traditional religions. Ganesh disguises himself as *Gareth*, only to claim later that he is G. Ramsay Muir. Further, politics provides a clue for understanding mimicry. *A House for Mr Biswas* is avowedly a fictional account of Naipaul's earlier life and a mirror of his relations with his father. Subsequently the novel narrates the paradoxes of exilic selves in the protagonist's existential search for a "portion of earth". To Mohun Biswas, Naipaul's most representative character, a house represents freedom—*his own portion of the earth*. Naipaul's writing highlights the experiences of the non-Western people who have been uprooted by historical currents and for whom *home* has lost its meaning. Mohun Biswas represents the typical disorder among the lives of the Indian expatriates living in Trinidad who constantly seek to find an order in the chaotic world. He has spoken of himself as being without a past, without ancestors, a country or a tradition. Their struggle to survive with dignity becomes not merely a regional or racial saga, but a universal saga of sad humanity.

The nostalgia for past, anguish of losing memory, love-hate relationship with the native past, and aspirations to mimic the Western culture mark the lives of the protagonists. *Miguel Street*, a collection of stories, is a series of brief portrayals of characters inhabiting Port of Spain. Here all are poor and all fantasize about a better life. The fantasy of these colonial daydreamers turns to mimicry. Similarly, *The Suffrage of Elvira* ridicules the typical mimicry of the colonials in the half-made postcolonial Trinidadian society. The creole Caribbean society is shown parodying democratic ideology of the West in the first general elections. The West becomes an unwelcome intruder which one can hardly escape but at the same time, to which one cannot feel attached heartily. The power of mimicry proves formidable. "Mimicry" allows the non-Western person to grasp at his or her aspirations. It also represents an attempt to adapt to a powerful, external reality while preserving something of one's own.

The second phase of Naipaul's career is marked by his broadening of outlook as now he goes beyond the enigma of the colonials in the Third World. He finds them caught in dilemmas and *ambivalence* wherever they move—may be in London also. *The Mimic Men* marks the switching over from essential Caribbean setting to the immensity of the typical ambivalence across the colonies. Tension fuels Ralph's tormented being and propels him to experiment all the means available to achieve something poignant. Politics, love, writing and cultural commitment fail to calm his colonial anguish during his stay in Isabella and after his escape to London too. Past and present, here and there, security and chaos, *self* and *other* interact and struggle to create the new out of the old. The metaphor of "shipwreck" aptly applies to perpetual expatriates like Ralph Singh. Though his earliest novels such as *The Suffrage of Elvira* and *Miguel Street* use irony to create comic effect, there has been, in *The Mimic Men* and *A Flag on the Island*, a darkening of the vision and utter sense of failure. The characters in *A Flag on the Island* demonstrate the common disorder afflicting Naipaul's West Indians. They are filled with a sense of their own insignificance, unreality and remoteness. Ralph Singh, an exiled colonial minister in the novel *The Mimic Men* experiences the fate of being a symbol of essential futility. He is a colonial seeking to develop a distinctive sensibility and to depict larger reality because he himself has been cut off and dispossessed of a coherent habitat by birth and circumstances. Exile is a position of distancing and craving for the past. This colonial ambivalence is discernible in *The Mimic Men*. Ralph's feeling of temporariness on the island stands in contrast to his unquestionable relationship with the island. This uncertainty has resulted from an upheaval of history. Ralph fails to re-negotiate his bond with the island. He undertakes a flight in which his search for order in England and the resultant disappointment takes him back to the beginning of his personal history. The London hotel provides him ample stimuli to re-imagine and reproduce his history of disorder. Naipaul's fictional works highlight the experiences of non-Western peoples who have been uprooted by historical currents. Given the formlessness of their lives, such people seek to find order. Naipaul's revisiting of themes like the pains of displacement, brutality, and emptiness in his earlier work suggests that the moment of decolonization has passed, and the moment of globalization has arrived.

The first four novels by V.S. Naipaul bear little surface resemblance to his later fiction. They are less dense, less intense and less allusive than the later novels, and in place of the gloomy vision of the third world embodied in such books as *Guerrillas* and *A Bend in the River*, there is a humorous appreciation for the vitality of the populous Caribbean world. These two Caribbean-African novels finally draw him suddenly into what Conrad had called "the heart of darkness", the gloom lurking inside the colonial Whites also. The distressed world of the West Indies, though ugly and bizarre, is seen as atavistic, pre-historic, a world beyond comprehension or control in *Guerrillas* and *A Bend in the River*. It is a long peep into the interiors of life which holds nothing, save a savagery of intention and rationale. In the novel *Guerrillas*, Naipaul's setting is a racially mixed Caribbean island where people sense that they are lost. Cut off from the land after the independence granted by Britain, people feel overwhelmed by outside forces. The novel seems to affirm the notion that independence has not brought any more freedom than the earlier colonial status and that the curse of marginality continues to upset the physical, social, mental, and moral lives of these people. The withdrawal of the colonial power from this island has only led to the taking over of the land by the Americans who have no cultural or historical links with the West Indians but only mercenary interests in the island's natural resources.

The discordant mixing of cultures and people lead the denizens and expatriates experience the ultimate vulnerability. Among the trapped and uprooted, an obsession to escape predominates. In *Guerillas*, Jimmy Ahmed, self-proclaimed revolutionary, seeks to establish a new order. Ironically, he symbolizes aspirations but he fails to fulfill them. It is through such complexities that Naipaul brings to the fore the convoluted patterns of human psyche and it is through *Guerrillas* that Naipaul marks a turning point in English colonial literature. The varied impacts of colonization on the colonized as well as the colonizers are evident in the characters like Jane, Jimmy and Bryant.

A Bend in the River is a pessimistic novel about a country very like Zaïre or Uganda, proclaiming the corruptibility and fallibility of mankind. Salim, the narrator is a Muslim, whose family, Indian traders, has lived in Africa since hundreds of years. Salim sets up a shop in a town on the bend of the river and gains success. But he has no future in a country ruled by the Big Man. Again Naipaul's protagonist is an expatriate, who realizes that his way of life is almost at its end and eventually he must give up everything. Here on, "bush" is Naipaul's metaphor for the country and the whole Third World. In V.S. Naipaul's fiction, there is always an area of darkness just beyond the edge of town; colonists arrive, empires rise and fall, and a new, not-so-brave world emerges, but always the *bush* remains. *A Bend in the River* highlights vulnerability of the expatriates—made homeless in former colonies by the withdrawal of the imperial order and the resulting threat of chaos. Their quest for survival, the dangers of their involvement in an alien setting, the after effects of hybridity and multiculturalism, and the common pattern of suffering are some of the key issues in the novel. The modern means of transportation, immigration and so-called liberalism contribute in bringing together so many heterogeneous races like various African tribes and the British and the Arabs. Naipaul comes out with utter gloom and cynicism while writing about the sense of futility and vanity of life owing to the obvious bewilderment of the natives and expatriates experiencing the disillusionment of decolonization. In a hopeless colonial milieu, nostalgia for the past, race, religion, place, home, culture, family or others, adds fuel to the fire. The stifled lives of individuals in a murky region of Africa become a metaphor for the paralyzed life in a so-called free state. It is a dark vision, to be sure, and it is a vision shaped by the author's own familiarity with the margins of society. He is now in the grip of a complex entangling vision of what happens in those unfortunate countries that have just toppled out of a tribal past, or freed themselves from colonial rule, but cannot reach the uncertain blessings of modernity. Naipaul's distrust of the colonizers, it seems, is commensurate only with his distrust of the colonized. Beyond this, Naipaul offers no intimations of hope or signals of perspective. It appears that the reality he grapples with allows him nothing but grimness of voice. His vision is fixed upon the brutal collision of cultures, the elaborate paralysis of *areas of darkness* and *wounded civilizations*, phrases used as the titles of his books on India. Evolving gradually, he has passed beyond India, or at least tho land mass of India, to a *universal darkness*.

Naipaul is also one of the greatest travel writers, and his absorption into the experience of rootlessness, and the alienating effects of colonial past on today's postcolonial people has taken him to Africa, South America, India and all over the world not in search of roots but ironically his pursuit to get himself rooted, simply confirms his rootlessness. *Half a Life* and *Magic Seeds*, the last two novels of Naipaul, explore the racial, political, linguistic, cultural, spiritual, or sexual tensions once more. In *Half a Life,* Willie Chandran—the protagonist—is not really different from Naipaul's other *shipwrecked* men, but the treatment of the theme is more harsh and broad-based. Willie moves to London, drifts in bohemian circles, publishes a book, marries Ana, a woman of mixed African descent, and moves with her to Africa, to her family estate. Willie has problems while coming to terms with himself, as the son of a Brahman, who has married an untouchable. His father is a rebel who ends at a monastery. Willie rebels against his own sense of history. In his wife's home country, in which the colonial system is breaking down, Willie is simply *Ana's London man*. After eighteen years, he decides to leave her, and tries to find his true identity. He has lived half a life, a shadow life, but Naipaul leaves Willie to continue with his existential search in the novel to come—*Magic Seeds*. The last novel seems to be an irascible outburst against modernity and postcolonial civilization across the world.

The four perceptible phases in the career of V.S. Naipaul may be well-sketched through the description of his preoccupations and travels during different periods of his life. In fact, a true understanding of Naipaul as a writer is impossible without having an idea about his travels which broaden his understanding at certain stages. His journey back to Trinidad provides him the stuff for *The Middle Passage*; India substantiates his Indian trilogy; Africa makes him penetrate deeper and deeper in the recesses of the African darkness and to produce *A Bend in the River*, and his visit to South America makes him available the sufficient stuff for *The Return of Eva Perón*. What he experienced and observed through his extensive travels is that the typical colonial disappointment, aspirations, tendency to escape, "halfness", meaninglessness and the characteristic ambivalence is a universal phenomenon, though with some circumstantial variations. Naipaul observes that the emptiness of the centre is a reflection of the emptiness of the periphery. Willie's circuitous journeys from India to London, London to Mozambique, Mozambique to India, and finally back to London signify the global postcolonial chaos. Moreover, the nomads—be they migrant people, exiles, refugees or voluntary expatriates like Naipaul—are offered fewer possibilities for belonging. The expatriates are bound to live ambivalent, marginal and displaced lives because of the differences of race, gender, class or circumstances.

Naipaul maintains his distinction as a diasporic writer because of his first hand observation of the postcolonial "universal civilization" and his tendency to fearlessly present the gloom of the colonized and the colonizer alike, without bothering about his critics who call him a conniver against the Third World. As he has stayed long in London, he finds his traditions, nativity and language eroding with the passage of time. Naipaul observes that every writer, in the long run, has a tradition of his own. But in his case, he has no tradition to stick to. Moreover, he has been successful in making a special room for himself as a postcolonial writer because of his "universality" and objectivity of expression.

Despite certain discernible paradigms marking V.S. Naipaul's fiction from *The Mystic Masseur* to *Magic Seeds*, there is a common connection between all of his works as they are all characterized by the novelist's obsession with the projection of his personal enigma as a homeless nomad seeking homeliness sometimes in India, and at others in Trinidad or England. But, by the end of his career, he seems to have developed a sense of equanimity and is no more nostalgic about his ties with the land of his forefathers or his own birthplace. Naipaul's later novels, historical essays, and social commentaries based on his extensive travels throughout Africa, Asia, South America, and the Caribbean, continue to explore the relation of colonialism to the loss of cultural identity, but without the streak of humour which characterized his earlier fiction writing. The later works, while being admired for their keen observation and clear descriptive style, have invited passionate criticism for their often bleakly negative appraisal of cultures ravaged by centuries of subjugation. Growing out of the shadows of personal gloom, he has ended up being a novelist with the vision of an objective sojourner articulating the postcolonial worldview without propagating any philosophy.

To conclude, V.S. Naipaul's fiction undergoes certain paradigmatic shifts especially in the presentation of the representative diasporic ambivalence among certain protagonists and other characters. His fiction is a parallel journey signifying his personal growth and ultimate mature perception. Starting from the issues pertaining to the narrow dismal environment of Caribbean island, he moves to the unexplored territories of the world with the passion of a navigator. His wholeness as the novelist may be measured through the review of fragmentary experiences he undertakes as a traveller. His treatment of the theme of "ambivalence" is penetrating and comprehensive as he shares the anguish of colonial expatriates throughout his career. His novels are not merely reflections of abstraction; rather, they are packed with thought. He is free of any romantic moonshine about the moral charms of primitives or the glories of bloodstained dictators. Nor does he propose a preference to Western superciliousness or nostalgia for colonialism. He is a tough-spirited writer, well-informed about the insipidness of much contemporary history and not especially hopeful about its consequences. By his own admission, V.S. Naipaul's situation is atypical and apprehensive. A novelist and journalist of Indian heritage, he grew up on Trinidad and became a resident of England. He appears a colonial seeking to depict larger reality, yet threatened with a possibility of being seen as a regional, West Indian writer; his writings seemingly lack a natural audience beyond his home island. But because he himself has been cut off, dispossessed of a coherent habitat by birth and circumstances, he has developed a distinctive sensibility. Naipaul's writings highlight the experiences of non-Western peoples who have been uprooted by historical currents. Both considerate and critical, he brings to light the failures of developing societies in the postcolonial era. Given the formlessness of their lives, such people seek to find order. How their struggles spread out becomes not merely a regional or racial narrative, but a human one. Writing as a dispossessed person, the one who has been culturally uprooted and forced to create his own world, Naipaul not only presents but also shares subjective perceptions. He finds personal reverberation with the worldviews of the dispossessed former colonial subjects who are busy in the pursuit of establishing their individual identity. Thus, his journey as a prominent diasporic novelist, perhaps, ends as a writer with a high sense of maturity, who according to Horace Engdahl, Permanent Secretary to Swedish Academy, calls to mind what Alfred Nobel said of himself: "My homeland is where I work, and I work everywhere."

Bibliography

Primary Sources

Naipaul, V.S. *The Mystic Masseur* (1957). London: Penguin Books, 1964.

——. *The Suffrage of Elvira*. London: Andre Deutsch, 1958.

——. *Miguel Street* (1959). London: Picador, 2002.

——. *A House for Mr Biswas*. Harmondsworth: Penguin, 1961.

——. *The Middle Passage: Impressions of Five Societies-British, French and Dutch in the West Indies and South America*. London: Andre Deutsch, 1962.

——. *Mr Stone and the Knights Companion*. London: Andre Deutsch, 1963.

——. *An Area of Darkness* (1964). London: Picador, 1995.

——. *A Flag on the Island*. London: Andre Deutsch, 1967.

——. *The Mimic Men*. (1967). London: Picador, 2002.

——. *The Loss of El Dorado: A History*. London: Andre Deutsch, 1969.

——. *In a Free State*. London: Andre Deutsch, 1971.

——. *The Overcrowded Barracoon and Other Articles*. London: Andre Deutsch, 1972.

——. *Guerrillas* (1975). Delhi: Picador India, 2002.

——. *India: A Wounded Civilization*. London: Andre Deutsch, 1977.

——. *A Bend in the River* (1979). Delhi: Clarion Books, 1980.

——. *A Congo Diary*. Los Angeles, CA: Sylvester & Orphanos, 1980.

——. *The Return of Eva Peron*. London: Andre Deutsch, 1980.

——. *Among the Believers: An Islamic Journey*. London: Andre Deutsch, 1981.

——. *Finding the Centre*. London: Andre Deutsch, 1984.

——. *The Enigma of Arrival*. London: Viking, 1987.

——. *A Turn in the South*. London: Heinemann, 1989.

——. *India: A Million Mutinies Now*. London: Heinemann, 1990.

——. *A Way in the World*. London: Heinemann, 1994.

——. *Beyond Belief: Islamic Excursions among the Converted Peoples.* London: Little, Brown, 1998.

——. *Reading and Writing: A Personal Account.* New York: New York Review of Books, 2000.

——. *Between Father and Son: Family Letters.* New York: Vintage, 2001.

——. *Half a Life.* London: Picador, 2001.

——. *The Writer and the World.* Ed. Pankaj Mishra. London: Picador, 2002.

——. *Literary Occasions: Essays.* Ed. Pankaj Mishra. London: Picador, 2003.

——. *Magic Seeds*, London: Picador, 2004.

——. *A Writer's People.* London: Picador, 2007.

Secondary Sources

Achebe, Chinua. *Morning yet on Creation Day.* Garden City, New York: Doubleday, 1975.

Ahmad, Aijaz. *In Theory: Classes, Nations, Literatures.* London and New York: Verso, 1994.

Anderson, Benedict. *Imagined Communities:Reflections on the Origin and Spread of Nationalism.* London and New York: Verso, 1983.

Ashcroft, Bill, Griffiths, Gareth and Tiffin, Helen. Eds. *The Post-Colonial Studies Reader.* London and New York: Routledge, 1995.

Ashcroft, Bill and Ahluwalia, Pal. *Edward Said: The Paradox of Identity.* London and New York: Routledge, 1999.

Baugh, Edward. Ed. *Critics on Caribbean Literature.* London: George Allen and Unwin, 1978.

Bakhtin, M. *The Dialogic Imagination.* Austin: University of Texas Press, 1981.

Bala, Suman. *V.S. Naipaul: A Literary Response to the Nobel Laureate.* New Delhi: Khosla Publishing House, 2003.

Ball, John Clement. *Satire & the Postcolonial Novel: V.S. Naipaul, Chinua Achebe, Salman Rushdie.* New York: Routledge, 2003.

Barnouw, Dagmar. *Naipaul's Strangers.* Bloomington: Indiana University Press, 2003.

Barry, Peter. *Beginning Theory: An Introduction to Literary and Cultural Theory.* Manchester: Manchester University Press, 1999.

Bhabha, Homi K. Ed. *Nation and Narration.* London: Routledge, 1990.

——. *The Location of Culture.* London and New York: Routledge, 1994.

Boehmer, Elleke. *Colonial and Postcolonial Literature: Migrant Metaphors.* Oxford: Oxford University Press.

Boxhill, Anthony. *V.S. Naipaul's Fiction: In Quest of the Enemy*. Fredricton: New Brunswick: York Press, 1983.

Brah, Avtar. *Cartographies of Diaspora: Contesting Identities*. London: Routledge, 1997.

Braziel, Jana Evans and Anita Mannur. Eds. *Theorizing Diaspora*. Malden: Blackwell, 2003.

Brathwaite, E. *Other Exiles*. London: Oxford University Press, 1975.

Brennan, Timothy. *Salman Rushdie and the Third World*. London: Macmillan, 1989.

Chatterjee, Partha. *The Nation and its Fragments: Colonial and Postcolonial Histories*. New Jersey: Princeton University Press, 1993.

Clifford, Geertz. *The Interpretation of Culture*. London: Fontana, 1993.

Dhawan, R.K. Ed. *Commonwealth Fiction*. 3 Vols. New Delhi: Classical Publishing Company, 1988.

Dissanayake, Wimal, and Carmen Wickramagamage. *Self and Colonial Desire: Travel Writings of V.S. Naipaul*. New York: Peter Lang, 1993.

Eagleton Terry. *Exiles and Emigres*. London: Chatto and Windus, 1970.

Fanon, Frantz. *Black Skins, White Masks*. 1952. London: Pluto Press, 1980.

——. *Studies in a Dying Colonialism*. 1959. Harmondsworth: Penguin, 1970.

——. *The Wretched of the Earth*. 1961. Harmondsworth: Penguin, 1971.

Feder, Lillian. *Naipaul's Truth: The Making of a Writer*. New York and Oxford: Rowman & Littlefield Publishers, 2000.

Goonatilake, Susantha. *Crippled Minds: An Exploration into Colonial Culture*. Mumbai: Vikas, 1982.

Gorra, Michael. *After Empire: Scott, Naipaul, Rushdie*. Chicago: University of Chicago Press, 1997.

Griffiths, Gareth. *A Double Exile: African and West Indian Writing Between Two Cultures*. London: Marian Boyars, 1988.

Guha, Ranajit. Ed. *Subaltern Studies: Writings on South Asian History and Society*. Vols. I–IX. Delhi: Oxford University Press, 1982.

Haley, Alex. *Roots*. London: Picador, 1976.

Hamner, Robert D. *V.S. Naipaul*. New York: Tyawne, 1973.

Hamner, Robert D. Ed. *Critical Perspectives on V.S. Naipaul*. Washington, D.C.: Three Continents Press, 1977.

Harris, Wilson. *The Tradition, The Writer and Society*. Port of Spain: New Beacon, 1967.

——. *The Womb of Space: The Cross-Cultural Imagination*. Westport C.T.: Greenwood Press, 1983.

Hayward, Helen. *The Enigma of V.S. Naipaul: Sources and Contexts*. London: Palgrave Macmillan, 2002.

Hobsbawm, E.J. *The Age of Empire*. London: Weidenfield and Nicholson, 1987.

Hughes, Peter. *V.S. Naipaul: Contemporary Writers*. London and New York, 1988.

Jain, Jasbir. *Problems of Postcolonial Literatures and Other Essays*. Jaipur: Printwell, 1991.

——. ed. *Writers of Indian Diaspora: Theory and Practice*. Jaipur and New Delhi: Rawat Publications, 1998.

Jan Mohammad, Abdul. R. *Manichean Aesthetics: The Politics of Literature in Colonial Africa*. Amherst: University of Massachusetts Press, 1983.

Jayaram, N. Ed. *The Indian Diaspora: Dynamcs of Migration*. New Delhi and London: Sage Publications, 2004.

Joshi, Chandra B. *V.S. Naipaul: The Voice of Exile*. New Delhi: Sterling Publishers, 1994.

Kamra, Shashi. *The Novels of V.S. Naipaul: A Study in Theme and Form*. New Delhi: Prestige Books, 1990.

Khan, Akhtar Jamal. *V.S. Naipaul: A Critical Study*. New Delhi: Creative Books, 1998.

King, Bruce. Ed. *Literatures of the World in English*. London: Routledge, 1974.

——. Ed. *West Indian Literature*. London: Macmillan, 1979.

——. *V.S. Naipaul*. Basingstoke: Macmillan, 2003.

Kirpal, Viney. *The Third World Novel of Expatriation*. New Delhi: Sterling, 1989.

Kumar, Amitava. *The Humour & the Pity: Essays on V.S. Naipaul*. New Delhi: Buffalo Books, 2002.

Lamming, George. *In the Castle of My Skin*. 1953. London: Longman Drumbeat, 1979.

——. *The Pleasures of Exile*. London: Michael Joseph, 1960.

——. *Natives of My Person*. 1972. London: Picador, 1974.

Levine, Laurence. *Black Culture and Black Consciousness*. New York: Oxford University Press, 1977.

Levy, Judith. *V.S. Naipaul: Displacement and Autobiography*. New York: Garland Publishing, 1995.

Mackenzie, John. *Propaganda and Empire*. Manchester: Manchester University Press, 1984.

Mahanta, Namrata Rathore. *V.S. Naipaul: The Indian Trilogy*. Delhi: Atlantic Publishers, 2004.

Manjit Inder Singh. *V.S. Naipaul: Nobel Prize Winner*. Jaipur: Rawat Publications, 1998.

Mannoni, O. *Prospero and Caliban: The Psychology of Colonisation*. New York: Praeger, 1964.

Mason, Nondita. *The Fiction of V.S. Naipaul*. Calcutta: The World Press, 1986.

Memmy, Albert. *The Coloniser and the Colonised*. New York: Orion Press, 1965.

Morris, Robert K. *Paradoxes of Order: Some Perspectives on the Fiction of V.S. Naipaul*. Columbia: University of Missouri Press, 1975.

Mustafa, Fawzia. *V.S. Naipaul*. Cambridge: Cambridge University Press, 1995.

Naipaul, Seepersad. *The Adventures of Gurudeva and Other Stories*. London: Andre Deutsch, 1976.

Nandy Ashis. *The Intimate Enemy: Loss and Recovery of Self under Colonialism*. Delhi: Oxford University Press, 1983.

Narasimhaiah, C.D. ed. *Commonwealth Literature: A Handbook of Select Reading Lists*. Delhi: Oxford University Press, 1976.

——. Ed. *Awakened Conscience: Studies in Commonwealth Literature*. New Delhi: Sterling Publishers, 1978.

Nayar, Pramod K. *Literary Theory Today*. New Delhi: Prestige, 2006.

Nixon, Rob. *London Calling: V.S. Naipaul: Post-Colonial Mandarin*. New York: Oxford University Press, 1992.

Padmanabhan Nair, K.N. *Irony in the Novels of R.K. Narayan and V.S. Naipaul*. Trivandrum, S. India: CBH Publications, 1993.

Panwar, Purabi. *V.S. Naipaul: An Anthology of Recent Criticism*. Delhi: Pencraft International, 2003.

Parry, Benita. *Delusions and Discoveries: Studies on India in the British Imagination, 1880–1930*. London: Allen Lane, 1972.

——. *Postcolonial Studies: A Materialist Critique*. London: Routledge, 2004.

Prakash, Gyan. Ed. *After Colonialism: Imperial Histories and Postcolonial Displacements*. New Jersey: Princeton University Press, 1995.

Rai, Sudha. *V.S. Naipaul: A Study in Expatriate Sensibility*. New Delhi: Arnold-Heinemann, 1982.

——. *Homeless by Choice: Naipaul, Rushdie, Jhabwala*. Jaipur: Printwell, 1992.

Ramadevi, N. *The Novels of V.S. Naipaul: Quest for Order and Identity*. New Delhi: Prestige Books, 1996.

Ramchand, Kenneth. *The West Indian Novel and its Background*. London: Faber and Faber, 1970.

——. *An Introduction to the Study of West Indian Literature*. London: Faber and Faber, 1976.

Ray, Mohit K. Ed. *V.S. Naipaul: Critical Essays*. Vol. I–III. Delhi, Atlantic Publishers, 2002.

Rushdie, Salman. *Imaginary Homelands: Essays and Criticism 1981–1991*. London: Granta, 1991.

Said, Edward W. *Orientalism* (1978). Harmondsworth: Penguin, 1995.

——. *The World, the Text and the Critic*. London: Faber and Faber, 1984.

——. *Culture and Imperialism* (1993). London: Vintage, 1994.

Sakaana, Amon Saba. *The Colonial Legacy in Caribbean Literature*. London: Karnak House, 1987.

Scott, Kilvert Ian, and Michael Thorpe. *V.S. Naipaul*. Harlow, Essex, UK: British Council, Longman Group, 1976.

Spivak, Gayatri Chakravorty. *In Other Worlds: Essays in Cultural Politics*. London: Metheun, 1987.

——. *The Post-colonial Critic: Interviews, Strategies, Dialogues*. London and New York: Routledge, 1990.

——. *A Critique of Postcolonial Reason: Towards a History of the Vanishing Present*. Calcutta: Seagull, 1999.

Theroux, Paul. *V.S. Naipaul: An Introduction to His Work*. London: Andre Deutsch, 1972.

——. *Sir Vidia's Shadow: A Friendship Across Five Continents*. London: Hamish Hamilton, 1998.

Thieme, John. *The Web of Tradition: Uses of Allusion in V.S. Naipaul's Fiction*. Caribbean: Hansib Dangaroo Press, 1987.

Thiong'O, Ngugi Wa. *Homecoming: Essays on African and Caribbean Literature, Culture and Politics*. London: Heinemann, 1972.

——. *Decolonizing the Mind: The Politics of Language in African Literature*. London: James Curry, 1986.

Thorpe, Michael. *V.S. Naipaul*. London: British Council, Longman Group, 1976.

Tinker, Hugh. *A New System of Slavery*. London: OUP, 1974.

Trivedi, Harish and Mukherjee, Meenakshi. Eds. *Interrogating Postcolonialism: Theory, Text and Context*. Shimla: Indian Institute of Advanced Studies, 1996.

Walder, Dennis. *Post-Colonial Literatures in English: History, Language, Theory*. Oxford: Blackwell, 2005.

Walsh, William. *V.S. Naipaul*. Edinburgh: Oliver and Boyd, 1973.

——. Ed. *A Manifold Voice: Studies in Commonwealth Literature*. London: Chatto and Windus, 1970.

White, Landeg. *V.S. Naipaul: A Critical Introduction*. London: Macmillan, 1975.

Williams, Eric. *Capitalism and Slavery*. London: Andre Deutsch, 1964.

——. *From Columbus to Castro: The History of the Caribbean, 1492–1967*. New York: Harper and Row, 1970.

Williams, Raymond. *Culture and Society, 1780–1950.* London: Penguin, 1958.

Wolfreys, John. *Introducing Literary Theories: A Guide and Glossary.* 2001. Delhi: Atlantic Publishers, 2005.

Young, J.C. *Colonial Desire: Hybridity in Theory, Culture and Race.* London: Routledge, 1995.

Articles

Ashok, M.R. "Colonial Consciouness in V.S. Naipaul." V.S. Naipaul: A Literary Response to the Nobel Laureate. Ed. Suman Bala. New Delhi: Khosla Publishing House, 2003. pp. 26–30.

Bharat, Meenakshi. "Cultural Maladies, Postcolonial Cures? 'Sick' Politics in *A House for Mr Biswas*." *V.S. Naipaul: An Anthology of Recent Criticism*. ed. Purabi Panwar. Delhi: Pencraft International, 2003. pp. 67–78.

Chaudhary, Helga. "V.S. Naipaul's Changing Vision of India: A Study of *An Area of Darkness* and *India: A Wounded Civilisation*." *Literary Half Yearly* 23, No. 1 (January 1982).

Chaudhuri, Amit. "Two Cheers for the Nobel Award: On V.S. Naipaul." V.S. Naipaul: An Anthology of Recent Criticism. ed. Purabi Panwar. Delhi: Pencraft International, 2003. pp. 187–190.

Choudhary, Tapas K. Roy. "Ambivalence, Colonial Text and Tagore." *Summerhill IIAS Review*. Vol. XII. No. 2, 2006. pp. 25–29.

Chitre, Dilip. "Naipaul and India: For him a Difficult Country." *New Quest*. 9 (May–June 1978).

Eastley, Aaron. "Joking With the Center: Naipaul's Ambiguous Treatment of Trinidadian English in The Mystic Masseur." *Journal of Contemporary Thought*. (Special number on Postcolonialism and the Discourse of Marginality). 1999, Summer. pp. 25–46.

Joshi, Chandra B. "'Very Much my Father's Book': Autobiographical Element in *A House for Mr Biswas*." *V.S. Naipaul: An Anthology of Recent Criticism*. ed. Purabi Panwar. Delhi: Pencraft International, 2003. pp. 79–92.

Kundu, Rama. "An Indian Who is not an Indian." *V.S. Naipaul: Critical Essays*. Vol. I. ed. Mohi K. Ray. Delhi, Atlantic Publishers, 2002. pp. 119–48.

Parekh, Bhikhu. "Some Reflections on the Indian Diaspora." *Journal of Contemporary Thought*. Baroda, 1993.

Parameswaran, Uma. "Home is Where Your Feet are, and may Your Heart be There Too!". *Writers of Indian Diaspora: Theory and Practice*. ed. Jasbir Jain. Jaipur and New Delhi: Rawat Publications, 1998. pp. 30–39.

Parrinder, Patrick. "V.S. Naipaul and Uses of Literacy." *Critical Quarterly*. 21, ii (1979), pp. 5–13.

Radhakrishnan, R. "Reading Said: Between Worldliness and Globality." *Journal of Contemporary Thought*. Baroda, 2003 (Winter). pp. 167–74.

Rai, Sudha. "Postcolonial Parables of Survival: V.S. Naipaul's *A Flag on the Island*." *V.S. Naipaul: An Anthology of Recent Criticism*. ed. Purabi Panwar. Delhi: Pencraft International, 2003. pp. 113– 25.

Shukla, Sheobhushan and Shukla, Anu. "Migrant Voices in Literatures in English." *Contemporary World Literatures in English*. II, 2005. pp. 1–18.

Singh, Gurbhagat. "Expatriate Writing and the Problematic of Centre: Edward Said and Homi Bhabha." *Writers of Indian Diaspora: Theory and Practice*. ed. Jasbir Jain. Jaipur and New Delhi: Rawat Publications, 1998. pp. 21–29.

Singh, Manjit Inder. *V.S. Naipaul*. Jaipur and Delhi: Rawat Publications, 2002.

——. "Contemporary Diasporic Discourse: Towards Understanding Cultural Dialogic." *Perspectives on Diaspora: Indian Fiction in English*. eds. Tejinder Kaur and N.K. Neb. Jalandhar: Nirmaan Publications, 2004.

Singh, Natwar K. "Unhappy Pilgrim." *New York Times Book Review*. 11 July 1965: 35.

Spivak, Gayatri. "Can the Subaltern Speak?" in Nelson, C and Grossberg, L. eds. *Marxism and the Interpretation of Culture*. Basingstroke: Macmillan Educational, 1998. pp. 271–313.

Tiffin, Helen. "Post-Colonialism, Post-modernism and the Rehabilitation of Post-colonial History." *Journal of Commonwealth Literature*, 23, I, 1988, pp. 169–81.

Williams, Patrick. "Edward Said (1935–2003)." *Contemporay Critical Theorists: From Lacan to Said*. ed. Jon Simons. Delhi: Atlantic Publishers, 2005.

Internet Sources

Chaudhary, Shoma. "A Fantasy of Nobility." *Tehelka*. 15 March 2007<http://www.tehelka.com/ channels/literary/2001/ Oct.12.

Chaudhuri, Amit. "Times Literary Supplement." 21 September 2001. *The Times of India*. 12 October 2005<http://www. complete-review. com/reviews/naipaulvs/half life. html.

Colin, Chris. "Half a Life by V.S. Naipaul." 12 June 2001. *Salon.com Books*. 14 April 2008 <http:www.Salon. Com/books/review/ 2001/12/06/Naipaul/-23k.

"Colonialism." *Stanford Encyclopedia of Philosophy*. Ed. Edward N. Zalta. Fall 2002. 30 September 2007<http://plato.stanford.edu/entries/colonialism/.

Dhondy, Farrukh. "Interview with V.S. Naipaul." 13 August 2001. *Indian Writers Don't Know Why Their Country Is In Such a Mess*. 15 July 2008<the courses01/rrtw/vsnaipaul.html.

Elizabeth, Hardwick. "Meeting V.S. Naipaul." 13 May 1979. *From the Archives of The New York Times*. 20 March 2007<http://www.nytimes.com/books/98/06/07/specials/naipaul-meeting. html.

Engdahl, Horace. "Prose in the Style of Naipaul." 14 December 2001. *The Nobel Prize in Literature*. 5 January 2007 <http:www.tehelka.com/channels/literary/2001dec./14/ir/b2140/speech/html-22k.

Evans, Adrian Rowe. "Interview with V.S. Naipaul." December 1971. *A Transition Interview*. 5 November 2006<http://links.jstor.org.

Express India. "V.S. Naipaul Kept a Mistress for Almost 24 Years." 21 March 2008. London. 10 October 2008<http://www.expressindia.com/latest-news/V-S-Naipaul-kept-a-mistress-for-alm o st-24-years/287179/.

Gilbert, Harriett. "VS Naipaul talks to BBC World Service about threat to Britain from 'council house culture.'" 23 September 2004. *BBC Press Office*. 25 October 2007.

Gussow, Mel. "V.S. Naipaul: 'It Is Out of This Violence I've Always Written.'" 16 September 1984. *The New York Times Archives*. 7 July 2006<http://www.nytimes.com/books/98/06/07/specials/naipaul-violence.html.

——. "The Enigma of V.S. Naipaul's Search for Himself in Writing." 25 April 1987 *The New York Times Archives*. 20 September 2007 <http: //www.nytimes.com/books/98/06/07/specials/naipaul-enigma.html.

——. "Travel Plus Writing Plus Reflection Equals V.S. Naipaul." 30 January 1991. *The New York Times Archives*. 5 February 2007 <http: //www.nytimes.com/books/98/06/07/specials/naipaul-travel.html.

——. "V.S. Naipaul in Search of Himself: A Conversation." 24 April 1994. *The New York Times Archives*. 25 August 2006<http: www.nytimes.com/books/98/06/07/specials/Naipaul/-38k.

——. "The Writer to be and his Mentor." 5 January 2000. *The New York Times Archives*. 25 August 2006<http:/www.nytimes.com/library/books/010500naipaul-interview.html.

Kakutani, Michiko. "Naipaul Reviews His Past From Afar." 1 December 1980. *The New York Times Archives*. 25 August 2006 <http://www.nytimes.com/books/98/06/07/specials/naipaul-afar.html.

Kumar, Amitav. "Amitava Kumar on V.S. Naipaul." 3 September 2001. *The New Statesman*. 5 January 2008<http://www.amitavakumar.com/articles/notebook.ht ml.

Manish. "Naipaul's *Magic Seeds*." 2 June 2008. *NYT Book Reviews*. 6 September 2008, para 4.

Merriam-Webster Online website. "Mimicry." 3 June 2008.

Mitra, Ashok. "Not Such an Enigma." 26 October 2001. *The Telegraph*. 8 August 2008.

Naipaul, V.S. "India After Indira Gandhi." 3 November 1984. *The New York Times Archives*. 22 August 2007<http://www.nytimes.com/books/ 00/01/16/specials/naipaul.html.

——. "Our Universal Civilisation." 5 November 1990. *Featured Author V.S. Naipaul: The New York Times Archives*. 22 August 2007 <http://www.nytimes.com/books/00/01/16/specials/naipaul.html.

——. "Interview with Farrukh Dhondy." 13 August 2001. *Tehelka*. 25 November 2007<http://www.tehelka.com/channels/literary2001/ 12 October.

Pais, Neal. "Naipaul's *Half a Life* a Prize-winning Exploration of Isolation." 22 February. 2002. *Daily Books Editor: The Michigan Daily*. 25 November 2007.

Phillips, Mike. "Growing pains." 25 September, 2004. *Guardian*. 24 October 2008.

Sachs, William L. "V.S. Naipaul and the Plight of the Dispossessed." 17 November 1982. *Religion Online*. 7 August 2006 <http: //www.religion-online.org/cgi-bin/research.dll/showarticle?item id,1354, 4.

Sheridan, Anne. "Half a Life: V.S. Naipaul." 2001. 4 March 2002. *Culture Vulture*. 5 May 2007<http: culturevulture.net/books/ *Half a Life*.html.

Suarez, Ray. "Author Conversation: V.S. Naipaul." 3 March 2000. *Online News Hour*. 7 October 2006<http://www.pbs.org/newshour/gergen/jan-june00/naipaul _3–3.html.

Theroux, Pal. "From the Critics." 2001. 3 March, 2002. *The Guardian*. 24 October 2008<http: www. members.tripod.com/brendajer/gnalid22–m.html.

——. "Into the Lion's Den." 1 September 2001. *Guardian*. 24 October 2008 <http://books.guardian.co.uk/print/0,3858,4248327-99930,00.html.

Thomas, Jessica Lee. "Naipaul revels in the space between extremes." *Half and Half*. 9 January 2008 <http://www.yalereviewofbooks.com/archive/spring02/review16.s html.

Tait, Theo. "Vicious Poke in the Eye." 4 November 2004. London Review of Books. 8 October 2006<http://www.lrb. co.uk/v26/n21/tait01_.html.

Index